Frontier Life in Ancient Peru

UNIVERSITY PRESS OF FLORIDA

Florida A&M University, Tallahassee
Florida Atlantic University, Boca Raton
Florida Gulf Coast University, Ft. Myers
Florida International University, Miami
Florida State University, Tallahassee
New College of Florida, Sarasota
University of Central Florida, Orlando
University of Florida, Gainesville
University of North Florida, Jacksonville
University of South Florida, Tampa
University of West Florida, Pensacola

FRONTIER LIFE IN ANCIENT PERU

The Archaeology of Cerro la Cruz

MELISSA A. VOGEL

University Press of Florida
Gainesville · Tallahassee · Tampa · Boca Raton
Pensacola · Orlando · Miami · Jacksonville · Ft. Myers · Sarasota

Copyright 2012 by Melissa A. Vogel
All rights reserved
Printed in the United States of America on acid-free paper

First cloth printing, 2012
First paperback printing, 2015

Library of Congress Cataloging-in-Publication Data
Vogel, Melissa A.
Frontier life in ancient Peru : the archaeology of Cerro la Cruz / Melissa A. Vogel.
p. cm.
Includes bibliographical references and index.
ISBN 978-0-8130-3796-7 (cloth: alk. paper)
ISBN 978-0-8130-6133-7 (pbk.)
1. Indians of South America—Peru—Chao River Valley—Antiquities. 2. Indians of South America—Peru—Chao River Valley—Politics and government. 3. Indians of South America—Peru—Chao River Valley—Migrations. 4. Indians of South America—Peru—Casma River Valley—Antiquities. 5. Indians of South America—Peru—Casma River Valley—Politics and government. 6. Chao River Valley (Peru)—Antiquities. 7. Casma River Valley (Peru)—Antiquities. I. Title.
F3429.1.C475V65 2012
985.'01—dc23
2011037548

The University Press of Florida is the scholarly publishing agency for the State University System of Florida, comprising Florida A&M University, Florida Atlantic University, Florida Gulf Coast University, Florida International University, Florida State University, New College of Florida, University of Central Florida, University of Florida, University of North Florida, University of South Florida, and University of West Florida.

University Press of Florida
15 Northwest 15th Street
Gainesville, FL 32611-2079
http://www.upf.com

To my friend and mentor, Carol Mackey, for her generosity,
wisdom, and sage advice,

and to my parents for their unwavering support of my career aspirations.

Contents

List of Figures ix

List of Maps xi

List of Tables xiii

Acknowledgments xv

1. Introduction: Geopolitical Boundaries in Andean Prehistory 1

2. A Time and Place of Transition: The North Coast of Peru, AD 900–1350 17

3. Archaeological Approaches to Peripheries 43

4. Investigating Peripheries: The Site of Cerro la Cruz . . . 59

5. Life on the Edge of the Casma Polity 84

6. The Geopolitical Landscape of the Peruvian Coast in Late Prehistory 149

7. Conclusion: Conquest and Abandonment 175

Notes 187

Glossary 193

References Cited 199

Index 223

Figures

1.1. View of Cerro la Cruz from the south   3
2.1. U-shaped *audiencia* with niches at the site of Chan Chan   24
2.2. Fragment of a Casma Incised olla from Cerro la Cruz (B3R10U1-58)   27
2.3. Drawing of a Casma Molded jar fragment from Cerro la Cruz   30
2.4. Serpentine Appliqué design on a sherd from Cerro la Cruz (SA01-8)   31
2.5. Fragment of a Serpentine Appliqué jar from Cerro la Cruz   32
2.6. Fragment of a Casma-style olla with rope design from Cerro la Cruz (B3R10U1-201)   32
2.7. Georeferenced 2007 Google Earth photograph of El Purgatorio in the Casma Valley   37
2.8. View of El Purgatorio Sector A   38
2.9. View of El Purgatorio Sector B   39
2.10. Georeferenced 1969 aerial photograph of Cerro la Cruz   41
4.1. Georeferenced 1997 aerial photograph of Cerro la Cruz   61
4.2. Ceramic workshop at the base of Compound D3   80
5.1. Compound B3 viewed from the south   88
5.2. Compound D3 viewed from the north   89
5.3. Close-up of Burial 1 in situ (B3R6U1)   93
5.4. Compound B3, Room 10, Unit 1 (B3R10U1) showing restricted access pattern   95
5.5. Compound B3, Room 28, Unit 1 (B3R28U1) with two niches and floor   96
5.6. Compound D3, Room 5, Unit 1 (D3R5U1) showing two niches and Floor 1   97
5.7. Face-neck jar showing Transitional style (B3R6T1-1,2,4)   111
5.8. Face-neck jar resembling the Moche style   112

5.9. Face-neck jar with possible Wari stylistic influence   113
5.10. Sherd showing part of a lizard with incised circle-and-dot motif   114
5.11. Drawing of a sherd with both Casma-style rope design and Chimú-style front-facing god (SA01-1)   115
5.12. Fragment with appliquéd *Spondylus* design   116
5.13. Drawing of a fragment of a kero   116
5.14. Tinaja rim with appliquéd dotted swirl (possibly spotted serpent or other animal tail)   117
5.15. Fragment of a grater   117
5.16. Test3U1 in ceramic workshop showing two firing pits   119
5.17. Fragment of a stirrup-spout mold found in ceramic workshop (SA01-18)   119
5.18. Fragments of mold found in ceramic workshop (SA01-20)   120
5.19. Fragment of mold found outside Wall 2 near ceramic workshop   120
5.20. Exterior of decorated mold found in ceramic workshop (SA01-9)   121
5.21. Interior of decorated mold found in ceramic workshop (SA01-9)   121
5.22. Drawing of decorated mold found in ceramic workshop (SA01-9)   122
5.23. Maker's mark on fragment from D3R1 (D3R1U2-57)   123
5.24. Maker's mark on rim from B3R10 (B3R10U1-172, 221)   124
5.25. Drawing of a wooden harpoon found in Test3U1   132
5.26. Stone pendant of spotted feline with protruding tongue found in Sector D   133
5.27. Decorated spindle whorl (SA01-2)   134
5.28. Plain spindle whorl found in Test2U1   134
5.29. Packet of hair found in Compound B3, Room 12, Unit 1 (B3R12U1)   137
5.30. Compound B3, Room 9, Unit 1 (B3R9U1) showing wall of Terrace 2 with floor   140

Maps

1.1. Map of the north coast of Peru showing the locations of Cerro la Cruz and El Purgatorio 2
1.2. Map of the Chao Valley showing the locations of Cerro la Cruz, Cerro Coronado, Huasaquito, and Cerro Pucarachico 13
2.1. Map of the lower Casma Valley showing the locations of El Purgatorio, Chankillo, and Pampa de las Llamas-Moxeque 36
4.1. Plan view of Cerro la Cruz showing sectors, compounds, and perimeter walls 64
4.2. Detailed map of Compound B3 showing excavation units, tripartite division of space, and access patterns 75
4.3. Detailed map of Compound D3 showing excavation units, tripartite division of space, and access patterns 76

Tables

2.1. Andean Chronology 18

2.2. Results of Accelerator Mass Spectrometry Dating 19

2.3. Sources of Information on the Casma Polity and/or Casma Style 28

2.4. Names for Variations on Casma Polity Ceramic Styles 30

5.1. Surface Ceramics by Section in Compounds B3 and D3 91

5.2. Phases of Compound Construction 104

5.3. Percentage of Each Vessel Form Based on Number of Rim Fragments 110

5.4. Textiles Analyzed and Their Contexts 129

6.1. Presence of Casma Ceramic Style Traits in the Southern Half of the North Coast 151

6.2. Valley Chronologies/Ceramic Styles Relative to Larger Andean Region Chronology 152

Acknowledgments

The funding for this project was provided by generous grants from the National Science Foundation and the Fulbright-Hays Program. My sincere thanks go to my mentor Dr. Carol Mackey and my graduate student David Pacifico for their tireless efforts to assist me with the revising and editing of this volume. I would also like to thank Dr. Jonathan Kent, Ms. Teresa Rosales Tham, Mr. Victor Vásquez Sánchez, and Dr. Alejandro Fernández Honores for their expertise in examining some of the faunal and botanical remains. I am greatly indebted to Ms. Susan Mowery for her skillful analysis of the human skeletal remains from Cerro la Cruz. I would also like to thank Dr. María Jesús Jiménez Díaz for her meticulous and thorough analysis of the textile fragments from Cerro la Cruz.

I thank the people of Buenavista for welcoming my interest in their town and the adjacent site and for their willingness to discuss the history of the area with me. Many Peruvian scholars contributed to the success of this project in the field; I am especially indebted to Luis Coronado, Rocio Sanchez, Silvia Saldivar, and Jorge Gamboa. I would also like to thank my invaluable copy editors, Camille Nelson and Angie Rogers, for their meticulous work; John Powell and Calvin Simmons for their assistance in modifying the maps and drawings; and Andrew King, who assisted with editing and organizational tasks. And I am truly grateful for the support and advice of my colleagues Dr. Mike Coggeshall and Dr. Kinly Sturkie.

Finally, I'd like to thank my family and friends for their enduring support and insistence that I could accomplish this within the time frame I had set for myself. Your love and encouragement helped make this a reality.

1

Introduction

Geopolitical Boundaries in Andean Prehistory

> The archaeologists have certain advantages. They deal with artifacts that not only are not language-bound but by their very nature lead to the classification of societies by similarity of function, not by differences of language and superstructure. Their work throws light on the essentials of economic and social structure at the artifact level of the tools used and the things produced, thus providing a material underpinning for later, chronicled records of the ways in which the products of the society were appropriated and distributed.
>
> Owen Lattimore, "The Frontier in History"

Archaeology offers us a window into the human past that history alone cannot provide. While the prehistoric past may lack the names, dates, and nuances that written documents can offer, this lack of clarity is often outweighed by the abundance of information that can be gleaned from the *other* material remains that people leave behind. Archaeologists tell stories about the distant past that make it more knowable, that bring it within reach. We can tell stories about people who are not represented in historical accounts, who would otherwise be invisible. This is the tale of a little frontier town from the Peruvian past that we now call Cerro la Cruz, and it augments the story of the people who built the town, members of the Casma polity, a group that until recently has remained somewhat neglected and ignored by archaeologists. Recent research on the north coast of Peru is slowly bringing this culture out of the proverbial darkness and into the light of a new understanding for this period in Peruvian prehistory.

This book examines the concepts of frontiers and border zones as types of peripheries and explores the potential insights that these areas can offer to the study of sociopolitical change. To illustrate this premise, I trace the movement of geopolitical boundaries on the north coast of Peru during

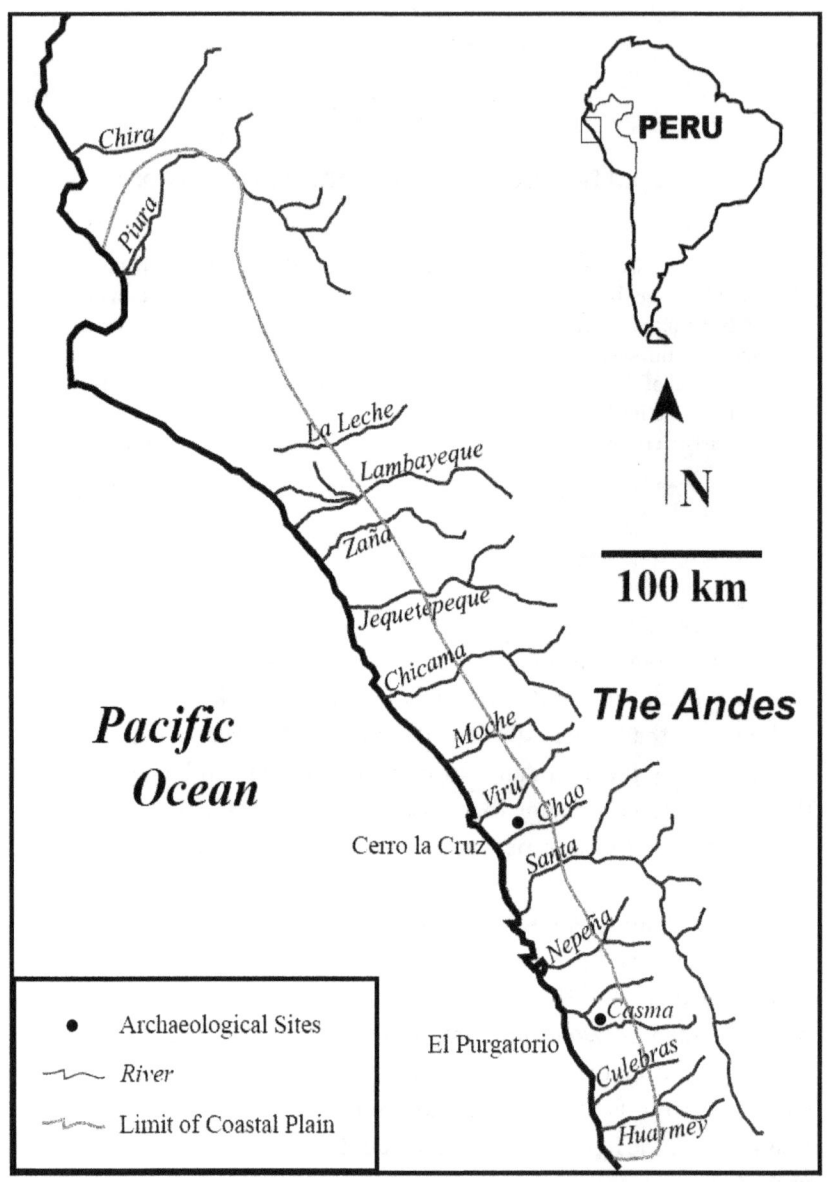

Map 1.1. Map of the north coast of Peru showing the locations of Cerro la Cruz and El Purgatorio (after Mathieu in Vogel 2005).

Figure 1.1. View of Cerro la Cruz from the south with modern fields in the foreground. Photo by author.

an important period of cultural transition (ca. AD 900–1300). Growing evidence suggests that the Casma polity, a previously understudied culture in this region, occupied a significant portion of the coastline, at least as far north as the Chao Valley (map 1.1). The investigation of a Casma hillside settlement, the site of Cerro la Cruz (figure 1.1), indicates that the Chao Valley may have served temporarily as the northern frontier and later as part of the border zone between the Casma and neighboring polities. Excavations at Cerro la Cruz were aimed at two major objectives: to identify the various cultural influences represented on the Casma periphery and to understand everyday life in an ancient frontier town. The results of the investigation at Cerro la Cruz are placed within the regional and temporal context in order to reconstruct the nature of the area's occupation and transformation over time.

Geopolitical Boundaries in Andean Prehistory

In the United States, the phrase "life on the frontier" may bring to mind images of the American West during the period of U.S. expansion, full of gunslingers, outlaws, or perhaps palisaded forts erected in "Indian territory." Similarly, "life in a border town" may evoke images of towns on the U.S.-Mexico border, shaped by both cultures and by people who embody the tension inherent in political boundaries. If one were asked to consider the frontiers and borders of the ancient world, one might envision the castles of medieval Europe, Hadrian's Wall in Scotland, or even the Great Wall of China. When asked to contemplate the rise and fall of great civilizations, one might recall the accomplishments of Alexander the Great, the vast expanse of the Roman Empire, or the domination of Asia by Attila the Hun. But while these civilizations and their achievements are well known, there are other ancient cultures whose accomplishments we are only beginning to understand. The study of these lesser-known cultures is providing new insights into frontier life, this time in South America.

The shape of precolumbian Andean frontiers and borders differs significantly from these Old World examples. More often than not, Andean geopolitical boundaries do not seem to have been marked by walls, and the lack of written documents makes the identification of these areas in the Andean past especially difficult. Similarly, what constitutes a boundary or fortification in the Andes does not appear nearly as impenetrable as the walls of a European medieval castle or walled town. For example, despite the enormous extent of the Inca Empire at its height and the substantial evidence for their militaristic might, the boundaries of their territory do not appear to have been marked by great walls or impressive fortresses but by culturally specific boundary markers such as mountain peaks, when they were marked at all.

After careful study, archaeologists have noted a number of patterns in Andean architecture, site location, and settlement distribution that permit the identification of both core and periphery areas, including frontiers, border zones, and fortifications, from the Andean past (e.g., Burger 2002; D'Altroy 2002; D'Altroy et al. 2000; Dillehay and Gordon 1988; Goldstein 2000; Lau 2001; Patterson 1987; Saloman 1986; Schjellerup 1997; Topic and Topic 1987). The specifics of these indicators differ somewhat by culture and through time, but the careful tracing of these spatial and artifactual patterns can reveal the dynamic movements of precolumbian geopolitical boundaries and allude to the events that caused their expansion and contraction.

Investigating Peripheries through the Archaeological Record

Peripheral areas such as frontiers and border zones are important arenas for archaeological exploration. Identifying and examining these areas can greatly contribute to our understanding of the development and collapse of complex societies. Frontier theory is an important dimension of core/periphery analyses that has received greater attention in recent years, shifting the focus from the core to the periphery. This new perspective on world-systems applications in archaeology provides unique insights into the dynamic movements of political boundaries and the cross-cutting social networks that tend to characterize such areas.

The study of frontiers and border zones not only has relevance for archaeological and historical interpretations of the past, but also holds implications for the modern world. Archaeological studies of political geography in the ancient world can make an important contribution both to our knowledge of the human past and toward understanding the processes of international conflict and change that affect our lives today. This is especially relevant at a time when the secular and religious governments of the world are engaged in violent cultural conflict.

In the Andes, research on prehispanic frontiers has focused primarily on the outlying areas of the Inca Empire, and with reason. The overwhelming majority of ethnohistorical data available in the Andes refers to the Inca Empire, since this polity dominated the Andean region at the time of the Spanish conquest. Much less investigation has been done on peripheral areas in earlier time periods, especially among political entities that are not thought to have reached a state level of organization. One such entity, the Casma polity, is uniquely situated both geographically and temporally to offer significant insight into the dynamics of political geography and Andean peoples' responses to sociopolitical change. The temporal span of the Casma polity covers a period of Peruvian prehistory, most of the Middle Horizon (ca. AD 600–1000) and the Late Intermediate period (ca. AD 1000–1470), about which our understanding has changed dramatically in the last few decades. Of special interest to Andean archaeologists, the transition between the Middle Horizon and the Late Intermediate period appears to be a time of great social and political transformation, as well as a time of increased cultural interaction between coastal and highland cultures. During this period long-distance trade expanded, the Moche and Wari polities collapsed, and the Casma polity expanded to its full extent. Governments composed of loosely allied, semiautonomous city-states, such as the Moche, were eventually replaced by more centralized, hierarchically organized empires such as the Chimú, who conquered most of the north coast during the Late Intermediate period. But in the coastal valleys from Chao south to Huarmey, there has been a gap in our understanding of the regional culture history, a gap we know now was filled by the Casma polity. As a frontier site settled by the Casma at the end of the Middle Horizon, which later became part of a border zone during the Late Intermediate period, the site of Cerro la Cruz provides an important opportunity to further the study of frontiers and border zones during a period of dynamic cultural transition.

Architecture and Spatial Organization as a Manifestation of Sociopolitical Change

Without historical records, the best indicator for tracing the movement of geopolitical boundaries is the built environment. This can be examined at different levels of scale and for changes over time that relate to sociopolitical events. Social and political change often co-occurs in human societies, though for analytical purposes, anthropologists often choose to separate these changes into discrete categories. From a political perspective, I expect fluctuations in leadership and control to have archaeological signatures, such as the expansion and stylistic modification of buildings as well as changes in their functions, including the construction of new buildings and the abandonment of other structures (e.g., Hyslop 1990; Isbell and McEwan 1991). In the social realm, how people choose to organize their living and working spaces shapes the ways in which they organize their lives as individuals and as a community (e.g., Rapoport 1994; Schortman and Nakamura 1991). Modification of spatial organization may reflect changes as simple as the availability of building materials or as complex as the adoption of a new belief system. These explanations are equally significant for understanding how people adjust to or create change. Using the site of Cerro la Cruz as a test case, this study examines the daily operations of a frontier population caught between polities and how this community dealt with changes in power, ideology, or political threats.

Spatial analysis has become an important tool for archaeologists to investigate the past, seeking to understand the meaning, significance, and intentionality behind architectural remains and the use of space (e.g., Lawrence and Low 1990; Steadman 1996). However, this approach has been applied only on a limited basis to the archaeology of the Andes. In the past, Andean archaeology was generally descriptive in its treatment of space, locating architectural and settlement patterns as a method for distinguishing cultural or ethnic groups and their territories. Although identifying these patterns remains an important aspect of architectural analysis, space can also be addressed in terms of cosmology (e.g., Hall 1996; Protzen and Rowe 1994; Zuidema 1983), social inequality (e.g., Moore 1992, 1996b; Pillsbury and Leonard 2004), and political power (e.g., Ashmore 1989; Moore 1996b). For example, in the Inca case, for which ethnohistorical data is available, researchers have used the direct historical approach to link spatial organization with cosmology and social organization, such as the meaning behind the puma shape of the capital city of Cuzco (Protzen and Rowe 1994; Zuidema 1983). Likewise, the Inca *ceque* system linked important landscape features and shrines to Cuzco's Coricancha, or Sun Temple, along radial lines, and this system had sacred, sociopolitical, and ideological implications (Hyslop 1990).

Nonetheless, analytical strategies that reach beyond description rarely have been applied to earlier groups, where the direct historical approach cannot be used to understand the archaeological record. More recent developments in approaches to spatial analysis (e.g., Ingold 1993; Moore 1996a, 1996b, 2005; Rapoport 1994; Smith 2003; Watson and Keating 1999) can provide provocative and creative means to explore earlier Andean perceptions of space and the changes in spatial organization over time. These innovative approaches analyze spatial organization as a means for social control and as an expression of power or ideology, taking into account how spaces would have been experienced as well as the agency involved in planning and utilizing these areas. Architecture and spatial organization can be seen in a variety of ways: as a means to legitimate power and reinforce authority, to replicate a cosmological order, to reinforce or circumvent social classes, to invite or to exclude. While description remains an important aspect of the analytical process, these newer approaches present a more holistic interpretation of ancient peoples' use of space and conception of their built environment.

Importance of Examining Geopolitical Boundaries in Archaeology

In this study, I seek to answer the question of why archaeologists, anthropologists, and other social scientists should examine the movement of geopolitical boundaries in the archaeological past. Adam T. Smith (2003) has already addressed this issue in detail, making a case for the relevance of archaeology's unique view of political landscapes, both prehistoric and historic. He critiqued modern political thought for abandoning the physicality of power and governance in favor of a postmodern focus on the "ephemeral State" (Smith 2003:21). As an alternative, he stressed the importance of understanding the spatiality of ancient states for interpreting the modern political world. In other words, Smith believes that analyses of modern politics would benefit from reflection on both the long-term development of political organization in human history (or prehistory) and the way in which that organization is manifested in the physical landscape. Like many anthropologists, he argued for a more holistic approach to the political, one which recognizes the importance of the spatial dimension for understanding power relationships, legitimization of rule, and the various forms the state has taken over the broad spectrum of time and space.

Smith also examined the constitution of authority through landscapes and the role of landscapes in political relationships. He argued that space is not preexisting, or prior to the social world, but that space emerges in relations between objects (2003:24–25). There is a phenomenological aspect to his approach, one that emphasizes the lived experience of ancient and modern peoples. Although his discussion tends to focus on the workings of government rather than on the everyday lives of its subjects, one could certainly extend his argument for the creation of space to include the activities of the populace and their relationship to the governing body, as I do here. Smith's case studies come from Mesoamerica, the kingdom of Urartu, and Mesopotamia from the Ur III period through the early Babylonian period (2003:26), yet the Andean world also offers a number of excellent opportunities to address these issues.

The analysis presented here focuses on just one subcategory of elements that comprise a political landscape: the geopolitical boundaries found on the periphery of any given polity. Smith's work is not only useful for stressing the importance and relevance of a study such as this for understanding both ancient and modern political organization. It is also useful for contextualizing the dynamics of these peripheral areas within the larger concept of the political landscape. He explained how geopolitical boundaries delimit a political unit in space as distinct from its neighboring polities, certainly a necessary task for prehistoric archaeological work. But he also emphasized the dynamic nature of both geopolitical boundaries and political structure itself. For example, he argued against imposing an absolute spatial ontology onto the Classic Maya political landscape, instead recognizing the use of a variety of political forms at different sites and in different times (Smith 2003:122). In the same way, the precolumbian Andean political landscape seems to present a number of different forms of governance over the course of at least three millennia of complex society. The development of these forms does not necessarily follow a linear path, and it is historically and culturally particular. This study presents a working model for one Andean polity still under investigation, the Casma of Peru's north coast. Understanding this case study may in turn influence our interpretation of other Andean polities, and of the development of complex societies in general.

The Site of Cerro la Cruz: A Case Study

The site of Cerro la Cruz was briefly investigated by two earlier projects (Cárdenas 1976, 1978; Silva 1991, 1992), which suggested that the site was an Early Chimú settlement based on the presence of walled compounds and some blackware ceramic sherds. This interpretation conflicts with the preponderance of Casma-style ceramics I recovered and the radiocarbon dates, which place the occupation of the site during the late Middle Horizon and into the Late Intermediate period (ca. AD 900–1300) and predate the Chimú imperial expansion to the south, which did not begin until at least AD 1300 (Mackey 2009).

Instead of confirming the Early Chimú hypothesis, the next three years of investigation showed that, based on ceramic style, architectural style, and radiocarbon dates, the site of Cerro la Cruz actually marked the northern periphery of the Casma polity. A polity—a distinct politically organized society that extends beyond kinship and ethnic ties but may or may not reach the level of a state—is identified by archaeological indicators such as ceramic styles, architectural styles, mortuary practices, and settlement patterns. Named for the valley to the south where their capital, El Purgatorio, was located, the Casma were one of three polities vying for power along the Peruvian coast during a transitional period between the Middle Horizon and Late Intermediate period. As mentioned above, this era has been interpreted as one of great political and social transformation. During this time, the Chimú state was just forming in the Moche and Chicama valleys to the immediate north, while the Lambayeque polity was already thriving on the far north coast, in an area that extended from the Jequetepeque Valley to the Motupe Valley (map 1.1).

Though the Casma polity preceded the Chimú chronologically, its contribution to state formation and cultural development in the region had yet to be studied. The possibility that the Casma had built Cerro la Cruz had never been tested, so one aspect of this research has been to untangle the archaeological evidence and determine which polity occupied the site. More important, the archaeological remains from Cerro la Cruz give a glimpse of what everyday life was like on the frontier between two large political powers struggling to dominate the north coast of Peru.

Several types of evidence recovered from the site of Cerro la Cruz indicate that it served as part of the Casma periphery. While the predominant forms of material culture conform to what has been identified as Casma style, some artifacts, especially ceramics, indicate a convergence of several cultural influences, as may be expected in a periphery. Defensive features such as perimeter walls with parapets, also common in frontiers and border zones, are found at the site of Cerro la Cruz, suggesting conflict or the potential for conflict with neighboring polities.[1] In addition, regional settlement patterns show that the site is located in a valley with a much lower population density and fewer sites than the Casma heartland farther south.

Research Objectives at Cerro la Cruz

The primary goal of the excavations at Cerro la Cruz was to understand the daily lives of ancient Peruvians in a Casma frontier town and how this site's occupation fit into the sociopolitical events of the time. With an emphasis on the built environment as a physical manifestation of power relationships, this study included the interpretation of continuity and change in the function, style, and meaning of architecture over time, as well as the exploration of the processes behind this continuity and change. This required a diachronic examination of the origin, expansion, and modification of the settlement. In previous research the site of Cerro la Cruz was considered to be primarily a fortification. This classification was based on four criteria: its defensive location, perimeter walls, parapets, and slingstones (Topic and Topic 1978). These architectural developments were linked to the need for defense against invaders, probably from the expanding Chimú state (T. Topic 1990:185).

In this study, however, the fortification premise is considered in light of the new data recovered at the site of Cerro la Cruz. Multiple explanations for the types and functions of architecture at the site are explored, including the administrative, ritual, productive, and consumptive aspects of the site's occupation. The research objectives were designed to explore what the expansion and modification of the architecture at Cerro la Cruz may indicate about sociopolitical change during the Middle Horizon and Late Intermediate period; to interpret the function and meaning of certain architectural features; to investigate the origins of the site and infer the degree of planning involved in its construction; to assess the degree of access control versus freedom of movement across the site; to utilize the ceramic sequence for the dating of architectural features and for indicators of cultural change; and to investigate indications of subsistence through analysis of organic remains and soil samples. Various lines of evidence, including architecture, spatial organization, ceramic and organic analysis, and other artifacts were used to reconstruct the cultural context and interpret the sociopolitical interactions that occurred during the site's occupation.

Everyday Life in the Andean Past

Excavations at Cerro la Cruz revealed a wealth of information on the everyday lives of ancient Peruvians living in the coastal deserts. One of the greatest benefits of working in such a dry climate is that it preserves nearly everything, from desiccated seeds and fruits, textiles and hair, to plaster and paint. The architecture still visible on the surface includes nine compounds (groups of rooms, patios, and/or plazas enclosed by a large exterior wall), four hilltop ceremonial structures, and numerous small residential terraces where commoners lived. Class distinctions between the site's residents are evident in the differential size and durability of construction, the type and quantity of ceramics present, and the differential quality of artifacts found in elite and commoner dwellings.

The compounds at the site of Cerro la Cruz were clearly multifunctional, incorporating space for public, domestic, and ritual activities. The relationship between the compounds and the other architecture at the site is most likely indicative of the social hierarchy of the inhabitants. Higher status families would have resided in compounds, while lower-status families would have made their residences on the outlying terraces. Just as the compounds contained areas for various functions (domestic, administrative, and ritual), so the outlying terraces may have served varied purposes such as areas for sleeping, workshops, and activity areas for the production of textiles, tools, and foodstuffs. A clear distinction appears to have been made between activities that took place inside compounds and those that took place outside.

The people of Cerro la Cruz continued the longstanding Andean tradition of trade between farmers and fisher folk. Although the site is located about 15 km from the sea, I recovered abundant remains of marine resources, including a number of mollusk species, fish, crab, and sea urchin. Agricultural remains were also recovered, including such staples as maize, squash, avocado, and cotton. Though local farmers may have occasionally ventured out to the sea for a day of fishing, most shellfish were probably traded into the site from people living closer to the ocean. I also recovered evidence for camelids, domesticated dogs, and rodents, although the species of rodent could not be determined.

In addition to procuring their own food, the people of Cerro la Cruz made their own cloth and at least some of their ceramics. Evidence for textile production included copper needles, spindle whorls, raw cotton, spun threads, and fragments of cloth. There was even a small ceramic workshop located on the east side of the site, where excavations revealed four firing pits, several molds, polishing stones, and wasters (poorly fired ceramics). Maker's marks on the inside of some vessels suggest that labor was recruited from different social groups. These simple symbols have been interpreted as indicators of distinct work groups who contributed ceramic vessels or, at other sites, adobe bricks as a form of taxation.

In addition to the many artifacts that helped us reconstruct the everyday lives of people at Cerro la Cruz, I found indications of the larger political struggle between the Casma and their neighbors. As the Chimú state grew in power and began to expand, the Chao Valley, perhaps along with its equally small northern neighbor the Virú Valley, became the border zone between the Casma and Chimú territories. In the end, the Casma appear to have lost the political battle, and perhaps an actual military battle as well. The site appears to have been not only abandoned, but also officially closed and ritually cleansed by a burning event, which is described in more detail in chapter 5. The site does not appear to have been settled by the Chimú or the Inca. Thus this periphery became incorporated into the core of the Chimú Empire during the second wave of expansion, which reached south past the Chao to the Casma Valley

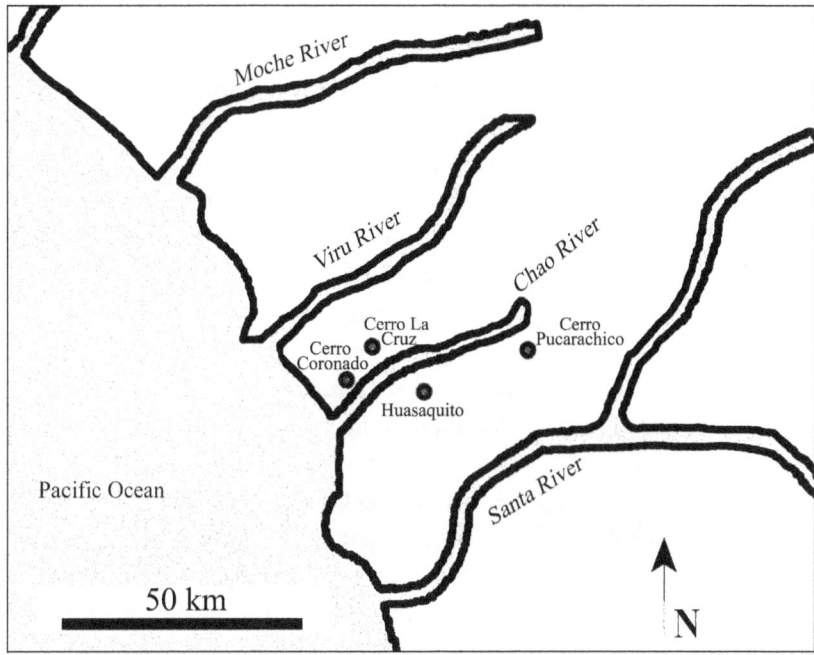

Map 1.2. Map of the Chao Valley showing the locations of Cerro la Cruz, Cerro Coronado, Huasaquito, and Cerro Pucarachico. Map by author.

(Mackey 2009). The Casma polity was subsumed under the dominance of the Chimú Empire, and in its turn the Chimú succumbed eventually to conquest by the Inca Empire.

This investigation of Cerro la Cruz builds upon our knowledge of Andean prehistory and the Casma polity and contributes to our understanding of frontiers and border zones as well as the development of complex societies in general. It addresses the study of peripheries from the perspective of a midsize site in a small valley on the north coast of Peru (map 1.2). Cerro la Cruz is a hillside settlement, one of four such Casma sites in the Chao Valley (figure 1.1, map 1.2). Data from this site combined with regional settlement patterns demonstrate the spread of the Casma polity, whose core was farther south in the Casma Valley, to what was most likely its northernmost extent at the end of the Middle Horizon. The Casma polity appears to have taken advantage of a period of instability on the north coast to incorporate the Chao Valley into its territory, only to later lose the valley to the Chimú state during its southward expansion.

Overview of This Work

The following chapters tell the story of a prehistoric fortified town, Cerro la Cruz, on the periphery of a little-known Andean polity, the Casma. The development of this town is traced along with the shifting geopolitical boundaries of its time and region. The everyday lives of its inhabitants are reconstructed and viewed as a window into the precolumbian Andean lifestyle and the Casma polity more specifically.

In order to further explain why the site of Cerro la Cruz qualifies as a frontier site and how it fits into the political geography of Andean prehistory, the next chapter provides a brief culture history of the north coast during the time of the site's occupation. I provide an overview of our current understanding of the relevant polities involved, primarily the Casma and the Chimú but to a lesser extent also the Wari, the Lambayeque, and the Moche. Chapter 2 also presents a concise summary of our current knowledge of the Casma polity, which is still being defined, as well as a brief overview of the ongoing research at the Casma capital city of El Purgatorio.

I begin chapter 3 by framing the problem of peripheries within the larger theoretical structure of world-systems analysis and its theoretical offspring, core/periphery interactions. I present the concepts of frontiers and border zones as utilized by political geography and archaeology, demonstrating the utility of Lightfoot and Martinez's (1995) frontier approach for the study of precapitalist states and polities. Chapter 3 also reviews other archaeological approaches to the study of peripheries, discussing political geography and briefly summarizing our current knowledge of frontiers in the Andean past, including their archaeological indicators. At the end of this chapter, the importance of the built environment for the frontier approach is revisited and my case study, the site of Cerro la Cruz, is introduced.

Chapter 4 situates the site of Cerro la Cruz within the geographic context of the Chao Valley and the natural resources available there. Here I provide a physical description of the site and analyze possible reasons for the site's location on a terraced hillside. Once the study of Cerro la Cruz has been oriented in time and space, I describe the methods used to investigate prehistoric frontiers and border zones in archaeology and how these were applied at Cerro la Cruz. These details are critical for understanding the validity of the case study and its applicability to case studies in other regions.

Once the context of this research has been described, the results of investigations at the site of Cerro la Cruz and the implications of this data for understanding the everyday lives of ancient Andean people are detailed in chapter 5. This chapter answers several central questions regarding life on the frontier and examines the archaeological evidence for the dynamic movements of the Casma frontier over time. The function and meaning of the site's compounds are discussed, including the evidence for an internal tripartite division of space. The perimeter walls and other noncompound architectural features are also examined. I synthesize the evidence for ritual, production, and consumption at the site and discuss the evidence for the site's previous characterization as a fortification. Finally, chapter 5 describes the evidence for the ritual termination event that accompanied the site's desertion.

In chapter 6 each of the valleys that comprised the Casma polity's territory is discussed individually and situated within the wider context of the regional culture history of the Middle Horizon and the Late Intermediate period on the north coast. The issue of interpolity relations with the highland Wari state is also addressed, as is the nature of the Casma polity's dynamic relationship with the emerging Chimú state. The intention of this chapter is not only to understand sociopolitical change during this transitional period on the north coast but also to suggest the potential benefits of cross-cultural comparison between this case study and other Andean or non-Andean societies for understanding peripheries and the people who inhabited them. The movement of geopolitical boundaries on the north coast of Peru can be compared to interpolity interactions in the Andean highlands and in other regions of the world.

The final chapter traces the trajectory of the site's establishment, occupation, and abandonment. I relate how the results of this investigation at Cerro la Cruz are relevant to our understanding of both Andean prehistory and other ancient peripheries. The importance of studying sociopolitical change in peripheral areas, even among lesser known prehistoric polities, is discussed as an important source of anthropological insights into state formation and development.

The study of peripheral areas such as frontiers and border zones can greatly contribute to our understanding of the forces behind the development and collapse of complex societies. These areas present a unique challenge to archaeologists since frontier sites often reflect the intersection of multiple social and political groups. Frontiers and border zones can also provide unique insights into the movements of political boundaries over time.

The research presented here utilized the site of Cerro la Cruz in the Chao Valley of Peru as a case study to investigate sociopolitical change on the periphery and the dynamic nature of geopolitical boundaries. To understand the multivariate aspects of life on the frontier, I employed stylistic and spatial analysis from a diachronic perspective on a regional scale to identify the various cultural influences represented in the archaeological record and to reconstruct the nature of the area's occupation and transformation over time. The artifacts recovered from Cerro la Cruz paint a picture of life on the frontier of the Casma polity, revealing the cross-cultural influences that shaped the lives and identities of the site's inhabitants. This study provides new insights into a relatively unknown cultural group, the Casma polity, during a period of cultural transition and political instability. In addition, this research enhances our knowledge of border zones and frontiers, and the roles they play in the interpolity dynamics of precapitalist states.

2

A Time and Place of Transition

The North Coast of Peru, AD 900–1350

In order to establish that Cerro la Cruz was a frontier settlement of the Casma polity, one must first consider the political and cultural landscape of its time. The north coast of Peru during the tenth, eleventh, and twelfth centuries AD was a place of great cultural transition. This era witnessed the fall of the Wari, an expansionist state in the Peruvian highlands, as well as the rise of the Chimú state on the north coast. Archaeologists used to believe that the Wari had conquered much of the north coast as well as the south coast during their reign (approximately AD 600–1000). However, more recent research on the north coast has failed to provide evidence of Wari occupation. Instead, more attention is now being paid to polities—such as the Lambayeque, the Chimú, and the Casma (e.g., Dulanto 2008; Mackey 2009; Vogel 2005)—that controlled the north coast from the late Middle Horizon and into Late Intermediate period. While much of this research is ongoing (e.g., Brown Vega 2008, 2009; Prządka and Giersz 2003; Prządka-Giersz 2009; Vogel 2011), it has the potential to essentially rewrite our current understanding of the events of this period. Keeping in mind that our understanding is in flux, this chapter provides a brief synopsis of north coast culture history as it is currently interpreted during the chronological periods that Cerro la Cruz was occupied, the Middle Horizon (ca. AD 600–1000) and Late Intermediate period (ca. AD 1000–1470). My focus is on the valleys that are most relevant to this analysis—those in the southern half of this region, which includes the Moche, Virú, Chao, Santa, Nepeña, and Casma valleys. Since previous ideas about Cerro la Cruz associated it with the Chimú polity, it is especially important to review the evidence for the Chimú imperial expansion. This is followed by an overview of both past and current research on the Casma

Table 2.1. Andean Chronology

Period name	Approximate dates
Preceramic period	?–1800 BC
Initial period	1800–900 BC
Early Horizon	900–200 BC
Early Intermediate period	200 BC–AD 600
Middle Horizon	AD 600–1000
Late Intermediate period	AD 1000–1470
Late Horizon	AD 1470–1532
Colonial period	AD 1532–1826

Note: After Rowe 1960; Silverblatt 1987; Keatinge 1988.

polity, with special attention given to the proposed Casma capital city of El Purgatorio.

The Temporal Setting: Andean Chronology

The division of Andean culture history into horizons and intermediate periods has been used to distinguish periods of relative stability dominated by a few major polities (the horizons) from those of instability and greater sociopolitical change (the intermediate periods) (table 2.1) (Covey 2008; Keatinge 1988; Rowe 1960). Several Andeanists have pointed out that the provisions upon which this chronology was developed are no longer supported by archaeological evidence (e.g., Mackey 1982; Topic 1991; Willey 1999). A revision of this chronology is in order for both Andean culture history on the north coast and conceptions of Andean sociopolitical change in general. However, until this chronology is replaced by another common standard, it serves as a useful framework for intersite comparison (Covey 2008:288).

Although the Chao Valley has been occupied continuously from the Preceramic period through the present day, the radiocarbon dates collected by this project (table 2.2) confirmed that Cerro la Cruz was occupied during only two periods of prehistory, the Middle Horizon and the Late Intermediate period, specifically from approximately AD 900 to 1300. The following sections discuss past chronological models for these periods and how they are being modified by the results of more recent fieldwork, so that the results of this research at Cerro la Cruz can in turn be placed within the context of the regional culture history.

Table 2.2. Results of Accelerator Mass Spectrometry Dating

Lab sample ID	Sample location	Material	^{14}C age (BP)	Calibrated ages 1-sigma	2-sigma
Z2044A	B3R3U1-L6	Charcoal	824 ± 45	AD 1165–1264	AD 1066–1282
Z2046A	B3R3U1-L8	Charcoal	1004 ± 31	AD 1001–1028	AD 984–1152
Z2047A	B3R6U1-L2	Charcoal	832 ± 30	AD 1190–1256	AD 1160–1276
Z2048A	B3R6U2X2-L3	Charcoal	944 ± 30	AD 1025–1158	AD 1020–1185
Z2052	B3R9U1X1-L5	Charcoal	833 ± 30	AD 1189–1256	AD 1160–1276
Z2051A	B3R9U1X1-L9	Charcoal	901 ± 30	AD 1042–1206	AD 1031–1217
Z2054A	B3R11U1-L4	Charcoal	1042 ± 35	AD 984–1019	AD 898–1035
Z2049A	B3R11U2-L5	Charcoal	943 ± 58	AD 1021–1162	AD 990–1220
Z2043A	D3C3U1-L2	Charcoal	749 ± 41	AD 1259–88	AD 1216–99
Z2045A	D3R4U1-L2	Charcoal	944 ± 54	AD 1021–1162	AD 996–1218
Z2053	D3R7U1-L1	Charcoal	813 ± 30	AD 1213–63	AD 1164–1279
Z2050A	D3R2aU1-L2	Charcoal	819 ± 30	AD 1211–61	AD 1163–1278

Note: Dates were calibrated with the program INTCAL-98 (Stuvier et al. 1998).

The Middle Horizon

The Middle Horizon has been characterized as "an era of profound cultural change" (Moseley 1992:209). Various factors, such as severe El Niño weather phenomena followed by an extensive drought (demonstrated by ice core evidence) and a proliferation of fortified and defensively located settlements, contribute to our understanding of this period as a time of shifting alliances and instability.

Traditional models had posited that a group of highland people called the Wari gained control over much of the north coast through military conquest, beginning around AD 600 (e.g., Isbell 1977; Isbell and McEwan 1991; McEwan 1990; Menzel 1964; Schreiber 1987, 1992). The Wari polity has been described as an "extensive" state (Moseley 1992:216) or even as an empire (e.g., Cook 1986; Isbell and McEwan 1991; McEwan 1990; Menzel 1964, 1977; Schreiber 1987, 1992; Stone-Miller and McEwan 1990/1991) that established administrative centers among dispersed local populations through the dissemination of a new agricultural technique, irrigated terracing. The military conquest model was generally supported throughout the 1960s, and notions of Wari state dominance on the north coast were rarely challenged until fairly recently (e.g., Bawden and Conrad 1982; Mackey 1982). However, further research at sites on the north coast has raised questions about the nature and extent of the Wari presence on the north coast (e.g., Jennings 2006; Topic 1991; Vogel 2003). The degree to which changes in ceramic and architectural styles on the north coast can be attributed to Wari state influence has been greatly debated (e.g., McEwan 1990; Pillsbury and Leonard 2004). Several authors (e.g., Conklin 1990; Mackey 1982; Pillsbury and Leonard 2004) have emphasized the continuity of north coast architectural styles, noting that features such as walled enclosures, once thought to have resulted from Wari influence, actually predate the Middle Horizon at sites such as Huaca de la Luna and Galindo and are the result of local architectural developments.

Instead of direct and complete authority, the relationship between coastal and highland populations may have been centered on trade and ideology (Jennings 2006; Shady 1982; Topic 1991), with either indirect Wari control (Isbell 1988) or multiple independent regional centers (Bawden and Conrad 1982; Mackey 1982) that were in contact with the Wari but not under their control. Politically speaking, the north coast was not dominated by any form of centralized control during this period, suggesting greater competition among lower-level elites and independent polities (Bawden 1996). The Wari polity did not survive beyond the Middle Horizon, and the capital city of Wari was abandoned by AD 1000 (Isbell 2008).

While the origins and development of the Casma polity are still under investigation (Vogel and Vilcherrez 2008, 2009; Vogel, Falcón, and Pacifico 2010), it seems likely that they arose in the Casma Valley during the Middle Horizon (Fung and Williams 1977; Vogel 2003; Wilson 1995). However, the absence of an earlier Moche occupation in the Casma Valley, despite its presence in neighboring valleys, is significant for probing the origins of the Casma polity (Collier 1962; Moseley 2001). At its height, the Moche polity consisted of two separate regions. The northern region was comprised of the Piura, Motupe, Lambayeque, Zaña, and Jequetepeque valleys, while the southern region included the Chicama, Moche, Virú, Chao, Santa, and Nepeña valleys (Castillo 2001:307). The debate over the political organization of the Moche state has developed significantly in the last two decades as more fieldwork has been conducted, but there is still no true consensus. There remains a distinct need for more field research in the southern Moche region, which has traditionally been characterized as a conquest state (e.g., Chapdelaine 2008, 2010). For the moment, the best model seems to be one of individual valley states united by culture and perhaps language, but without a strong, centralized authority.[1]

It appears that during the Middle Horizon, the Moche polity retreated from the southernmost valleys but still occupied the northern half of their territory as well as the important Moche Valley site of Huacas de Moche into the seventh and eighth centuries AD (Chapdelaine 2010). Bawden (1996:264–75) credits the Moche polity collapse to three major factors: environmental catastrophe, foreign pressure from the Wari polity, and internal social stress. One possible source of this internal stress, at least in the southern valleys, could be the emergence of the Casma polity.

About the time of the Moche collapse, another important polity emerged on the far north coast and continued to develop contemporaneously with the Casma polity. Centered in the Lambayeque region, the Sicán polity (also referred to as the Lambayeque polity and often, in the past, confused with the Chimú state) has been the subject of extensive research by Shimada's Sicán Archaeological Project since 1978. Although the exact origins of the polity are still unclear, Shimada has developed a three-phase chronology from approximately AD 800 to 1375 that traces the rapid rise of Sicán to a period of impressive cultural florescence known as the Middle Sicán period (Shimada 2000). The Sicán polity is credited with the revivalist building of enormous platform mounds, the expansion of trade networks into Columbia and the Amazon, and the development of innovative metallurgical techniques. Shimada (2000:61) argued that this was a centralized state with distinct social classes and that it maintained control over multiple modes of resource exploitation. While its demise may have begun with internal dissension, the Sicán/Lambayeque state did not collapse until, like the Casma, it was conquered by the Chimú during the fourteenth century AD.

The Late Intermediate Period

By the beginning of the Late Intermediate period, the Moche and Wari polities had both collapsed. Moseley (2001) pointed out the significant environmental changes that took place and their effects on human adaptation, especially the extended drought that began shortly after AD 1100 and continued until AD 1500. This drought was particularly important in coastal valleys such as the Chao, which have a limited water supply in years of average rainfall and would therefore have been even more vulnerable to such a long period of drought.

The emergence of the highly centralized Chimú state at the end of the Middle Horizon represented a dramatic change from the previous few hundred years of dynamic political tension. The Chimú consolidated first the Moche, Chicama, and Virú valleys (approximately AD 900–1300), then, through the conquest of the Lambayeque polity to its north and the Casma polity to its south, it became the largest and most stable polity in the Andes at the time (Mackey 2009; Moore and Mackey 2008). Chimú political organization was by far the most centralized form of government yet practiced on the coast and perhaps in the Andean region—exceeded only by the Inca Empire, which struggled long and hard to conquer them. Based on Spanish accounts documenting indigenous oral histories, we can date the Inca conquest of the kingdom of Chimor to ca. AD 1470 (Mackey and Klymyshyn 1990; Moore and Mackey 2008; Rowe 1948). Once the Inca captured the north coast, no other local polity was able to gain a foothold there before the Spanish conquest of Peru, which was only sixty years later.

Although we still know relatively little about the Casma polity, evidence from the site of Cerro la Cruz and the large center of El Purgatorio in the Casma Valley suggests that this culture survived through the fourteenth century, far into the Late Intermediate period (Vogel 1999, 2000, 2011; Vogel and Coronado 2001; Vogel and Vilcherrez 2009 [2007]). The polity was at least partially subsumed under the Chimú Empire by AD 1350, and it completely collapsed shortly thereafter. Exactly how this decline took place, though, requires further study at Casma polity sites in their core area, the Casma Valley.[2] The frontier site of Cerro la Cruz provides an important opportunity to investigate how sociopolitical change occurring during the late Middle Horizon and Late Intermediate period affected Casma communities on the north coast of Peru.

The Emergence of the Chimú Empire

Thankfully, our understanding of the Chimú polity and its sociopolitical organization is much more complete than that of the Casma polity, if not entirely comprehensive. Many Andean archaeologists have contributed to our knowledge of Chimú culture, religion, sociopolitical organization, and imperial expansion.[3] This section concentrates on the most salient topics for understanding the Chimú-Casma connection: the geographic and temporal range of the Chimú Empire, its identifying characteristics (especially its architectural and ceramic styles), and its political organization. My bias is toward the development and expansion of the imperial phase, the period most relevant to the research at Cerro la Cruz.

Geographic and Temporal Extent

The Chimú developed the largest and most centralized state on the north coast of Peru, eclipsed only by the Inca, who conquered them in approximately AD 1470 (Mackey 2009; Mackey and Klymyshyn 1990; Moseley 2001). Ethnohistorical sources state that at its fullest extent, the Chimú Empire stretched from the Tumbes Valley in the north to the Chillon Valley in the south. This constitutes a distance of approximately 1,000 km, encompassing two-thirds of the coastal population (Moseley 1990:1). However, archaeological evidence indicates the presence of Chimú state power from the Motupe Valley to the Casma Valley but remains ambiguous for the outermost valleys (Mackey 2009; Mackey and Klymyshyn 1990:207, 219). The beginnings of the Chimú state can be traced back to approximately AD 1000 in the Moche Valley, where the capital of Chan Chan is located. Mackey and Klymyshyn (1990) also include the Chicama and Virú valleys when describing the central area, or core of the empire.

Chimú Style: Architecture and Ceramics

From a stylistic viewpoint, distinctive indicators of Imperial Chimú group affiliation have been identified in architecture, ceramics (both fineware and utilitarian wares), iconography, textile technology, and mortuary practices. Many of these stylistic attributes evolved from long-term cultural continuities on the north coast but were codified into a distinct Chimú style during the consolidation of the state. For example, the trademark architectural feature of Chimú architecture is a U-shaped structure with niched walls called an *audiencia* (figure 2.1). Other typical Chimú-style architectural features include high-walled adobe compounds with baffled entries, pilastered doorways, entry plazas, restricted access patterns, and labyrinth-like passageways (Keatinge 1982:199; Moore 1996b; Moseley 1975).

In terms of ceramic style, press-molded blackware is typical of Chimú

Figure 2.1. U-shaped *audiencia* with niches at the site of Chan Chan. Photo by author.

fineware, while carinated rims are the hallmark of utilitarian ollas (Collier 1955:111; Topic and Moseley 1983). Chimú-style ceramics are predominantly mold-made and, thereby, mass produced. Stirrup-spout bottles are a common vessel form, often with a small monkey or lug located at the juncture of spout and stirrup. Surface decoration generally involved low-relief press molding, one of the most common being stipples of various sizes. Vessels may be highly burnished but are rarely slip painted (Donnan 1992:96). Flat-bottomed plates appear to have originated on the north coast with the Chimú state. Other popular vessel forms include jars, bowls, and spout-and-handle bottles (Donnan 1992:96).

Unlike the Moche style that preceded it, Chimú art is rarely narrative, focusing instead on repeated patterns of zoomorphic, anthropomorphic, or geometric forms (Pillsbury 1997:182). Its iconography becomes highly restricted as the Chimú state becomes an empire, focusing on only four major deities from the state religion: the staff god, the two-tasseled headdress god, the goddess, and the moon animal (Mackey 2001). Mackey (2001:138) pointed out that Chimú imagery is much more standardized than that of earlier north coast styles, and that its deities take on a more human appearance. Chimú-style ceramic vessels also depict maritime themes such as fish, waves, pelicans, and *Spondylus* shells (Pillsbury 1997).

This artistic canon applies to other media as well, including textile designs, metal objects, and adobe friezes on compound walls. Ethnohistorical documents confirm the importance of the sea and the moon goddess in north coast religion at the time of the Inca conquest, which may explain the predominance of maritime themes (e.g., Anton 1972:67, McClelland 1990:75; Rowe 1948). But these themes also reflect larger regional continuities which can also be found in the late Moche and Lambayeque art styles (Mackey 2001:134).

Chimú Political Organization

Scholars have also given a great deal of attention to the political organization of the Chimú state. It appears to have been the second most centrally organized polity in the precolonial Andes, surpassed only by the Inca Empire, which followed it and made use of its administrative achievements to rule the north coast. The Chimú state religion is reflected in the production of ceramics, textiles, wooden implements, and metal objects depicting a limited pantheon of deities. Evidence for state-sponsored ceremonies is also found in the architectural models that show rituals taking place in large enclosed plazas, such as those found in the capital city of Chan Chan.

According to ethnohistorical documents (Rowe 1948; Cabello Balboa [1586] 1951; Calancha 1638), expansion to the north and south occurred in two major waves. However, archaeological evidence recovered from Chimú administrative centers has revised the chronological sequence for imperial expansion. Radiocarbon dates from the site of Farfán in the Jequetepeque Valley suggest that the northern valleys were conquered around AD 1300 (Mackey 2009), soon followed by the southern expansion through the Casma Valley. Mackey and Klymyshyn's (1990) research at the site of Manchan indicated that the Chimú state conquered the Casma Valley by AD 1350 (Mackey 2009). In addition, no Chimú administrative centers have been found in the valleys south of the Casma Valley, so the degree to which the southernmost valleys were integrated into the empire remains questionable (Mackey 2009; Mackey and Klymyshyn 1990:207). Radiocarbon dates from the Lambayeque Valley indicate that the northernmost valleys were not conquered until after AD 1350 (Shimada 1990:313) and may thus represent a third stage of expansion (Mackey 2009).

Defining the Casma Polity: Previous Research

Determining how the lesser-known Casma polity fits into this regional culture history is an ongoing project, but our knowledge of this culture is growing rapidly and adding to the dispersed contributions of previous scholars. Prior to the completion of this research at Cerro la Cruz, only surface survey and test excavations had been completed at any Casma polity site. Few publications refer to the Casma as a polity instead of just a ceramic style (e.g., Collier 1962; Conlee et al. 2004; Daggett 1983; Fung and Williams 1977; Mackey 2009; Tello 1956; Vogel 2003, 2011; Vogel and Vilcherrez 2009 [2007]; Wilson 1995). One goal of this research is to amplify and define our understanding of the Casma polity. This section synthesizes what is known about the Casma polity and style to form a preliminary model for the constitution of the Casma polity and to identify archaeological indicators of a Casma polity presence.

Geographic and Temporal Extent

Thus far the Casma polity appears to be coastal, occupying only the *chala*[4] and low-altitude *yungas*.[5] However, further investigation must be conducted to verify what connection, if any, the Casma polity maintained with the highlands. Mackey and Klymyshyn (1990) suggested that the Casma polity extended from the Chao Valley south to the Huarmey Valley, a distance of approximately 300 km. This would make the Chao Valley (possibly along with its equally small neighbor, the Virú Valley) the northern border between the Casma polity and the emerging Chimú state. If this is correct, Cerro la Cruz may have been first a frontier outpost and later part of a border zone for the Casma polity, linked to a southern core in the Casma Valley.

The temporal limits of the Casma polity's existence also remain largely undefined. Researchers have generally referred to it as a Middle Horizon (ca. AD 600–1000) culture (Daggett 1983; Mackey and Klymyshyn 1990; Tello 1956; Wilson 1988, 1995) that persisted into the Late Intermediate period (Fung and Williams 1977). These temporal designations are based primarily upon relative dating of the Casma Incised and Casma Molded ceramic styles found at various sites, but not in combination with other lines of evidence or absolute dating techniques. In contrast, the research at the site of Cerro la Cruz focused exclusively on a Casma polity site, using multiple artifact classes and producing absolute dates in association with these artifacts. In addition, ongoing research at the Casma capital city of El Purgatorio has produced radiocarbon dates of approximately AD 700–1400 (calibrated, 2-sigma, see Vogel 2011:Table 2.23).

Casma Incised and Casma Molded Ceramic Styles

Nearly all the information currently published regarding the Casma polity focuses exclusively on the ceramic styles, which nevertheless require further definition and clarification (tables 2.3 and 2.4). Tello (1956) was the first to coin the term "Casma style" during his survey of the Casma Valley. He was also the first to describe the site of El Purgatorio, the proposed capital of the Casma polity. His classifications of ceramic styles have since been revised and refined, but his pioneering survey provided the foundation upon which further research was based. Collier (1962) then divided the Casma style into two types, Casma Incised and Casma Modeled (also known as Casma Molded; figures 2.2 and 2.3), and equated

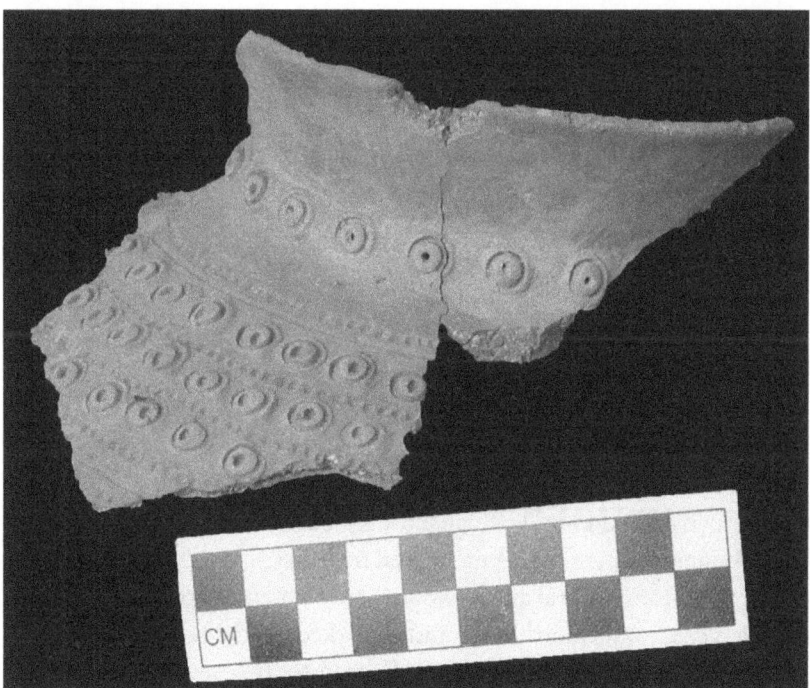

Figure 2.2. Fragment of a Casma Incised olla from Cerro la Cruz (B3R10U1-58). Photo by author.

Table 2.3. Sources of Information on the Casma Polity and/or Casma Style

Author	Subject of publication	Information on ceramic style
Tello 1956	Survey of Casma Valley	Photographs, drawings, and description
Collier 1962[a]	Survey of Casma Valley	Drawings and description
Fung and Pimentel 1973[b]	Chankillo site in Casma Valley	Brief description
Fung and Williams 1977	Survey of Sechín Valley	Photographs and description
Cárdenas 1976/1978 (illustration in 1979 and 1998)	Survey of Chao Valley	No drawings or descriptions in 1976/1978, but a few in 1998
Daggett 1983	Survey of Nepeña Valley	Drawings and description
Wilson 1988[c]	Survey of Santa Valley	Drawings and description—name differs
Mackey and Klymyshyn 1990[d]	Chimú Empire in Casma Valley	Brief mention, no illustrations
Wilson 1995[e]	Survey of Casma Valley	Named but no illustrations

[a]Divides Casma Incised and Casma Molded ceramic styles.
[b]Links Casma culture with Casma ceramic style.
[c]Refers to the Casma polity as the "Black-White-Red State."
[d]Suggests extent of Casma territory is from Chao to Huarmey Valleys.
[e]No name given to state.

them with Kroeber's (1944) "Sechín style." Collier also related Tello's Santa and Huaylas Yunga styles to the Black-White-Red style (1962:415), which Collier considered to be Tiahuanaco-derived.

Although neither the Casma Incised nor Casma Molded style has been studied in depth, several archaeologists have noted its presence at Middle Horizon sites on the north coast and remarked on its characteristics. Fung and Williams (1977) linked Casma Incised to Thompson's (1966) Huarmey Incised style, as well as to a Nepeña Valley style that Proulx (1968,

Information on architectural style	Information on site layout	Information on settlement patterns	Information on political organization
Brief description of El Purgatorio, no drawings/maps	—	—	—
—	—	—	—
—	—	—	—
Brief description, no drawings	3 site maps	Map of sites on Sechín branch	Secular state
—	—	Map of all sites in valley	—
—	—	Does not list the sites surveyed, only a map	—
Brief description, no drawings	3 site maps	Maps and description	State, El Purgatorio as capital
—	—	Mention seven Casma sites but no map or names	Unified polity, El Purgatorio as capital
—	—	Maps and description	El Purgatorio as capital

1973) referred to as Huari Norteño B. There appear to be local variations on the Casma style in each valley, but I focus primarily on descriptions of ceramics found in the heartland of the Casma polity, the Casma Valley, for comparison with those found at the site of Cerro la Cruz, on the periphery.

In his work on the Casma Valley, Collier (1962) described Casma Incised pottery as redware, primarily ollas decorated with incision, punctation, stamped designs such as circles and dots, and various appliquéd

Table 2.4. Names for Variations on Casma Polity Ceramic Styles

Ceramic style	Provenience by valley	Publication
Corral Incised, San Nicolas Molded, San Juan Molded, Black-White-Red, Guañape	Virú	Collier 1955
Tanguche, Black-White-Red	Santa	Wilson 1988
Huari Norteño B, Nepeña Black-White-Red	Nepeña	Proulx 1973
Serpentine Appliqué	Nepeña	Daggett 1983
Sechín	Sechín	Kroeber 1944
Casma, Santa, Huaylas Yunga	Casma	Tello 1956
Casma Incised, Casma Modeled, Black-White-Red	Casma	Collier 1962
Huarmey Incised	Huarmey	Thompson 1966

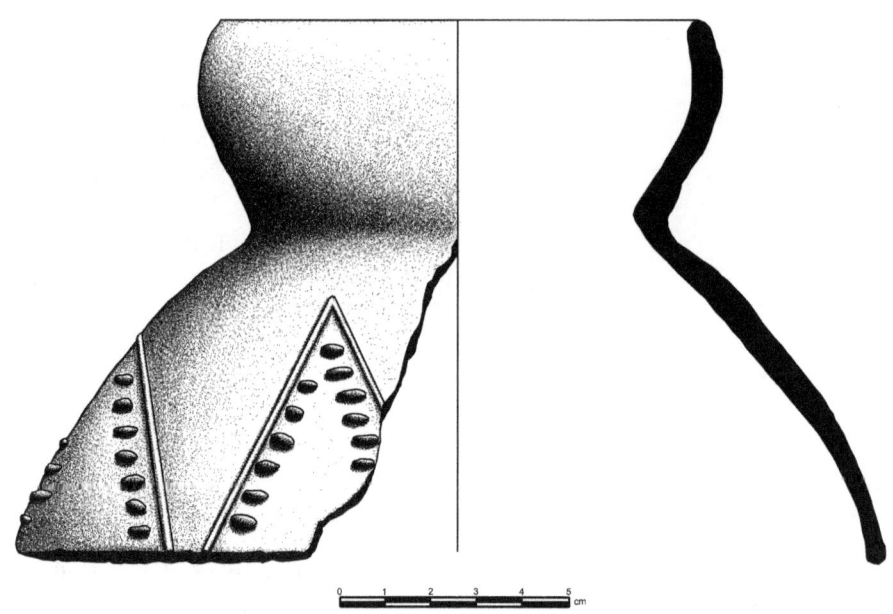

Figure 2.3. Drawing of a Casma Molded jar fragment from Cerro la Cruz. Figure drawn by author.

Figure 2.4. Serpentine Appliqué design on a sherd from Cerro la Cruz (SA01-8). Photo by author.

bumps, serpents, and zoomorphic adornos (modeled figures that have been applied to the vessel), such as the common "rope design" around the neck (figures 2.2–2.6). Daggett (1983) generally agreed with this description based on the sample she gathered from the Nepeña Valley. Her sample included 200 rims, but she did not specify from which sites they were collected. She stated that the distinguishing feature of Casma Incised jars was the treatment of the rim. Flared rims were the most common type in her sample, followed by lipped-flare rims and, lastly, short, incurving rims (Daggett 1983:213). She also described small, thick handles attached to the shoulders of jars and rim decorations such as appliquéd nodules, rope designs, and short incised lines. One important detail Daggett mentioned is that adornos most frequently take the shape of a bird.

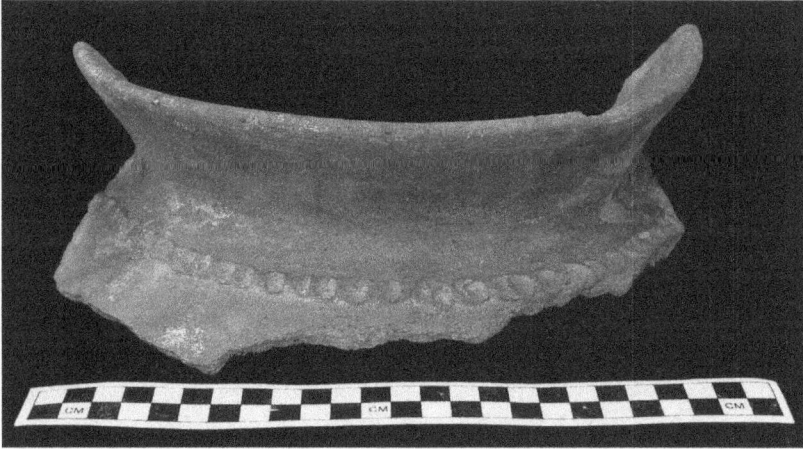

Figure 2.5. Fragment of a Serpentine Appliqué jar from Cerro la Cruz. Photo by author.

Figure 2.6. Fragment of a Casma-style olla with rope design from Cerro la Cruz (B3R10U1-201). Photo by author.

Daggett classified a portion of her sample as a separate type called Serpentine Appliqué, whereas I would include these designs as a subset of the broader Casma style.[6] She described Serpentine Appliqué as a red-brown utilitarian ware similar to Casma Incised in several ways: the primary vessel form is the jar, similar handles are also applied to the shoulder, and the rims fall into the same three categories. Serpentine Appliqué style differs from Casma Incised only in the type and placement of design and in the slight burnish that some sherds show. Designs consist of appliqués in a crescent or S shape on which small circles are incised, giving a spotted serpent appearance (figures 2.4 and 2.5). These appliqués are placed on the shoulder but do not extend from rim to handle as they do on Casma Incised jars. Daggett notes that Serpentine Appliqué is found with red press-molded ware and a Black-White-Red painted ware, but in limited distribution. Black-White-Red painted ware is probably also a fineware variation of Casma style, but examples of this style were not found in our investigation at Cerro la Cruz.

Fung and Williams (1977) remarked on the ubiquity of Casma Incised ceramics in their survey of the Sechín branch of the Casma Valley. They conducted a settlement pattern survey of ten sites with limited excavation. Their interest focused primarily on Initial period and Early Horizon sites, but they also provided a more comprehensive discussion of the Casma polity, identifying possible Casma sites and architectural features and speculating about their political organization. Significantly, Fung and Williams (1977) pointed out that many of the simple designs incorporated into the Casma style have antecedents in Chavín-style designs of the Early Horizon. Indeed, the principal design element of Casma Incised style consists of a deeply impressed dot within a circle (figure 2.2), sometimes referred to as an "eye" or "jaguar spot." This design seems to have extremely long-term continuity and widespread distribution along the coast of Peru, further complicating attempts to refine the definition of the Casma style.

Architecture and Settlement Patterns

Fung and Williams linked several architectural elements to Casma architectural style. These elements include carefully planned compounds with internal subdivisions, platforms, and rectangular patios connected by a system of terraces (Fung and Williams 1977:138). They attributed to the Casma polity the sites of Huanchay[7] and Cahuacucho, both of which are located on terraced hillsides. Fung and Williams also noted construction techniques at various sites that correspond to those found at Cerro la Cruz, including thick stone walls and walls that appear to be made of adobe but actually have stone foundations (1977:126). Moreover, structures in some cases are agglutinated, or connected to one another, but in other cases are free standing.[8]

Previously, Wilson (1995) was the only author to discuss Casma polity settlement patterns, although he never refers to the Casma polity by name. According to his survey, the periods dominated by the Casma polity (the Choloque and Casma periods) were the most populous periods in the prehistory of the Casma Valley (see also Thompson 1964:95). He estimates 245 occupations for the Choloque period (ca. AD 650–900) and 387 occupations for the Casma period (ca. AD 900–1100). Wilson suggests that these periods show a "distinct hierarchy of site size and function," with the site of El Purgatorio as the first-tier settlement in the Casma Valley (1995:204). His findings are discussed in more detail in the interregional comparison in chapter 6, but one important result must be mentioned here as a possible archaeological signature of the Casma polity: the increase in fortified and defensively located sites associated with the Casma periods in the Casma Valley. This may be a pattern for Casma polity site location, a pattern illustrated by the location and fortifications of Cerro la Cruz.

Opinions on the population size of the Casma polity vary widely among scholars. Due to the absence of large pyramidal mounds or evidence for a Moche occupation during the Early Intermediate period (ca. 200 BC–AD 600), Collier (1962) argued that the Casma Valley was largely unoccupied during this time. Yet immediately following this period there seems to be a Middle Horizon peak in population on the southern north coast, which could be due to the growth of the Casma polity (Proulx 1973:66; Thompson 1964:92). Wilson (1995) also associated the Casma polity with a peak in the population of the Casma Valley but does not give specific population estimates.

Casma Political Organization

Conceptualizations of Casma polity political organization are also conflicting. Whether this was a highly centralized political organization or a loose confederation of local elites from different valleys is still under investigation. My impression based on the data collected thus far is that the Casma polity was more hegemonic than territorial, that they recruited and incorporated local elites into an alliance rather than conquering each valley. However, this interpretation requires further exploration in other valleys for confirmation.

Fung and Williams (1977) proposed that the Casma polity dominated the Casma Valley by the beginning of the Middle Horizon, perhaps even earlier. They contrasted the absence of pyramidal mounds, which are considered ceremonial structures, with the presence of rectangular compounds, which they presumed to be administrative. Fung and Williams characterized Casma political organization as more secular, in which, "in contrast to earlier times, religion and the priesthood were overshadowed by the government" (1977:138; my translation). They asserted that this secular orientation is reflected in the settlement pattern, which is centered on administrative or defensive sites in strategic locations.[9] The pattern thus described by Fung and Williams (1977)—lack of pyramidal mounds, proliferation of rectangular compounds, defensively located administrative centers with few ceremonial structures—conforms to my observations of the location and spatial organization at the site of Cerro la Cruz. This pattern also agrees with my observations at the Casma capital city, the site of my current field research, which is described below.

The Casma Capital City of El Purgatorio

Perhaps the most critical aspect of creating a preliminary model for the composition of the Casma polity is to examine the capital city, which is thought to have been located at the site of El Purgatorio in the Casma Valley (Collier 1962:416; Conlee et al. 2004:211; Mackey and Klymyshyn 1990:198; Tello 1956; Thompson 1974:19; Wilson 1988:334, 1995:204). This characterization is based primarily on the abundance of Casma-style surface ceramics and the immense size of the site. Prior to my current project, El Purgatorio had only been described briefly in various surveys of the Casma Valley (Collier 1962; Mackey and Klymyshyn 1990; Tello 1956; Thompson 1964, 1974; Wilson 1995), and only limited previous test excavations had been undertaken by Thompson (1974). Due to the site's location along a prehispanic road, Tello also suggested that the site may have served as a *tambo*, or way station, during Inca times. We are currently

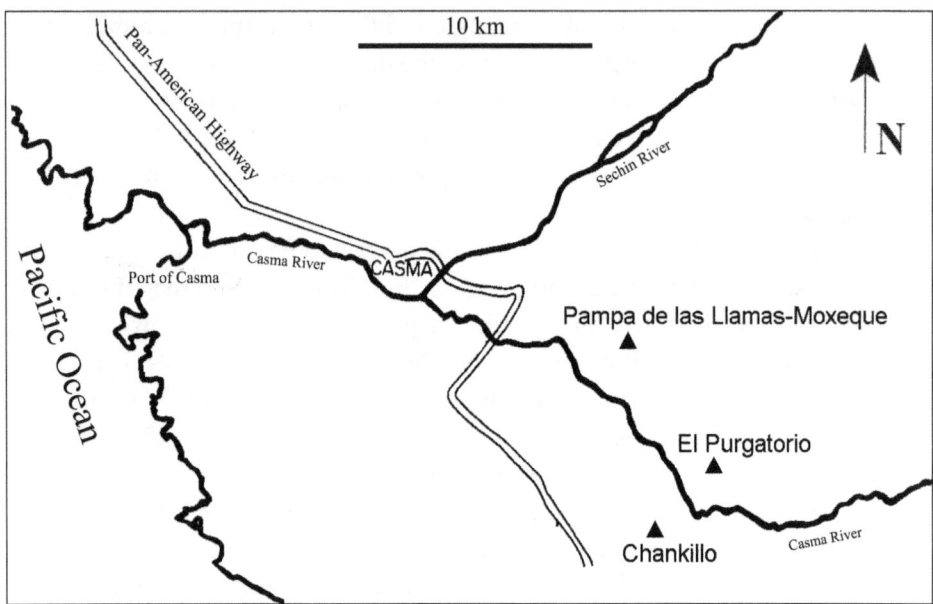

Map 2.1. Map of the lower Casma Valley showing the locations of El Purgatorio, Chankillo, and Pampa de las Llamas-Moxeque (after Mackey and Klymyshyn 1990).

investigating the site of El Purgatorio to obtain further information on the structure, extent, and impact of the Casma polity on Peruvian prehistory (Vogel 2011; Vogel, Falcón, and Pacifico 2010). The results of this research are contributing to a wealth of evidence for the Casma as a polity and illuminating the connections between Casma polity sites.

El Purgatorio is a truly monumental urban site, located in the lower Casma Valley, toward the southern end of the north coast of Peru at an altitude of approximately 180 m above sea level (map 2.1). Situated between the Nepeña Valley to the north and the Culebras Valley to the south, the Casma is the most extensive of the three valleys, with the greatest amount of arable land. Covering approximately 5 km², El Purgatorio is the largest site in the Casma Valley from any time period (figure 2.7). It sits on the northeast side of the Casma River within sight of two important Formative period sites, Chankillo and Pampa de las Llamas–Moxeque (map 2.1).

The site consists of four sectors, stretching across the base of Cerro Mucho Malo (also known as Cerro Purgatorio) on its western and southern sides as well as up its valley-facing slopes. The majority of the

Figure 2.7. Georeferenced 2007 Google Earth photograph of El Purgatorio in the Casma Valley. QuickBird/Digital Globe, Inc. Image 07MAY26155810-S2AS-005726208010_01_P001. Courtesy of Digital Globe, Inc. and The Center for Ancient Middle Eastern Landscapes, Oriental Institute, University of Chicago.

Figure 2.8. View of El Purgatorio Sector A with Cerro Mucho Malo in the background. Photo by author.

monumental architecture, which consists of several large compounds with complex internal structures, is located on the western side of the mountain in Sector A (figure 2.8). Although these compounds are freestanding, some have annexes (attached rooms or patios) or other associated structures filling in the spaces between compounds. In Sector B, numerous habitational terraces extend a considerable distance up and on top of the hillside, which is crowded with densely packed smaller structures and at least one small cemetery (figure 2.9). On the south side of the hill supporting Sector B is a third zone, Sector C, which consists of three looted cemeteries, a few additional compounds, several agglutinated room clusters, and a number of smaller associated structures. Finally, Sector D is located on the hilltop above the southern end of Sector C, filled with smaller stone structures resembling the commoner residences in Sector B and littered with Casma style ceramics. In both size and variety of architecture, El Purgatorio shows evidence for a large and socially stratified population, with a minimum of two but more likely three social classes (i.e., elites, intermediates, commoners).

Analysis of the construction techniques at El Purgatorio revealed that the site's builders utilized a mixture of adobe and uncut stone, the same pattern noted in my research at Cerro la Cruz, with an important

Figure 2.9. View of El Purgatorio Sector B showing residential terraces. Photo by author.

distinguishing feature: layers of organic material (composed of maize stalks and cobs, reeds, leaves, etc.) as construction fill. Tello (1956) noted, and my project confirmed, a scattering of Casma-style ceramics over the entire site surface in all three sectors. When approaching the site, one is confronted by an almost labyrinthine conglomeration of walls, but no major mounds are present—only a few medium-sized platforms are located within the compounds. These platforms are often fronted by a rectangular plaza in a pattern I call the platform/plaza complex. Although there are at least eight of these complexes, the relatively small size of the platforms is remarkable in a valley known for some of the earliest large mounds in Peru.

Unlike the Casma frontier site of Cerro la Cruz, El Purgatorio is not surrounded by perimeter walls or any other obvious traces of fortifications. However, the two sites show many architectural similarities in the form of large walled compounds and terraced slopes crowded with residential structures (figure 2.10). Both sites manifest a spatial division between the areas dominated by the compounds (more elite and public architecture) and the zones of small residential terraces (for commoners). There are similar construction techniques at both sites: a combination of adobe and uncut stone construction and the use of the case-and-fill technique, in which two opposing walls of stone or adobe are filled in with layers of dirt, rock, and compacted organic matter. However, the quantities of adobes used and the extent of construction are far greater at El Purgatorio, differences which are not surprising given that this site is approximately five times the size of Cerro la Cruz. In addition, similar vessel forms have been recovered at both sites: ollas, bowls, face-neck jars, tinajas, and so on. But the variants of the Casma Incised and Casma Molded styles at El Purgatorio tend to be more ornate in their decoration.

Our research at El Purgatorio is beginning to identify a pattern for Casma polity mortuary practices. So far we have located at least four cemeteries at El Purgatorio, as well as burials placed in the architecture of the site after its abandonment (Vogel and Vilcherrez 2009). The primary criteria I used to identify burial style were body position, the style and placement of associated ceramic vessels, and radiocarbon dating. Using these criteria, Casma-style burials are tightly flexed, usually found in a seated position but occasionally on their side, and often associated with one or more of the Casma-style vessels (Molded, Incised, or Black-White-Red). Frequently a ceramic or gourd bowl is found atop the individual's

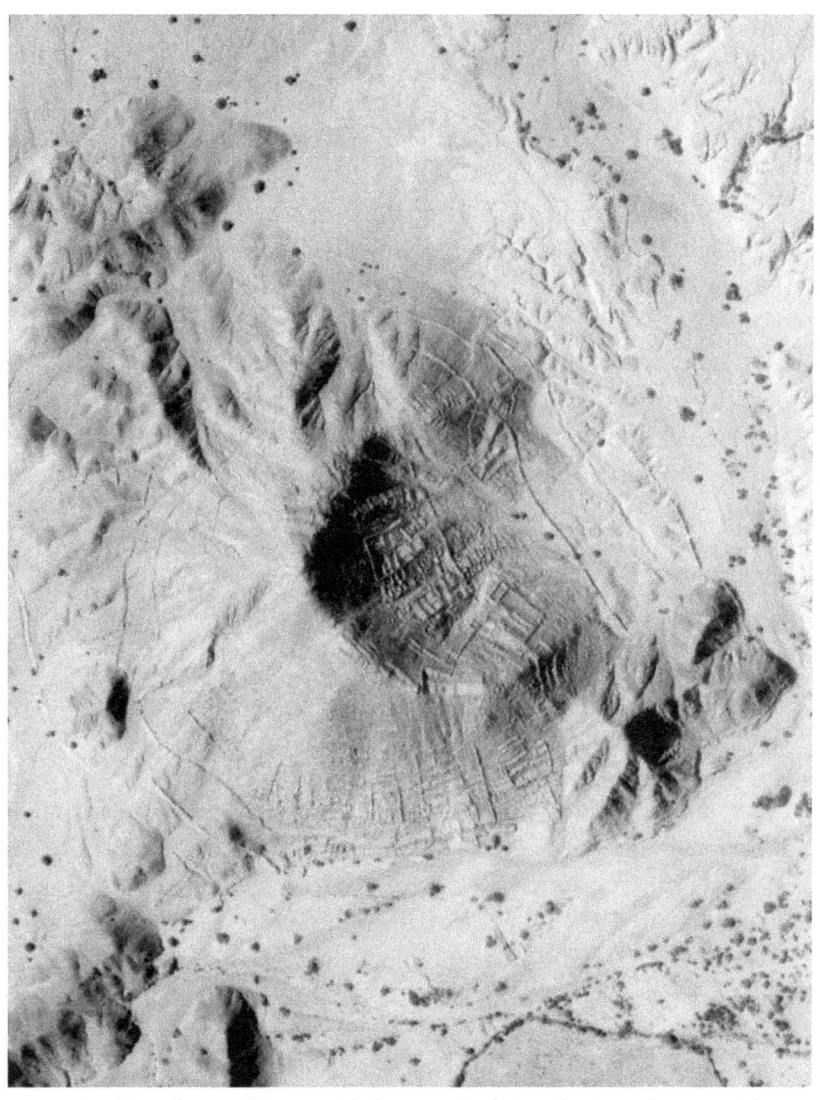

Figure 2.10. Georeferenced 1969 aerial photograph of Cerro la Cruz. Photograph by Servicio Aerofotográfico Nacional del Perú (#170-69-712).

head. For those Casma-style burials that could be dated thus far, 2-sigma calibrated radiocarbon dates place them mostly in the Late Intermediate period. While some of the Casma-style burials show clear indications of thin textile wrappings, the remnants of these textiles usually crumble to dust and are rarely well preserved enough to be removed along with the body. Nevertheless, the impressions left behind suggest that Casma people wrapped their dead in textile shrouds for burial, but probably not in layer upon layer of textiles.

Due to the persistence of these patterns in the material culture, I now use the following data sets as archaeological indicators of the Casma polity: ceramics in the Casma Incised, Molded, or Black-White-Red styles (figures 2.2–2.6) and an architectural style consisting primarily of rectangular compounds with enclosed patios and small platforms such as those found at the site of El Purgatorio or within Compound B3 at the site of Cerro la Cruz. In some cases, adobe walls with stone foundations replace the uncut stone construction. Settlement patterns are currently not well understood but seem to include defensively located and fortified sites, often located on terraced hillsides. Such is the case for the hillside site of Cerro la Cruz in the Chao Valley, which is described in chapter 4.

Summary

To create a foundation for my argument that Cerro la Cruz was a frontier site on the periphery of the Casma polity, this chapter situated my case study in the relevant temporal and cultural context. A concise overview of our current understanding of the Middle Horizon and Late Intermediate period on the Peruvian coast was presented so that the evidence for events at Cerro la Cruz may be placed within the framework of the regional culture history. In addition, I described previous research on the Casma polity as well as my ongoing investigations at the Casma capital city of El Purgatorio in the Casma Valley. Now that the site of Cerro la Cruz can be seen in light of the political landscape of its time, the next chapter explains the theoretical approach that I applied to the research design and interpretation of the results.

3

Archaeological Approaches to Peripheries

To place the research at Cerro la Cruz within the appropriate theoretical framework, a brief summary of archaeological approaches to peripheries is necessary. In this chapter, I explain the origin of the core and periphery concepts in world-systems theory (e.g., Algaze 1993a, 1993b; Broda, Carrasco, and Matos 1987; Burger and Matos 2002; Champion 1989; Chase-Dunn 1990; Chase-Dunn and Hall 1991; Gottman 1980; Hall 1999; Haselgrove 1987; Hedeager 1987; Hudson 1969; Rowlands, Larsen, and Kristiansen 1987; Schortman and Urban 1992, 1994; Urban, Schortman, and Ausec 2002). I then proceed to describe how the frontier approach was derived from critiques of world-systems theory and to define the difference between frontiers, border zones, and boundaries. I discuss how these areas are identified archaeologically, as well as the important role that the built environment plays in the investigation of frontiers. I then turn my attention to the Andes, briefly describing the political geography of the Peruvian coast, followed by an overview of previous research on Andean frontiers. Finally, I explain how the frontier approach is relevant to my research at Cerro la Cruz. The overall purpose of this chapter is to show the origin of the frontier approach and to contextualize my research within a larger theoretical framework.

Frontiers and Peripheries in Relation to World-Systems Theory

Archaeologists working around the globe and in widely divergent time frames have attempted to apply world-systems theory and concepts, which were developed for analyzing modern world-systems, to precapitalist world-systems with varying degrees of success.[1] Hall and Chase-Dunn

(1993) suggested that the major motivation for the archaeological interest in world-systems has to do with our current historical moment, in which the modern world-system is shifting through such processes as globalization and the effects of multinational corporations. They pointed out that scholars are examining earlier major transitions to gain insight into where things might be going and, in some cases, for inspiration on how to push change in a positive direction (Hall and Chase-Dunn 1993:122).[2] Indeed, the search for connections between the past, present, and future of human civilizations motivates entire disciplines, such as archaeology and history. We hope that by learning from the past we may better our future.

Developed originally by Wallerstein (1974, 1989, 1990, 1991, 1992) to examine interregional interaction on a large spatial scale, the primary goal of world-systems analysis is to understand how intersocietal interactions affect social evolution (Hall 1999:4). World-systems theory assumes that peripheral areas supply core areas with raw materials, core areas are politically and economically dominant, and social and economic development in all regions is constrained by their roles in the system (Trigger 1989:332). The core is the economic center or heartland of a world-system, while the periphery is on the fringe of such a system at the farthest extent of the economic network. The periphery may or may not be geographically most distant from the core(s); it may be situated politically or economically on the fringes of its respective world-system. Thus core/periphery relations refer to the interregional interactions between the various parts of a world-system.

Although world-systems theory was originally designed to describe relationships between modern, predominantly capitalist states, archaeologists have subsequently employed it in their studies of numerous precapitalist societies. World-systems theory has been applied to such diverse subjects as the effects of hinterland migration into urbanized areas of Asia and Europe from 4000 BC to AD 1500 (Modelski and Thompson 1999); the earliest civilizations of Mesopotamia (Algaze 1993b); exchange, empires, and boundaries in Roman Europe (Wells 1999); the relationship between the Aztec Empire and the Mesoamerican world-system (Smith 2001); and the collapse of prehistoric world-systems in native North America (Peregrine 1999). In the Andes, world-systems theory has been applied primarily to the Inca Empire (Kuznar 1999).

While many scholars have critiqued Wallerstein's original conceptions of world-systems, especially when applied to precapitalist societies (e.g.,

Blanton and Feinman 1984; Edens 1992; Schneider 1977; Schortman and Urban 1992; Stein 1999; Urban and Schortman 1999; Smith 2001; Stanish 2003:170–71), the critique offered by Lightfoot and Martinez (1995) has proved especially useful for this case study. Rather than take a traditional approach to core/periphery interactions, they chose to examine a specific type of periphery, the frontier, as a way to achieve a more comprehensive understanding of the past. Lightfoot and Martinez's approach to frontiers rests on a critique of traditional models for core/periphery relations as core-centered and usually restricted to macro-scale perspectives in both temporal and spatial dimensions.[3]

These core-centered models describe frontiers as "passive recipients of core innovations" and include the expectation that clear boundaries will be visible in the material culture of these areas (Lightfoot and Martinez 1995:471). Lightfoot and Martinez instead suggested that frontiers are "zones of cross-cutting social networks" in which cultural change is visible and active (1995:474) and where creolization (the process by which two or more cultural traditions are combined to produce a new cultural tradition) can be productively studied. Furthermore, Lightfoot and Martinez argued for a multiscalar approach that recognizes both the agency of frontier inhabitants and the unique contributions they offer for the study of interethnic interactions and the "construction, negotiation and manipulation of group identities" (1995:474). Their approach lends itself to the study of factional competition and cooperation and to the consideration of periphery residents as active agents in shaping their own lives.

This alternative interpretive framework is not so dependent on the original limitations of world-systems theory, and it attempts to balance perspectives from both the core and the periphery. Frontier theory has proved much more suitable for the interpretation of the data presented here than has traditional world-systems analysis because it allows for the study of peripheral areas in their own right, and not purely in relation to the core. Peripheral areas are recognized both for their relationship to the core and for their relationships with neighboring polities. Emphasis is placed on the residents of the frontier as active agents in the process of cultural change. The study of these areas can in turn inform research and interpretation at the core, which in the case of the Casma polity is ongoing.

But Lightfoot and Martinez (1995) are not alone in their criticism of traditional core/periphery models. Stein (1999, 2005) made a similar argument that many world-systems analyses have been inappropriately and uncritically applied to smaller scale societies and that too much weight has been given to the dominant role of the core. He critiqued the manner in which the world-systems concept has been applied to historical and archaeological cases. Stein (2005:6) concurred with Lightfoot and Martinez that a more relevant theoretical framework must be multiscalar, and that it must view the organization of culture contact at both intra- and interpolity levels. He added that the balance of power between cores and peripheries is variable; it cannot be assumed that more developed cores always dominate their less developed peripheries (Stein 2005:6). Instead, it is important to investigate the polity's internal dynamics (e.g., political, economic, social, and ideological processes) as well as the external processes (e.g., long-distance trade or colonization) in order to understand the overall network organization (Stein 2005:7). This heterarchical and more holistic approach to the study of peripheries (including both frontiers and border zones) is especially well suited to regions and time periods where archaeological knowledge of the polities involved is asymmetrical and still evolving, such as the north coast of Peru ca. AD 900–1350, and was therefore quite appealing for this study of the Casma polity frontier.

Frontiers are associated with complex societies at various levels of political organization. To avoid the use of simplistic evolutionary schemes that force diverse, dynamic forms of political organization into static categories (e.g., chiefdom, state, empire), I generally refer to the archaeological cultures mentioned here as polities. A polity is a culturally distinct political organization, usually identifiable primarily by archaeological indicators such as ceramic and architectural style, settlement pattern, and subsistence base. The level of political organization in these polities may or may not reach the level of the state, but certainly extends beyond kinship and even ethnic ties. In the Andes, this translates to a level of political organization beyond an individual ayllu, the basic unit of Andean social organization. However, a polity could consist of several ayllus joined in alliance.

Defining Frontiers, Boundaries, and Border Zones

Frontiers and border zones have been defined variously as appropriate to individual case studies. For the purposes of this research, a frontier is defined as the outermost extent of any given polity's territory, which may or may not border another polity's territory. That is, a frontier could be the limit of incorporated territory after which the land is not currently claimed by a particular group (i.e., a "no-man's land"), or it could border another group's territory. Frontiers can become economic as well as political boundaries, but they need not do so. They are dynamic, shifting with the movement of political and economic ties. Frontiers can also function to separate emerging power cores, as was frequently the case in the premodern world (de Blij 1973:148). In fact, the current politicogeographical situation in which the entire world has been divided into states with precise borders is a relatively recent phenomenon.

The words "frontier" and "boundary" are often used interchangeably, although this is not technically correct. A boundary is seen as the vertical plane that divides adjacent polities. But some languages do not even have separate words for frontiers and boundaries (Kristof 1973:270 [1959]). De Blij (1973) believes this is due to the fact that frontier characteristics can still be recognized in areas where a boundary does exist and where, therefore, those areas have technically become border zones. A border zone is defined as the larger area where territories governed by two or more separate polities meet or intersect. A subtle but significant difference exists between these two concepts in that a frontier can also be a border zone, but a border zone is not necessarily a frontier. De Blij prefers to distinguish these concepts by describing frontiers as outer-oriented, meaning their attention is directed outward toward unincorporated lands. In contrast, border zones are inner-oriented and more closely tied to developments at the core, although the degree of the core's direct control over the border zone may vary.

Frontiers and border zones are by definition dynamic, meaning they are constantly shifting and being renegotiated. Even if the area that comprises the border zone remains stable for hundreds of years, this temporary stability is renewed every time adjacent polities choose not to expand or choose to renew their political ties with opposing polities. Of course, if one polity does succeed in expanding its territory, the boundary will shift accordingly, and its characterization as frontier or border zone may change.

There is also a slight distinction between a border zone and a boundary. The boundary itself may or may not be marked on the ground; therefore, the concept of a border zone is useful for less clearly defined boundaries. To clarify, a boundary is merely a "line in the sand" that divides two polities, while the border zone is the general region where the territories of two polities intersect. In some cases, we are fortunate to have clear indications of these boundaries, such as the Great Wall of China or Hadrian's Wall in Scotland. But in many precapitalist states, boundaries were not necessarily marked in ways that are obvious to modern people. In fact, few of the world's boundaries are actually marked on the earth's surface even today. For example, a distinctive landmark such as a mountain may be locally understood as the extent of a particular group's territory because it is the home of a particular spirit or deity (e.g., D'Altroy 2002; Hyslop 1990). In the Andes, culturally specific indicators such as *ceque* systems (Hyslop 1990) and mortuary monuments (Isbell 1997) may have served as territorial markers. In addition, it has been suggested that the few "Great Walls" on the Peruvian coast, such as the "Great Wall" of the Santa Valley (Kosok 1965; Proulx 1973; Topic and Topic 1978; Wilson 1988), may have served as boundary markers or fortifications. However, these Great Walls are few compared to the number of polities that have occupied coastal territory over the course of at least three thousand years of complex society.

Archaeological Indicators of Peripheries

If there are no clear delineators such as walls or fences, then frontiers and border zones must be located archaeologically by examining the regional spatial distribution of archaeological styles within the relative chronology of the region. Such examination may yield not only the presence of multiple cultural influences but also the absence of total domination by any one of these cultural influences, the combination of which may indicate a frontier or border zone. The more difficult task may be to determine whether styles are being replaced, traded, or influenced by outside groups. This type of "fuzzy" boundary might prove frustrating for the investigator, but it may more accurately reflect the complexity, multiplicity, and dynamics of social and political interactions that occurred in frontiers and border zones.

In order to differentiate frontiers from border zones, the locations of peripheries must first be determined. Once sufficient survey data have been collected and archaeological indicators have been established for the relevant polities, archaeologists can identify the locations and types of peripheries for any given region and time period. Then the characterization of these peripheries can be confirmed and investigated further through excavation and analysis. Several important characteristics are common to these peripheral areas and are especially relevant for the identification of these areas in the archaeological record. These characteristics include the following: lower population density and therefore fewer sites as compared to the core area; proliferation of fortifications and defensive features, such as perimeter walls and defensively located sites; co-occurrence of various material culture styles or other evidence for interactions with outside groups; and evidence for a common identity or political affiliation with the core. These characteristics must be contextualized within the culture history of the region in order to distinguish the relevant polities for that temporal and geographical sphere. For prehistoric periods, patterns of artifact and architectural style are used to identify these polities.

The Importance of the Built Environment for Investigating Frontiers

The primary means to approach the study of frontiers and border zones is through the built environment because it is a physical manifestation of power relationships. The built environment includes architecture, the space it encloses, and to some extent the space immediately surrounding it, especially landscape features created by human activities. This analysis addresses spatial organization on two scales: the intrasite level refers to the organization of space and architectural features at the site of Cerro la Cruz, and the intersite level refers to the larger regional scale of Peru's north coast. At the larger scale there are both within-valley and between-valley comparisons.

Anthropologists have shown that the built environment both reflects and reinforces relationships within and between communities (e.g., Bourdieu 1973; Donley 1982; Rapoport 1994). Regional analyses have used similarities in architectural style and organization among sites as evidence for state control of outlying areas and peoples in such cases as the Tiwanaku polity (e.g., Goldstein 1993; Kolata 1991; Kolata and Ponce 1992) and the Chimú polity (Moore 1992). In other words, there are political and social aspects to consider in the construction of walls and architectural compounds, and power relations may play a large role in architectural design (Bender 1998; Moore 1996b, 2005). For example, spatial organization in a particular locale may be the result of individuals controlling their own land or of elites coordinating the labor of others. Site location can also be selected for purposes of controlling or tracking the movement of travelers (Madry and Crumley 1990). The creation of a single structure may involve a wide range of decisions, such as the purpose of the structure, the number of people it is meant to hold, and the message the builders wish to convey to those who see it. Thus in many ways power relationships are embedded in the spatial realm, and they may be expressed in the form of architecture. To understand the nature of these power relationships, architectural features must be interpreted within the context of the culture and time in which they were created. They are part of a larger landscape that is culturally and socially situated (Moore 2005). From a diachronic perspective, archaeology can explore the ways in which people have adapted to fluctuating social and political conditions. Applying frontier theory to smaller sites and lesser known polities can not only enrich and revise our vision of the past but also give us greater insights into the true fabric of the daily lives of the ancient people who are, after all, the true object of our studies.

One significant feature of the built environment that relates to power relationships is the construction of perimeter walls. For example, the high exterior walls of Chimú royal compounds may have been intended as expressions of elite power and as a means to mediate between people and the "larger mythological environment" (Conklin 1990:63). Similarly, perimeter walls and causeways that connect outlying communities with major centers may be attempts to maintain boundaries during times of political instability, such as the collapse of Classic Maya civilization (Kurjack and Andrews 1976).

The three perimeter walls at the site of Cerro la Cruz comprise one of the most significant features of its built environment. Problematizing the function of the perimeter walls was an important aspect of this study, which acknowledges the defensive capability of some walls while questioning what other purposes these walls may have served. In many parts of the world, the presence of perimeter walls alone marks a site as fortified. It often follows that the site is labeled a fort or a military outpost. But in the Andes, the situation is often more complex. For example, the use of the term *fortaleza* (fortress) for an Inca hilltop complex at the site of

Ollantaytambo is actually misleading, since the complex was primarily a sacred district (Protzen 1993:73). Similarly, Hyslop (1990:152) argued that the walls of Inca enclosures served various nonmilitary functions, including supporting structures, restricting access and providing privacy, and separating sacred aspects of the landscape from the surrounding environment. Ghezzi (2006) has shown that, even as far back as the Early Horizon, the hilltop "fortress" at the site of Chankillo in the Casma Valley was actually a temple-fortress complex, complete with the first solar observatory in the New World (Ghezzi and Ruggles 2007, 2008). Thus site functions cannot be inferred from the presence of one architectural feature, and multiple functions need not be mutually exclusive.

Walls can also be viewed through the lens of social relations and their mediation by physical barriers (Samson 1992). Walls can define areas of authority and symbolize possession, constrain the movements of people and animals, and even impart knowledge of "illegal" entry or exit (e.g., Redman 1986:51–52; Samson 1992).[4] Walls can separate the sacred from the profane, and they can serve to regulate the behavior that occurs within but not outside them (Moore 1996b). They can symbolize power, create privacy, and send messages to outsiders about the status, wealth, or identity of those who live within them. But most important, walls "are neutral without the social relations necessary to make them work" (Samson 1992:32). Therefore, there are several possible explanations for the function and significance of perimeter walls, which are likely to serve multiple purposes.

Now that the necessary concepts and their corresponding theoretical framework have been introduced, they can be applied to the archaeological past of the Andean culture area, with specific reference to the Peruvian north coast.

Political Geography and the Andean Archaeological Record

While Wallerstein focused primarily upon economic interactions within world-systems, it should be noted that political relationships also play an important role. The interaction between economic and political systems has been readily apparent to political geographers, who have reinterpreted many world-systems concepts as one aspect of adopting a broader scope and a more holistic approach to politicogeographical analysis. This approach includes analysis of all the networks of power relations, whether economic, political, religious, and so on (Claval 1980:64). The reinterpretation of world-systems theory and its application to political geography has proved especially useful to archaeologists for the investigation and explanation of culture change.

The geography of the Andean region had a profound effect on political expansion prior to the Spanish conquest, and this was certainly true for the Casma polity. The site of Cerro la Cruz is located in the coastal desert *chala*, which supports vegetation only along beaches, rivers, and associated irrigation canals (except during El Niño).[5] Just beyond Cerro la Cruz is the middle valley *yungas*, a low-altitude (500–2,300 m above sea level) zone that includes cacti and scrub vegetation (Topic and Topic 1983:240). Both the *chala* and the *yungas* require irrigation to support agricultural activities. As one travels into the higher altitudes, one encounters at 2,300–3,500 m the *quechua* zone, which is generally frost free and amenable to rainfall agriculture, and at 3,500–4,000 m the *suni* zone, a frost-prone grassland most useful for pastoralism (Topic and Topic 1983:240). These ecological settings can be found in each river valley along the northern coast of Peru. Each river valley is then generally separated from the next on its northern and southern borders by chains of foothills extending west intermittently from the Andes Mountains toward the Pacific Ocean. As a result of this topography and the dependence of coastal populations on rivers as their only water source, archaeologists tend to use river valleys as the primary unit of spatial analysis on the Peruvian coast.

As Topic and Topic (1983) noted, this geographical setting also affected political expansion in a distinct manner. Political expansion tended to occur on a valley-by-valley basis because of the topography, in which "densely populated areas occur as islands surrounded by seas of sparse or nonexistent population" (Topic and Topic 1983:249). Coastal polities tended to expand north and south because these areas were more highly populated and the routes easier to cross.[6] They could not expand west because of the Pacific Ocean, and they were less likely to expand east into the lower-populated *yungas* or the fringes of the *quechua* on the western slopes of the Andes because they could expect to receive less return on their investment. These constraints affected the growth of both the Casma and Chimú polities, and they help to explain the settlement pattern found in the Chao Valley.

Frontiers in the Andean Past

Of course, this is not the first study to examine an Andean frontier, so a brief review of previous research on Andean frontiers is in order. Andeanists, like most archaeologists, have traditionally preferred macro-scale, core-centered models of cultural systems to explain culture change, such as those that have been developed for the Inca Empire and, more arguably, the Tiwanaku and Wari "empires" (e.g., Bauer 1992; Isbell 1977; Kolata 1993; Schreiber 2001). These models represent one way of investigating world-systems, but one which subsequently needs to be supplemented and contextualized within the particulars of each region at a smaller scale. As theoretical and methodological resources continue to expand, our analyses can reflect a more sophisticated and nuanced interpretation of the past than was possible earlier, and which may prove a more suitable fit for the data we have recovered.

In the last two decades, Andean archaeologists have begun to turn their attention from monumental sites and capitals to sites in peripheral areas (e.g., Burger and Matos 2002; Earle et al. 1987; Goldstein 2000; Janusek 2004; Jennings 2006; Lau 2001; Malpass 1993; Malpass and Alconini 2010; Nash and Williams 2005; Schreiber 1992, 2001). Yet relatively few frontiers in the Andean past have been explored at any depth. The major exceptions to this are the various borders of the Inca Empire at the time of the Spanish conquest (e.g., Alconini 2004, 2005; D'Altroy 1992, 2002; Hyslop 1990; Kuznar 1996, 1999; La Lone 1994; Malpass 1993; Malpass and Alconini 2010; Patterson 1987; Salomon 1986).

The Frontiers of the Inca Empire

Due to the wealth of ethnohistorical documents from the Spanish conquest, the majority of research on Andean frontiers concerns the Inca Empire. The Inca maintained control over the vast reaches of their empire through both direct and indirect means, depending on the level of local infrastructure and the degree of hostility exhibited by conquered peoples. For example, Salomon (1986) has examined the northern Inca frontier in Ecuador (cf. Lippi and Gudiño 2010). Here the Inca appear to have maintained open relations with local lords, yet they required a line of forts along the eastern edge of the Quito basin to confront the fierce resistance of people living along the eastern slopes. Along the eastern borders of the Inca Empire, Schjellerup (1997) has found several small forts in Huánuco, but none farther south. D'Altroy (2002:261) suggested that this lack of fortifications implies a more peaceable relationship between the Inca Empire and these jungle peoples, but one attained only after conquest had failed. On the southeastern frontier of the empire, Alconini (2004, 2005, 2010) has found evidence for shifting power relations between the Yampara, the Chiriguano-Guaraní, and their Inca conquerors.

D'Altroy (D'Altroy 2002; D'Altroy et al. 2000) has also investigated the Inca frontier in northwest Argentina and found a string of forts beyond which he believes Inca expeditions explored but did not incorporate any territory. The southern frontier has been considered more difficult to define. Dillehay and Gordon (1988) have explored this area and suggested that economic and cultural ties with local people in Chile extended beyond the Inca Empire's military and political limits (e.g., Rossen, Planella, and Stehberg 2010). All of these studies point to the agency of local people on the frontiers, but Patterson (1986, 1987) has addressed this issue directly in his various works on the Inca, emphasizing resistance and contestation of power. He states that the expansion of the Inca state "promoted uneven development among the border peoples and those living outside the frontier area," causing ethnocide in some areas and ethnogenesis in others (Patterson 1987:120). These varying processes were repeated again during the Spanish conquest, when non-Inca peoples lost the rights they had claimed under the Inca Empire to a colonial regime that recognized Inca hegemony as first and foremost over their previously occupied territories (Silverblatt 1987).

Pre-Inca Andean Frontiers

The shortage of literature on pre-Inca frontiers is likely due to the difficulty in defining such areas. For preconquest South America, there are no written records of territorial growth or loss, or even precise knowledge of how political and/or social groups identified themselves. Spanish chronicles of the Inca Empire's political organization and history of conquest are useful as analogies for earlier polities, but must be applied with care and ample supporting evidence. However, a few recent attempts have been made to investigate pre-Inca peripheries and are worth a brief mention here for comparison to the site of Cerro la Cruz.

Long considered to be the first locus of civilization in the Andes, the "Chavín Horizon" may be the earliest period during which core/periphery analysis is appropriate. Burger and Matos (2002) discussed a site called Atalla, which they considered to be located on the periphery of the Chavín polity. Although the exact nature of Chavín political organization is highly debated, they contend that Atalla played an important role in the Chavín interaction sphere because of its proximity to sources of cinnabar, a highly valued mineral in prehispanic Peru. Burger and Matos argued for an asymmetric power relationship between the site of Atalla and the core at the site of Chavín, largely due to the small size of both Atalla and its population.

Moving forward in time to the Early Intermediate period (ca. 200 BC–AD 600), Lau's (2001, 2005) study of the central highland site of Chinchawas demonstrated the effects that a fluctuation in power relationships between cores has on the periphery. Lau determined that Chinchawas served as a periphery to two different highland entities over time, as power shifted from the Recuay polity to the Wari polity. He also examined local peoples' responses to both internal and external socioeconomic factors during this transition (Lau 2002:3).

Advancing chronologically to the Middle Horizon, the recent literature shows that archaeologists are now paying greater attention to areas on the Wari and Tiwanaku peripheries (e.g., Janusek 2004; Jennings 2006; Nash and Williams 2005; Schreiber 1992, 2001). For example, unlike the authors of the studies mentioned above, Goldstein (2000) considered but ultimately rejected the world-systems perspective as inappropriate for explaining the presence of cross-cultural stylistic traits on ceramics and textiles found in the Moquegua Valley. Moving from analysis of particular sites to the big picture, Jennings (2006) examined how models of the Wari periphery have been constructed over the course of the last century. He made a convincing argument that a "dominant interpretive tradition" has framed our interpretations of the Middle Horizon and influenced how archaeologists explain Wari influence on their own periphery (Jennings 2006:267). This dominant narrative makes it difficult for new interpretations to take hold in the disciplinary discourse, despite the addition of new data from the Wari periphery. Nevertheless, all of these studies contribute to our understanding of the rise and fall of complex societies at various stages of development.

The expansion and retraction of Andean polities and their territories comprises not only the linear development of Andean culture history but also the cyclical ebb and flow of the centralization and dispersal of power and wealth. Archaeologically, we can detect the traces of these sociopolitical tides in the form of patterns of material culture and changes in those patterns (e.g., Conkey and Hastorf 1990; DeBoer 1990; DeBoer and Moore 1982; Dietler and Herbich 1998; Donley 1982; Earle 1990; Janusek 2002, 2003; Menzel 1964; Morris 1995; Willey 1999). Such patterns include everything from style in art forms of numerous media (e.g., ceramic, metal, textile, wood, stone) to spatial organization and construction techniques, settlement size and distribution, and mortuary practices and religious beliefs. As archaeologists, our job is not only to find the patterns but also to find the irregularities in those patterns and then try to explain both if possible. As this is an exceptionally difficult task when dealing with prehistoric societies, it is not surprising that some archaeologists tend to focus on the patterns and ignore or suppress the irregularities. In those cases where boundaries are not clearly visible, examining frontiers and border zones can be one way of correcting this tendency by confronting the inconsistent, anomalous, and troublesome aspects of the archaeological record.

Application of the Frontier Concept to the Site of Cerro la Cruz

It was evident from the early stages of my research at Cerro la Cruz in the Chao Valley that the typical approaches of world-systems theory and core/periphery relations would not adequately explain the site. Once my team's excavations revealed that the site was not established by the Chimú state[7] (as was previously thought) but by a polity from the Casma Valley, I realized that I would need to reexamine my approach. It was no longer clear what role the site had played in the geopolitical landscape of the Middle Horizon. Indeed, more work is currently underway to clarify whether the Casma polity could be considered part of a world-system and, if so, what shape that may have taken (e.g., Vogel 2011; Vogel, Falcón, and Pacifico 2010).

Nonetheless, the models for frontiers and border zones that have evolved from more traditional world-systems and core/periphery analyses do appear to be highly applicable to the site of Cerro la Cruz and are, therefore, useful as explanatory frameworks. This is because the frontier approach is not so dependent on the original limitations of world-systems theory; it allows for the study of peripheral areas in their own right, not solely in relation to the core. Research at frontier sites like Cerro la Cruz can in turn inform research and interpretation at the core, which in this case is the Casma Valley. The study of Cerro la Cruz can teach us not only about intrapolity dynamics among the Casma people, but also about interpolity relationships between the Casma and neighboring polities, with special attention given to the residents of Cerro la Cruz as active agents in the process of cultural change.

This realization prompted me to ask three major questions: whether the Chao Valley was a frontier or border zone in the past, what relationship it had with the larger polities of the time period, and how those relations changed over time. Cerro la Cruz would have been peripheral not only to the Chimú state but also to the site's founders, the Casma polity. The recognition that Cerro la Cruz lies in a unique position between these two polities, the Casma and the Chimú, and that it was occupied during an important temporal transition from the end of the Middle Horizon into the Late Intermediate period opened the possibility of exploring the dynamics of frontiers and border zones. From this perspective, one can observe the rise of one polity at the expense of another, as well as the interpolity interactions that transpired during the site's occupation. In the case of the frontier site of Cerro la Cruz, this means the formation of the Chimú Empire at the expense of the Casma polity and the displacement of local elites after the Chimú conquest. While many aspects of the Chimú polity have been more thoroughly investigated and are presumably more fully understood than those of their Casma counterparts, taking the frontier approach to Cerro la Cruz could produce insights that inform our interpretations of both polities. Furthermore, research on Andean frontiers, especially on those frontiers that date prior to the Inca state, has shown that we do not need an exhaustive knowledge of the core in order to gain significant knowledge of earlier Andean polities from their peripheries (e.g., Burger and Matos 2002; Earle et al. 1987; Goldstein 2000; Janusek 2004; Jennings 2006; Lau 2001; Malpass 1993; Malpass and Alconini 2010; Nash and Williams 2005; Schreiber 1992, 2001). In fact, research on these areas can produce unique insights into larger-scale interpolity dynamics that may be less visible at the core. Thus I deemed the frontier approach especially useful for investigating life at the site of Cerro la Cruz, adding further knowledge to our understanding of the Casma polity and providing the beginnings of an ongoing investigation of the Casma polity's place in the larger Andean world.

Summary

Frontiers have long been areas of investigation for archaeologists, historians, political geographers, and other social scientists. These locales often provide fruitful arenas for investigating the agents and mechanisms of culture change. In this chapter, I presented the theoretical history behind the concepts of frontiers and border zones as utilized by critics of world-systems theory, and I attempted to define them as useful tools for archaeological analysis. First I situated these concepts within the framework of core/periphery interactions, which themselves were developed out of world-systems analyses generated in economics. I then described the archaeological indicators of peripheries and demonstrated the importance of these areas for understanding cultural change. Next I discussed the application of these concepts to political geography and the built environment and then described several frontier case studies from the Andean world. Finally, I explained the reasoning behind my decision to apply the frontier approach to the site of Cerro la Cruz, which I argued to be a prime candidate for this type of analysis.

Now that the site of Cerro la Cruz has been situated in its theoretical and culture historical frameworks, I can move on to a description of the work that was carried out by my project. The methodology discussed in the next chapter provides the context for the results of my research at Cerro la Cruz. Those results can be found in chapter 5.

4

Investigating Peripheries

The Site of Cerro la Cruz

The methodology for investigating prehistoric peripheries focuses primarily on the spatial dimension and the kinds of changes that occur over time in the specified region. To distinguish frontiers and border zones in these peripheral areas, archaeologists employ political geography in combination with material culture as indicators of the cultural groups or polities associated with such areas. Political geography examines the relationship between the physical environment and political entities, including the effects of geography on politics and the effects of politics on geography. In other words, archaeologists attempt to determine what territory fell under which polity's control at a given point in time, as well as how control of that territory shifted over time between polities. Archaeologists use architectural style, artifact style, and the distribution of these styles as the primary means to attribute individual sites to polities.

In order to characterize a site as a border zone or frontier settlement, the spatial analysis must focus not only on the site but also on the geographic area in which it is located. Eventually researchers also must consider the larger regional context as part of the study of the spatial realm because the definition of a frontier or border zone is dependent on that area's relationship to the entire territory under a polity's control as well as to neighboring polities. The result of the investigation of border zones, then, is a multiscalar nested analysis of space; it begins with the locus, in this case the site of Cerro la Cruz, and extends out to the valley (the Chao), the neighboring valleys (the Virú and the Santa), and finally to the larger regional context, the north coast of Peru. Thus it is essential to situate the site of Cerro la Cruz within the geographic context as well as within the temporal context (described in chapter 2). Although archaeological sites are often the most obvious signs of past cultural activity, the land itself also frequently bears the mark of human interaction with the physical environment, both in the past and in the present. Just as a site contains stratigraphic layers of cultural occupation, so too the landscape becomes a palimpsest of hundreds or even thousands of years of interplay between humans and the space around them. The examination of the geographic setting of Cerro la Cruz not only considers the impact of humans on their physical environment but also permits the culturally constructed features of the Chao Valley to inform archaeological interpretation of cultural activity in that area. Therefore, this chapter describes the physical environment of the site of Cerro la Cruz and the Chao Valley. This chapter also explains the previous hypotheses regarding the site's function and details the methodology used in the investigation of the site.

The Geographical Setting: The Chao Valley

Most of the Peruvian coast consists of an arid, treeless desert. This certainly describes the north coast of Peru, located between the Pacific Ocean to the west and the Andean Cordillera to the east. It consists of a series of river valleys, from the Piura Valley in the north to the Huarmey Valley in the south, which carry water from the highlands across the desert plain to the sea (map 1.1). The Chao Valley is located in the southern half of this area, at approximately 8.28° N, 78.38° W (map 1.2). The area encompassed by the Chao Valley measures approximately 1,558 km2 (Carcelen and Angulo 1999:1), so small that it is often referred to in conjunction with the slightly larger Virú Valley to its north (i.e., Virú-Chao).

The Chao River begins at Cerro Ururupa, 4,050 m above sea level in the Andes Mountains (Alva 1986:48). The three major tributaries of the Chao River, the Huamanzaña, Chorobal, and Cerro Blanco Rivers, converge about 2 km southeast of Cerro la Cruz, creating one of the largest areas of irrigable land in the valley (ONERN 1973). This area, from Cerro Huasaquito to the town of Chao, also contained the majority of irrigation canals prior to the installation of the Chavimochic canal discussed below. For this reason, the Hacienda Buenavista was built here and later developed into the modern town of Buenavista, which is adjacent to Cerro la Cruz (figure 4.1).

The topography of the valley is narrow and uneven, sloping sharply from the highlands, or upper valley, down to the flatter, lower valley on

Figure 4.1. Georeferenced 1997 aerial photograph of Cerro la Cruz. Photograph by Servicio Aerofotográfico Nacional del Perú (#455-97-2928).

the coast. Climatic conditions change as one travels down the valley: beginning with humid montane prairie in the highlands, becoming brushy steppes, and ending in arid desert closest to the ocean (Alva 1986:49). There are only a few isolated hills on the otherwise flat valley floor, including Cerro Coronado, Cerro la Cruz, and Cerro Blanco. Of these, Cerro la Cruz is the largest.

Fauna and Flora

The vegetation[1] of the Chao Valley belongs to four basic types: "huarango" trees (*Acacia macracantha*), "bichayo" (*Capparis ovalifolia*), "zapote" fruit-bearing bushes (*Capparis angulata*), and "algarrobo" trees (*Prosopis* sp.) (Silva 1992). Kent (1998:3) adds to this list several species of cacti (primarily *Cereus macrostibas*), "huayabillo" (*Cryptocarpus* sp.) vines and fruits, and "molle" trees (*Schinus molle*). He also points out that "carrizo" reeds (*Arundo donax*), "caña brava" reeds (*Ginerium sagittatum*), and "sauce" (*Salix* sp.) are found along drainages, all of which provide useful raw materials for construction and tool manufacture (Kent 1998:3). The periodic increased availability of these resources following El Niño–Southern Oscillation (ENSO) events would have made them extremely valuable to the residents of the Chao Valley, who might otherwise have had a more difficult time obtaining wood and other plant resources. In years of normal or low precipitation, some of these resources may have been imported from neighboring valleys or the highlands.

In terms of wild animal species, contemporary mammalian fauna include fox (*Duscicyon sechurae*), deer (*Odocoileus virginianus*), and rodents (Rosales 1999:4). Several species of birds are present, especially ground owls called "lechuzas" (*Speotyto cunicularia*) and "chucluy" (*Crotophaga sulcirostris*) (Kent 1998:3). Toads (*Bufo spinolosus*), snakes, and lizards (*Dicrodon guttulatum*) have also been observed, and local residents have occasionally captured river crayfish (*Chryphiops caementarius*) (Kent 1998).

Land Use in the Chao Valley Prior to 1997

As of the 1970s, only 2,000 ha of land were under cultivation within the Chao Valley. This is approximately one-fifth of the total cultivable area, and, therefore, the modern population was small and dispersed (Alva 1986:48). In the early 1970s, the Oficina Nacional de Evaluación de Recursos Naturales (ONERN) conducted surveys of all the coastal valleys of Peru for agricultural development. These surveys documented irrigation canals, major roads, towns, and contemporary land use patterns, including soil quality and typical local vegetation (ONERN 1973). According to the survey conducted in Chao, no major mineral resources existed in the valley, but a few areas have been mined for gravel and sand.

At the time of the ONERN survey, the land nearest Cerro la Cruz was either uncultivated, abandoned, or in fallow, but farther south were fields of sorghum, chili peppers, avocados, and maize, with bean fields farther southwest. The majority of the crops grown in the valley at the time were maize, beans, and sweet potatoes, yet the overall soil quality was low except where enhanced by irrigation (ONERN 1973:44, 46, 64). By the time of my research in 1999–2001, the cultivation zone had advanced all the way to the base of the hill, in some places destroying the outermost walls of the site.

The Chao Valley is one of the driest on the north coast, with annual precipitation ranging from 7 to 40 mm and an average temperature of 20.3°C or 68.54°F (Carcelén and Angulo 1999:1). According to Kosok (1965), the Chao River flowed during only three months of the year, providing insufficient water resources for expanding the area of irrigable land.[2] To support the population at Cerro la Cruz (at least in part) through agriculture probably would have required the maximization of the Chao River's variable and unreliable water resources. To resolve this problem, the Peruvian government developed the Chavimochic Project to increase water resources in several north coast valleys. "ChaViMoChic" stands for Chao, Virú, Moche, and Chicama, the four valleys which now receive water from the Santa River since the construction of this major canal system in the early to mid-1990s.

This brief history of the use and availability of such resources as arable land and water in the valley is important for understanding the subsistence base likely to have been utilized by the original residents of the site of Cerro la Cruz as well as to suggest that there were likely other reasons, besides scant natural resources, for establishing a regional center in such a difficult environment.

The Site of Cerro la Cruz

Cerro la Cruz is located on the north side of the Chao Valley, approximately halfway between the Pacific Ocean and the Andes Mountains (map 1.2). It was initially registered in 1976 by a team of archaeologists under the direction of Mercedes Cárdenas (1976). The site was named Cerro la Cruz in reference to a cross that the local population had placed on top of the hill. Encompassing an area of approximately 40 ha, the hill of Cerro la Cruz rises from the floodplain of the valley floor 100–150 m, and its slopes are steep enough to require terracing in order to support structures (figure 1.1). The topography of the site consists of an arid hill with two small ravines that may channel water under exceptional conditions, such as ENSO events (Silva 1992:36).[3] The ridge at the top of the hill forms a horseshoe or U shape (figure 2.10).

Nestled within the U formation are the remains of several large structures (figures 2.10 and map 4.1). The southern face of the hillside has an even larger quantity of structural remains. A small number of structures are sparsely distributed across the northern aspect of the hillside, which

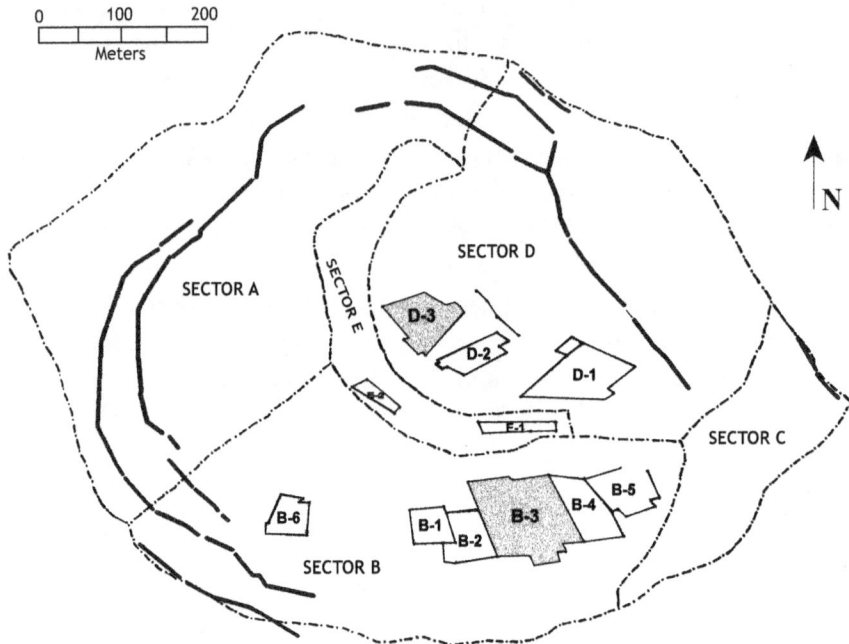

Map 4.1. Plan view of Cerro la Cruz showing sectors, compounds, and perimeter walls. Shaded areas indicate the compounds in which excavations were conducted. Map by author.

is also significantly less modified by terracing. This northern sector is bounded on the western side by a ravine and on the eastern side by a ridge that forms the northern arm of the U. Although the builders of Cerro la Cruz created terraces to support structures, the overall crescent shape of the hill is still quite apparent. The investment of labor appears to have been in creating functional space on these terraces rather than in drastically modifying the shape of the hillside. Nevertheless, the terraces themselves are dramatically visible from a distance and transform the natural slope of the hillside into a stepped pattern. The three perimeter walls surrounding the site of Cerro la Cruz comprise one of the most significant features of its built environment (map 4.1). Determining the function of these walls was an important aspect of the Cerro la Cruz project, acknowledging the defensive capability of some walls while questioning what other purposes they may have served.

Previous Ideas about the Chao Valley and Cerro la Cruz

Archaeological research in the Chao Valley has been infrequent, limited primarily to partial survey and dispersed test excavations (Kosok 1965; Cárdenas 1978; Topic and Topic 1978; Wilson 1988), and there has not yet been a comprehensive archaeological survey of the valley. Only one other potentially contemporaneous site has received serious archaeological attention, the site of Santa Rita B, approximately 10 km up the valley from Cerro la Cruz (e.g., Rosales 1999; Rosales and Kent 2000; Rosales et al., Informe Final 2008). Rosales and Kent directed a long-term project there, and they argue that Santa Rita B was occupied continually over the last three thousand years. The site's location at the throat of the valley (where the foothills of the Andes Mountains begin) is conducive to controlling the movements of people and pack animals between the highlands and coast (Kent 1998:3). They have found evidence to suggest that several large enclosures at Santa Rita B were used as camelid corrals, as well as abundant marine shells to suggest a strong trade connection with people living down valley on the coast. Since Santa Rita B was probably occupied at the same time as Cerro la Cruz, the Santa Rita B Project has been able to contribute valuable data to our understanding of the larger cultural context of the Chao Valley.

Several archaeologists have included Cerro la Cruz in their general surveys of the north coast and ventured ideas regarding its cultural affiliation, age, and function (Kosok 1965; Cárdenas 1978; Topic and Topic 1978, 1987; Silva 1991, 1992). The first description of Cerro la Cruz comes from Kosok's (1965) landmark survey of the north coast. In fact, the only two sites he mentioned from the Chao Valley are Cerro la Cruz and Huasaquito, the latter of which is located on the southern bank of the river slightly east of Cerro la Cruz (map 1.2). Other than referring to these two sites as major ruins, his comments simply described the architecture of both sites as consisting of concentric rows of "closely packed stone structures" (Kosok 1965:185). However, the aerial photographs he published preserve the best views available of each site. My visit to the site of Huasaquito confirmed the presence of Casma Incised and Casma Molded ceramics, suggesting that it may also have been a Casma polity site.

The first archaeologists to conduct formal research at Cerro la Cruz were from the team directed by Mercedes Cárdenas (1976, 1978). Because her survey covered numerous sites in a short period of time, her remarks on Cerro la Cruz were brief but significant. Her project excavated three test units at Cerro la Cruz. Based on ceramic style, Cárdenas concluded that there was an Early Horizon occupation and then a much greater Chimú occupation in the Late Intermediate period. However, the incised designs she described for the Early Horizon ceramics greatly resemble those of the Casma Incised style, and she did not provide absolute dates to support the Early Horizon interpretation. I disagree with the Early Horizon interpretation but realize that it may stem from the long-term continuity of Casma-style design elements, since the incised circle-and-dot motif found in the Casma Incised style is also known from the Early Horizon Chavín style.

In fact, Cárdenas's radiocarbon dates (AD 720 ± 60 and AD 880 ± 70, uncalibrated) place the site of Cerro la Cruz squarely in the Middle Horizon[4] (Cárdenas 1978). The Middle Horizon dates do not support Cárdenas's identification of the site as belonging to the Chimú polity, which did not fully take shape until AD 1000 and did not expand beyond the Moche, Chicama, and Virú valleys until approximately AD 1300 (Mackey 2009). I believe the inconsistencies in Cárdenas's conclusions are a direct reflection of the complexity of material culture deposited at a frontier site such as Cerro la Cruz and the relative lack of information about coastal ceramics available in the 1970s.

The Fortification Hypothesis

One of the major ideas investigated in this research concerns the characterization of the site of Cerro la Cruz as a "fortification" by Topic and Topic (1978). John Topic and Theresa Lange Topic have studied Andean militarism for over thirty years. They specify four major attributes of defensive structures: parapeted walls, moats outside the walls, slingstones, and defensible locations with restricted access (Topic and Topic 1987:48). In their 1977–80 survey of several north coast valleys, Topic and Topic located several fortified sites in the Chao Valley (1987:619). They dated these sites to the Middle Horizon and early Late Intermediate period, and they suggested the sites were later conquered by the Chimú state (Topic and Topic 1987:54). They proposed that fortifications such as the site of Cerro Coronado in the Chao Valley were never completed but were related to the first phase of the Chimú expansion (Topic and Topic 1987:54). Based on my brief survey of Cerro Coronado, I would suggest that this site may have been a Casma polity fortification, which was abandoned at the same time as the site of Cerro la Cruz due to the Chimú conquest of the valley. This interpretation is supported by the date of AD 1130 ± 60 obtained by Cárdenas (1978:30) for Cerro Coronado, a date too early for the site to have been constructed as a result of Chimú state expansion.

In their survey of the Virú Valley, Topic and Topic concluded that "there is no evidence of local fortifications during the Middle Horizon in either the lower or middle valley" (1987:54). However, they did find fortifications dating to the Late Intermediate period that were probably built by the Chimú state, including some built in a drainage that allows access to the Chao Valley (T. Topic 1990:184). This pattern of Middle Horizon fortifications in the Chao Valley but not in the Virú Valley supports the idea that the Chao Valley was the frontier zone between the Casma polity and the emerging Chimú state. The Late Intermediate period fortifications in the Virú Valley may have been built by the Chimú state when the Chao Valley became a border zone between the Casma and Chimú polities.

Theresa Lange Topic described the site of Cerro la Cruz as a "fortress" with three concentric defensive walls and parapets "consisting of benches and breastworks" (T. Topic 1990:185). Outside of a structure that was termed a "dry moat," piles of slingstones were documented and interpreted as evidence of a siege by Chimú forces (T. Topic 1990:185). Since Topic and Topic only found slingstones outside the walls, they suggested that the site had been taken without a battle. However, our survey noted slingstones within and on top of the walls, which would have served defensive purposes for the residents of the site. While the presence of slingstones on both sides of the walls does not necessarily indicate that a battle took place, it does suggest that the inhabitants of Cerro la Cruz were preparing to fight.

Shelia Pozorski and Thomas Pozorski completed an informal survey of the Chao Valley in the late 1970s (Thomas Pozorski, personal communication 1999). They reported being impressed with the high terraces at the site of Cerro la Cruz but noticed a relative lack of midden deposits, especially when compared to the nearby site of Huasaquito, which is considered to be a "twin site" to Cerro la Cruz. Thomas Pozorski observed a "ceremonial road" just inside the innermost wall of the site of Cerro la Cruz (Thomas Pozorski, personal communication 1999). Because this benchlike structure hardly rises above the surface level, I suspect the ceremonial road described by Pozorksi and Pozorski is the same feature Topic and Topic referred to as parapets.

The Strategic Location Hypothesis

The most thorough study of Cerro la Cruz prior to this project was completed by Silva (1991, 1992) as part of the Chavimochic Archaeological Survey of the Chao Valley. Silva's work included drawing maps from aerial photographs, groundproofing these maps during survey, excavating four stratigraphic trenches in Structure E-1, and excavating two test pits in Sector D. He proposed several ideas regarding the site's occupation, some of which have been supported by the evidence recovered in my project.

Silva argued that the construction of such well-organized architecture would have required a strong political organization. He viewed the site of Cerro la Cruz as a population center controlled by a local, relatively low-ranking cacique, or indigenous ruler. He pointed out that the placement of the site near the intersection of routes running north-south and west-east make it a strategic location for controlling trade. Furthermore, he referred to the site of Cerro la Cruz as a frontier settlement, as do I—although we disagree on the identity of its occupants. Silva credited the establishment of the site to the Early Chimú polity, whereas I argue that it was established by the Casma polity. He did not mention the Casma Incised style in either of his publications and may not have been aware of it. His suggestion that Cerro la Cruz was an Early Chimú site contrasts with our current understanding of the culture history of Chimú expansion, in which the Early Chimú polity occupies only the Moche and Chicama valleys. Nevertheless, there are many other points on which Silva and I agree.

Reasons for the Location of the Site of Cerro la Cruz

I argue that the Casma carefully chose the location of the site of Cerro la Cruz and that this choice involved several considerations. These concerns can be divided into four overlapping categories: control, protection, visibility, and subsistence. Control issues involve monitoring the passage of people and goods through the valley not only for purposes of trade and taxation but also for defense. Protection of the site includes both defense from invaders and protection from the flooding caused by ENSO events. The third category, visibility, refers to the prominent position of the site on a large hill, which is not only a good vantage point for viewing the surrounding area, but which can also be seen from some distance away. In the final category, subsistence factors consist of the availability of water resources in conjunction with arable land.

To address the first category, control, an examination of the Chao Valley's geography suggests a number of possible reasons for the location of Cerro la Cruz. The Chao Valley is both the shortest (west to east) and the narrowest (north to south) in the region, allowing for quick passage from the coast to the highlands or between the Virú Valley (the valley immediately north) and the Santa Valley (the valley immediately south). The site of Cerro la Cruz is situated beside the Chao River at the intersection of routes stretching both north-south and west-east. Citing these geographic advantages, Silva (1992) suggested that the site functioned as a strategic location for trade, both between the coast and the highlands and between the Virú and Santa valleys. In a similar vein, during his extensive survey of the Santa Valley, Wilson (1988) noticed many roads connecting the Chao Valley with its neighbors, which may be further evidence of intervalley trade and communication. These roads would have also served the valley's occupants defensively during an invasion.

The problem with the control hypothesis lies in the difficulty of dating roads. These routes could predate or postdate the occupation of Cerro la Cruz, or the site's inhabitants could have built them for their own use. Nevertheless, if these roads were in use during the site's occupation, they would have been beneficial to the site's residents; who may have built them is of secondary importance. Evidence for trade to support this idea would consist of exotic artifacts (that is, items not native to the valley).[5]

In terms of protection, the site's builders had a variety of reasons for constructing Cerro la Cruz the way they did: the flooding of the lower elevations during El Niño years, the need for defense, and the desire to control passage all warrant the selection of an elevated location for the site. Thus it is not surprising that they chose to occupy a large hill, centrally located in the middle valley, constructed terraces on it, and built their homes, administrative buildings, and ritual areas on its slopes. Evidence for defense can be found in the site's perimeter walls, parapets, and slingstones. The perimeter walls also assist in flood control, along with smaller retaining walls.

As far as visibility is concerned, the imposing size and strategic position of the site allow it to dominate the surrounding area, commanding a view for kilometers from its summit and demanding the attention of those who approach it. Anyone standing on the hilltop or even on the upper slopes of the site could monitor the passage of people through the valley, either for purposes of control or for protection. Two other sites which may have been occupied by the Casma polity, Cerro Coronado to the west and Huasaquito to the east, can be seen from Cerro la Cruz (map 1.2). These three sites form a visual chain up the valley, possibly in conjunction with a fourth site at Cerro Pucarachico,[6] such that signals could have been sent quickly from one site to another in the event of approaching danger. In addition, the construction of terraces, large compounds, and perimeter walls that could be seen from a distance would likely have made a distinct impression on anyone approaching Cerro la Cruz. Compound B3 in particular stands out from the other structures on the southern slope. Unfortunately there is no way to confirm these conclusions archaeologically, aside from the experience of the modern observer, but such strategies for visibility remain viable possibilities.

The final category, subsistence, addresses everyday, practical concerns such as the availability of food and water resources. As mentioned above, the confluence of the three major tributaries of the Chao River about 2 km southeast of Cerro la Cruz creates one of the largest areas of irrigable land in the valley (ONERN 1973). Of course, this water could have been used for drinking, washing, and other tasks as well, while the mud and clay from the riverbanks would have been useful for making adobe bricks. Building the site on the hillside leaves the maximum amount of arable land open for farming. Archaeological signatures to support this idea include the presence of water, remnants of irrigation canals, remains of food grown locally, and the virtual absence of architecture on areas of flat land.

In fact, in all four categories the selection of the hillside for large compound structures is especially significant. If the inhabitants of Cerro la Cruz were not concerned with control of movement through the valley, defense from invaders, protection from flooding, enhanced visibility, and availability of land and water resources, it would have been much easier to build such large structures on flat land than to carve terraces out of a steep hillside. Whether all of these possibilities are equally valid is more difficult to judge.

Problems Inherent in the Study of Peripheries

Certain methodological concerns arise in the study of all peripheries. As areas of culture contact and shifting sociopolitical alliances, archaeological remains recovered from peripheries are likely to indicate a conflicting mixture of culture influences. This mixture can be confusing and ambiguous at first glance, albeit reflective of the cross-cutting social networks found in frontiers, border zones, or other areas of great trade and cultural interaction. Depending on how long the area remained on the periphery, the longevity of a site's occupation may exacerbate the difficulty of sorting out these various cultural influences. This is because the archaeological evidence of sociopolitical change over time may be manifested as layers of accumulated material or may have been destroyed or obscured by the remains of later periods of occupation. In other words, archaeologists would expect to find evidence of contact with neighboring groups during the Casma polity occupation within the same layer of cultural remains. However, an earlier level of occupation by the Casma polity might be destroyed or covered over by the remains of a later Chimú or Inca occupation at the same site. These site deposition processes are relevant for all archaeological sites, but frontiers and border zones may prove especially problematic because of the fluctuating and dynamic nature of their occupation.

The lack of previous archaeological research in the Chao Valley adds to the difficulties of studying a frontier settlement like Cerro la Cruz. Researchers have not yet established a ceramic sequence for the Chao Valley as a whole, and the Casma polity has received only limited archaeological attention (e.g., Fung and Pimentel 1973; Fung and Williams 1977; Mackey and Klymyshyn 1990; Wilson 1995). This is a problem because distinguishing the styles of artifacts and architecture found at Cerro la Cruz is a critical step toward establishing who inhabited the site and recognizing the other cultural groups with which they interacted. Nevertheless, many of the problems encountered at the site of Cerro la Cruz are not so different from those found in most peripheries or at any site belonging to a culture that has received little archaeological attention.

Style as Identity: Architecture and Ceramics in the Andes

Archaeologists use the style of artifacts and architecture as a means for identifying the cultures that created them. But the link between the object and its creator is not always straightforward. One important consideration for the study of style is the degree of control over craft production exercised by an outside party, usually elites or the state, rather than by the producer (e.g., Costin 1998; Helms 1993; Shimada 1994). Taking ceramic style as an example, both Moche and Chimú fineware ceramics show clear evidence of standardization and elite control over production (Bawden 1996; Mackey 2001; J. Topic 1990). Mass production of mold-made pottery was common to both polities, and the iconography depicts repeated variations on a limited number of themes and subjects (e.g., Castillo 1989; Donnan 1978; Donnan and McClelland 1999; Mackey 2001). Workshops have been found in many administrative centers: at Moche sites such as Mocollope (Russell 1990; Russell, Leonard, and Briceño 1994), Galindo (Bawden 1996), and Pampa Grande (Shimada 1994) and at the Chimú sites of Chan Chan (J. Topic 1990) and San Jose de Moro (Castillo et al. 1997). Moving work areas out of individual family homes into workshops within or near elite residences demonstrates direct elite supervision of ceramic production. In fact, fineware ceramics seem to have been used as a form of currency between elites of the same and different polities (Donnan and McClelland 1999; Shimada 1994), one reason it is especially important to identify which ceramic styles are considered "fineware."

Utilitarian wares, on the other hand, may have been made either in elite-controlled workshops or by family-run cottage industries. When objects are made for consumption by someone other than the producer, the link between style, producer, and sponsor is especially important for interpreting cultural identity, because the identity of the producer may or may not correspond to the object's style, which may be dictated to some extent by the sponsor (Costin 1998; Moseley 1990). The degree of autonomy enjoyed by Andean artisans and architects may have varied widely and is difficult to determine archaeologically.

Several artifact classes have proven especially useful for the study of cultural identity in the Andean past, architecture and ceramics in particular. Included in the architecture category are artistic embellishments, such as murals and friezes or other decoration found on walls, floors, and doorways. The style of architecture, ceramics, textiles, and other artifacts can provide a wealth of information regarding the cultural identities of the people who created and used these objects and structures, including some aspects of ideology and social status. In terms of status, certain materials and types of objects are known to be associated with individuals of higher status. For example, on the north coast of Peru, adobe and plastered walls as well as roofed areas were reserved for elites, while quincha[7] architecture is indicative of commoner dwellings. Similarly, precious metals and stones, fine textiles, fineware ceramics, and other prestige goods are also believed to have been restricted to the upper classes. Ideology can also be accessed to some extent through the investigation of style. Iconography is especially useful for gaining insights into cultural beliefs as well as practices.[8]

In Andean archaeology, artifact classes are not equally useful for determining cultural identity. For example, Rodman (1992:319) uses ethnographic data to emphasize the importance of textiles as "significant markers of cultural identity" in the Andes for her study of ethnicity at the site of San Pedro de Atacama. In contrast, Janusek (2002, 2003) privileges serving vessels as important vehicles for the expression of social identities, yet advocates a multivariate approach, one that relates stylistic variation to many other data sets, including spatial organization, dietary remains, and mortuary patterns.[9]

The artifact classes most relevant to this case study include architecture and ceramics, because they are the most abundant and well-preserved remains at the site of Cerro la Cruz. However, not only is the importance of other artifacts such as textiles, wood and stone objects, and human remains acknowledged, but these artifacts are also employed as secondary sources. These artifacts are considered supplementary due to their lower frequency and poor preservation at Cerro la Cruz, yet they remain significant contributors to the overall interpretation of the site.

Research Design for the Site of Cerro la Cruz

To begin any spatial analysis, an archaeologist must document how the space is organized, divided, or enclosed. In the case of Cerro la Cruz, an examination of the architecture must include an understanding of the overall site layout and how space utilization developed diachronically. My excavation strategy was designed to map the spatial organization of the site, understand construction techniques, and elucidate the construction sequence as well as any changes or continuities in space utilization over time. During the 2000 season, we documented the architectural remains that were visible on the surface. In 2001, the second phase of the investigation focused on excavations of living floors, access patterns, and superimposed structures to expose any changes in architectural design and style. Excavations also included the retrieval and analysis of artifactual evidence for daily activities and cultural affiliation.

Reconnaissance and Preliminary Survey

Initial reconnaissance at Cerro la Cruz showed that the surface was littered with relatively well-preserved ceramics and remarkable standing architecture. I was surprised that the site was not more disturbed, considering its location next to the modern town of Buenavista (figure 4.1). I did find, however, that a 1998 ENSO event had damaged the site and certain key areas had been looted. After comparing the site's current appearance with aerial photographs from 1942 (Kosok 1965:184, Figure 10) and 1969 (figure 2.10), the effects of agricultural expansion were clear, as can be seen in comparison to a photograph from 1997 (figure 4.1). The dramatic difference in the area following the construction of the Chavimochic canal suggested the need for further investigation before more of the outer walls were destroyed.

The preliminary survey also suggested that the site's perimeter walls, both segmented and continuous, might have served multiple purposes. These purposes range from the retention of soil on the steep hillside to the direction of movement around the settlement, as in the case of the path or "ceremonial road" that runs along the uphill side of most of the remaining perimeter walls. In support of this multipurpose functionality, a resident of the town of Buenavista reported that the current inhabitants of the area have repaired a segment of one of the lowest walls to protect their fields from flooding during ENSO events. Evidently, this series of short wall segments helps break the flow of water down the *quebrada* (ravine).

Survey and Mapping

In the summer of 2000, we created a digital base map of the site, along with the detailed interior maps of two compounds selected for excavations, Compounds B3 and D3 (maps 4.1–4.3). I selected these compounds

Map 4.2. Detailed map of Compound B3 showing excavation units, tripartite division of space, and access patterns. The dotted lines indicate the division of the compound into upper, middle, and lower sections. Map by author.

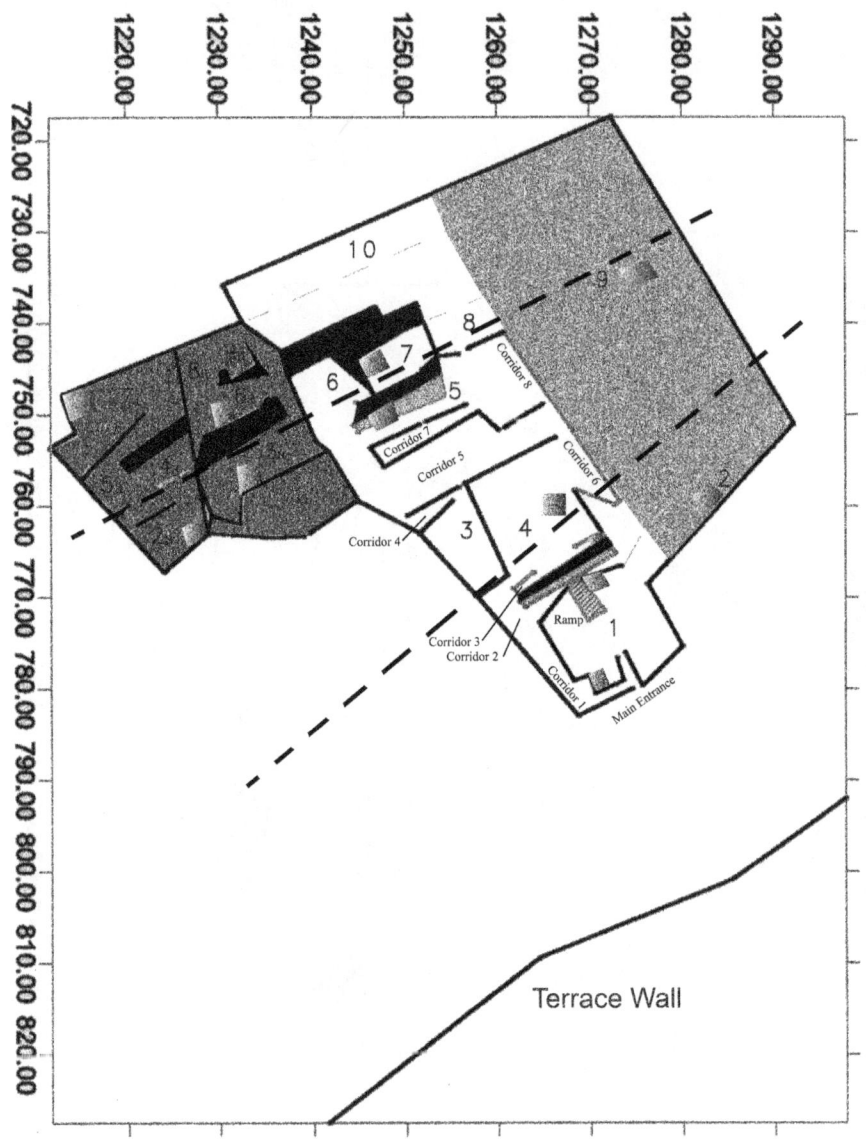

Map 4.3. Detailed map of Compound D3 showing excavation units, tripartite division of space, and access patterns. The dotted lines indicate the division of the compound into upper, middle, and lower sections. Map by author.

for three reasons: their excellent state of preservation, the abundant surface remains, and their central location among the densest architectural remains on the site's southern and eastern slopes, respectively.

The architecture at Cerro la Cruz shows a distinct contrast between more formal, organized enclosed space (within compounds) and the irregularly shaped terraces distributed around the compounds. Although I cannot say with complete certainty, the layout and distribution of the compounds suggest a higher degree of planning than the terraces, which seem to have been constructed in a less controlled, more organic fashion. I chose, therefore, to focus on the internal spatial organization of Compounds B3 and D3. The detailed mapping of these compounds shaped my hypotheses concerning the use of space in what appear to be ceremonial, public, and domestic areas. My observations during the mapping process influenced my selection of areas for strategic excavation to determine the functions of individual rooms and structures. Similarly, careful examination of the perimeter walls revealed several possible gateways, especially on the north and west slopes, which indicate the pattern of access into the site of Cerro la Cruz.

During the 2000 season, we also completed a surface collection of diagnostic ceramics and botanical remains in Compounds B3 and D3. The purpose of this collection was to document quantities of surface scatter and to examine qualitative characteristics such as vessel forms and styles. Rather than collect the thousands of body sherds on the surface, we sorted sherds by paste type and took a count on a room-by-room basis.[10] This surface collection of diagnostic ceramics and organic remains contributed to my hypotheses for the functions of rooms, which were tested during excavation. Although I compared the surface data to the excavation data, they were analyzed separately in recognition of the greater effects deposition and erosion processes have on surface artifacts. I treated surface organic remains as only suggestive of what excavations might reveal, since modern plant and animal remains were mixed with preconquest remains on the surface. For example, we found both large modern corncobs and tiny prehispanic corncobs on the surface; these clearly dated to different time periods.[11]

Sampling Strategies

To understand the duration of occupation and the history of deposition at the site, strategic sampling was applied to the two sectors that contained the majority of cultural remains, Sectors B and D (map 4.1). As mentioned above, I selected one compound in each sector to obtain data for comparison, Compounds B3 and D3. Outside of the compounds, I selected the locations of five test units to acquire data for comparison with that from the compound interiors. The goal of this comparison was to locate differences and similarities in spatial organization and function between areas outside of compounds and those enclosed within. Finally, in an attempt to determine the relationship between the construction of the perimeter walls and the compounds, I selected locations for the excavation of two trenches between the concentric perimeter walls. These trenches were intended to serve two goals: to provide stratigraphic profiles showing the layers of accumulated cultural remains and to test for the presence of subsurface architectural remains between the walls. Unfortunately, these areas did not produce useful stratigraphic profiles. I expected the comparison of these trenches to reveal any depositional differences between the two areas and to help create a chronological sequence for the site's occupation, but there was almost no stratigraphy to recover. Instead, the chronological sequence was developed through an analysis of the events recorded in the compound architecture, with the assistance of radiocarbon dating. However, the second goal of testing for the presence of subsurface architecture was achieved, albeit with differing results.

Excavation Methods

The interior mapping of Compounds B3 and D3 that was completed during the 2000 season resulted in the division of rooms into nine categories (maps 4.2 and 4.3). The categories are based on each room's location on the hillside and possible function. I created these categories during the mapping process when I noticed a difference in architectural style and the distribution of surface artifacts that suggested a tripartite division of space within the compounds. My proposition was that rooms in the left, or First Section, served domestic functions; the middle, or Second Section, was for public or administrative uses; and the right, or Third Section, was a sacred or ceremonial space. Of course, excavation was required to test this idea. I then split the rooms in these three numbered sections into three groups (lower, middle, and upper) based on their location on the slope, for a total of nine categories. Thus a room could be categorized as lower, middle, or upper First Section; lower, middle, or upper Second Section; or lower, middle, or upper Third Section (maps 4.2 and 4.3).

In the 2001 season, 2 m × 2 m units were excavated in rooms from each category of both compounds to determine whether there was a consistent link between room location and function as suggested by the tripartite division of space explained above. The resulting excavations included seventeen units in thirteen rooms of Compound B3 and twelve units in eleven rooms of Compound D3. All units and significant features within these units were added to the base map during the 2001 season.

In addition to the compound excavations, two units (Test1 and Test2) were excavated on the western side of the site, nearly at the end of the terraced area. There are no compounds around this bend in the hillside, and these structures were more isolated from the central structural zone. Test1 was placed on the terrace immediately inside of Wall 3 for comparison with Test2, which was situated on a terrace higher up the slope. The goal was to determine what sorts of activities had been taking place outside of the compounds and whether the height of a terrace along the slope would correlate with any difference in activity or deposition.

During the 2000 season mapping process, I had noticed dense surface debris from a wide variety of vessels in the area directly east of Compound D3 (figure 4.2). In 2001, I investigated the area as the possible location of a ceramic workshop. Two units (Test3 and Test4) were excavated in this area to test this idea. Finally, one unit (Test5) was excavated against the eastern side of Wall 3 (in Sector D) to find the base of the wall and locate any adjoining architectural remains.

Nearly all excavation units began as 2 m × 2 m squares, but some were extended to uncover features or follow walls. All units were excavated to the sterile level, with the singular exception of unit B6R6U2X2. In the case of B6R6U2X2, we found a wall at a depth of 1.465 m below datum. Unfortunately, we could not expose this wall further without destroying the upper level of the platform. Therefore, we were unable to reach the sterile level in this portion of the unit.

We used shovels to clear the surface debris, then we continued excavation according to natural levels using trowels and brushes until it appeared that the sterile level had been reached. If the sterile level did not

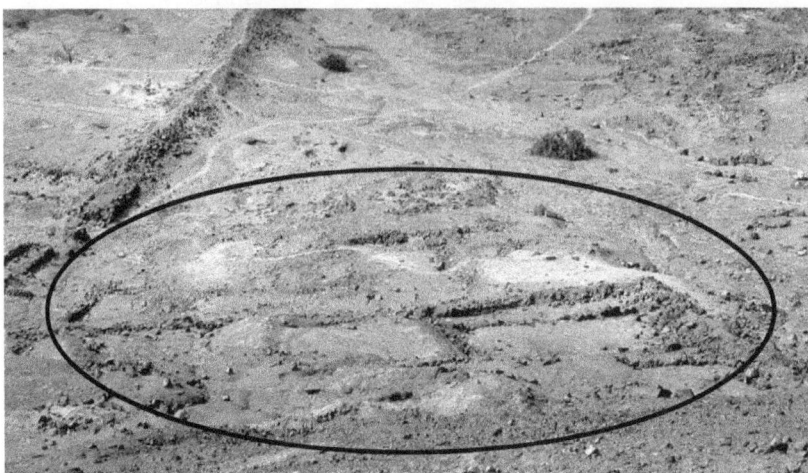

Figure 4.2. Ceramic workshop at the base of Compound D3. Photo by author.

include bedrock, we used shovels to confirm that no further cultural remains lay below the sterile soil. We screened all unit soil with 1/8-inch mesh. The only exceptions to this procedure were the two trenches, which were excavated with shovels and whose soil was not screened. Since the purpose of the trenches was to reveal stratigraphy and locate subsurface architecture, we collected only unusual or especially significant artifacts. In fact, artifacts were relatively scarce in the trenches, as were architectural remains.

In general, the excavation strategy focused on retrieving data from a strategic sampling of features within the compounds to determine change and continuity in the structure and function of rooms as well as trenching between segments of the site's perimeter walls to determine the relation of the walls to the enclosed structures. This methodology focused on understanding the relationship between sociopolitical change and the modification of architecture and spatial organization. For example, similar patterns of spatial organization would suggest that the same group of people built all of the compounds, while chronological controls such as stratigraphy, superimposition of architecture, and radiocarbon dating were used to determine the sequence of construction. Simultaneously, we collected artifacts to investigate the possibility of cross-cutting social networks and how they may have affected the occupation of the site. Because material culture styles can serve as indicators of cultural affiliation, I examined the styles of the artifacts recovered (such as ceramics or textiles) to identify the site's inhabitants and to determine the groups with whom those inhabitants interacted.

Although nearly a thousand years have passed since the site was occupied, the artifacts of frontier life are relatively well preserved, due in part to the dry climate of the desert coast and in part to the fortuitous location of the site on a hillside, which is not suitable for farming and is therefore relatively safe from being plowed. Unfortunately, the same cannot be said for the site's cemetery, which appears to have been located under the adjacent modern town of Buenavista. This realization was truly disappointing, since skeletal remains and mortuary practices can contribute many important clues to the identities of a site's occupants. However, material culture recovered from the habitation site can be used to explain much about the people who lived there.

The primary data sources for my identification of Cerro la Cruz as a Casma site included architectural style and spatial organization, ceramic style, textile style and technology, and skeletal analysis of the single burial excavated in Compound B3. These data sets were interpreted using direct historical analogy, including both Inca and Chimú ethnohistory, ethnographic analogies to modern Andean peoples, and some archaeological analogies to other research on identity in the Andes.

Post-Excavation Analysis

Artifacts such as ceramics, tools, ritual items, and food remains provide evidence for subsistence practices and indicate functions for individual rooms within the compounds. Special attention was given to exotic materials that may have been traded, as evidence for interaction with other regions. Analysis of artifacts and spatial data also provides evidence for higher-level interpretations of site functions and cultural identities. For example, the presence of ceramic molds suggested pottery production; drinking and storage vessels signified the consumption of maize beer; and the style of serving vessels indicated the cultural identity of the individuals involved in production and consumption. Maize beer, or *chicha*, is known from both ethnohistorical and ethnographic data to be a central component of many ceremonial activities in the Andes, especially feasting. Archaeological evidence for the production of *chicha* includes corncobs, large storage vessels called tinajas, drinking vessels called keros, and residues of the fermented beverage, which have been found in some of these vessels. Additionally, the size of the vessels may indicate the number of people participating in feasting and drinking activities. In this manner, sociopolitical events ranging from sponsored feasts and ritual intoxication to changes in power or social control may be reflected in the style and quantities of storage and serving vessels, and the controlled production of such products as ceramics and maize beer.

I analyzed the ceramics in terms of style (including design, iconography, vessel form, and function), technology, and density of distribution. While there is currently no ceramic sequence for the Chao Valley, the ceramic sequences for the neighboring valleys of Virú and Santa are well known (Collier 1955; Strong and Evans 1952; Wilson 1988), as is the Chimú ceramic sequence for the Moche Valley (Donnan and Mackey 1978; Topic and Moseley 1983). The ceramics from Cerro la Cruz, therefore, may be dated comparatively.

I compared the site layout and architectural style with data from other north coast sites, dating to the Middle Horizon and Late Intermediate period, to search for indicators of cultural affiliation and chronology. For example, typical Wari-style architecture features D-shaped structures and agglutinated rooms while the Chimú style favors U-shaped structures called *audiencias* (figure 2.1) and baffled entryways. The presence of any of these architectural features may indicate some form of cultural influence, whether imposed by an outside group or voluntarily incorporated. The absence of any of these known architectural signatures may indicate a unique cultural style or a local variation on a foreign style.

Although we did not find much midden depth at Cerro la Cruz, we did take consistent soil samples for comparison of organic remains between structures at the site. We collected soil samples from each level of natural strata in all excavation units and analyzed them for evidence of subsistence as well as to estimate the climatic and environmental conditions over time. We recovered organic remains from soil samples using both dry sieving and flotation methods in order to compare the relative utility and productivity of each method.[12] The results show that both methods were effective at retrieving identifiable botanical remains. Fortunately, the level of organic preservation at the site was also sufficient for radiocarbon dating.

Artifacts were catalogued, and some preliminary analysis was conducted at the project's laboratory in the town of Chao. Further analysis of organic remains was completed at the University of Trujillo, skeletal and ceramic analysis was conducted in the project laboratory in the town of Huanchaco, and textiles were taken to a textile expert for analysis in the town of Pacasmayo.[13] With written permission from Peru's National Institute of Culture, twelve carbon samples and thirteen adobe samples were transported to the United States for analysis. The results of these analyses and their interpretation are subsequently presented in chapter 5.

5

Life on the Edge of the Casma Polity

The site of Cerro la Cruz, like many other sites on the arid Peruvian coast, contains an abundance of well-preserved artifacts and architectural features that have remained standing since the time of the site's occupation. This rich archaeological record can help us to understand the daily lives of ancient Peruvians in a Casma frontier town. As described in chapter 4, I designed the research program at Cerro la Cruz to answer the following questions: Who were the residents of Cerro la Cruz and how did they make their living? How did they build the site and for what purposes? What did they eat and where was that food produced? This study also addressed issues such as how the Casma were organized socially and what evidence there is for their political leadership or religious activities, and perhaps catch a glimpse of how they viewed their world. In this chapter, I interpret the archaeological remains recovered from Cerro la Cruz to determine what this data can tell us about the lives of the site's inhabitants. The site's architecture and spatial organization, ceramics, botanical and faunal remains, textiles, and other artifacts are used to reconstruct a picture of life in this fortified town. These features and artifacts are described, followed by the interpretations that can be gleaned from them.

The Perimeter Walls and Other Fortifications

The terraced hillside of Cerro la Cruz has previously been interpreted as a fortification, surrounded by three defensive walls, with parapets consisting of "benches and breastworks" (T. Topic 1990:185) and topped by slingstones. These walls are built of stone and/or adobe, encompassing an area of approximately 40 hectares. Walls 2 and 3 are constructed primarily of uncut stone from the hillside stacked in layers with no evidence of mortar or plaster. Some of the wider segments of Wall 2, such as those on the eastern end, show case-and-fill construction, in which two lines of stacked stones are separated by rubble fill, approximately 2 m wide. Only Wall 1 used adobe in its construction. The fragments of Wall 1 on the southern side of the site are built with adobe casing on either side of rock fill, with more adobes on top of the fill, while the eastern fragments consist of adobes and some soil fill. Rather than using only solid adobe bricks, a costly labor expenditure, the builders interspersed adobes with layers of soil fill, a less stable but cheaper and quicker construction technique. It is likely that the outermost wall was covered in adobes and plaster more for appearance than defense since adobe walls are easier to scale and more costly to make than uncut stone walls. All the larger wall segments are tapered, wider at the bottom to support the weight of the rock.

The site map (map 4.1) shows the relationship between the compounds[1] and the concentric perimeter walls of Cerro la Cruz. By the time of my field research, Wall 1 had been almost completely destroyed, most likely by the rare but often devastating floods that can accompany ENSO events. The extremely fragmentary condition of this wall makes it impossible to determine whether it once enclosed the entire site. Although Wall 2 and Wall 3 are much better preserved, they do not enclose the compounds on the southern side of the mountain. While it is certainly possible that at least one of these walls once continued on this side and has since been destroyed, I found no remnants of these walls, nor were they visible in 1969 aerial photographs. This exposure of the southern compounds challenges the notion of a purely defensive function for the perimeter walls.

The heights of the walls vary significantly as they follow the undulating slopes of the hill. The outermost wall, Wall 1, is the tallest at approximately 2 m, and most of the remaining fragments are on relatively flat ground. Walls 2 and 3 appear much larger and more intimidating when viewed from the downhill side, while on the uphill side they are at times only knee high. However, the eastern end of Wall 2 is significantly taller (at approximately 2 m), probably also because it rests on flat ground at the base of the hill. Wall 3 is farther upslope and never more than 0.65 m high.

Our survey counted four deliberate gateways and seven unintentional breaks in Wall 2 while Wall 3 showed seven deliberate gates and eight unintentional breaks (map 4.1). Wall 1 is so completely destroyed that counting gates is not possible. Distinguishing between gateways (deliberate breaks) in the walls and unintentional breaks (where the wall has been washed downhill) is somewhat difficult. The best criteria for an intentional gateway are finished corners on at least one side of the opening. However, it is possible that some gates were widened by erosion and thus no longer appear intentional. There are paths along the uphill sides of Walls 2 and 3, and at some points, these paths are defined by a line of stones approximately a meter away from the wall.

There are also sparse remains of canals, which Theresa Lange Topic (1990) views as a dry moat. I argue that these canals may have served a dual purpose: as canals when the river was flowing or during sporadic flooding, and as a dry moat the rest of the year. Outside the canal/dry moat, more piles of slingstones had been found by Topic and Topic, which they considered to be evidence of a besieging force attacking, perhaps in Chimú times (T. Topic 1990:185). Unfortunately, none of the outer piles of slingstones remain, having been plowed under or removed during the agricultural expansion onto the site. However, there are scatters of fist-sized stones on the surface between Walls 1 and 2 on the eastern side of the hill, as well as on top of Wall 2 along the western slope. The site's residents probably made these piles for defensive purposes.

Due to the expansion of agricultural fields onto the site, it was impossible to demarcate the site using the distribution of surface artifacts or indications of subsurface architecture, so I used the perimeter walls to delimit the site's boundaries. However, it is likely that during the site's occupation structures existed outside of Wall 1 that have since been destroyed. Based on the results of the trench excavations, there appears to have been relatively little architecture erected between the perimeter walls. Instead, most likely smaller, less permanent structures were erected in this area, as suggested by the evidence that was found for *quincha* architecture, at least on the eastern side of the hill. However, the presence of any architecture, especially between Walls 1 and 2, could imply that the walls were built in succession as the settlement expanded outside Walls 2 and 3, the more interior walls (map 4.1). This expansion may have required the building of Wall 1, the most exterior perimeter wall, for defensive or delimiting purposes or to protect against occasional floods.

My comparison of the 1969 and 1997 aerial photographs (figures 2.10 and 4.1) revealed that several canals, which were dry and located in areas not being farmed at the time of the earlier photographs, are now being used. This suggests that many of the canals being used to irrigate modern fields were built directly on prehispanic canals, a fairly common practice on the Peruvian coast. This modern land use pattern illustrates Silva's

(1991) point that the location of the site on the hillside left the arable land free for agricultural production. This decision was particularly wise in light of the fact that the Chao Valley is an area with few reliable water resources and irrigable land is at a premium.

Architectural Investigations: The Compounds and Their Features

When the architectural differences between the five sectors of Cerro la Cruz were examined, it became clear that the site's more elaborate architecture is situated in Sectors B and D, where all of the compounds are located—six compounds in Sector B and three compounds in Sector D (figure 4.1). There are also four structures along the ridgetop in Sector E which appear to have served primarily ceremonial functions. Sectors A and C contain only some scattered, relatively small terraces. I assigned structures a number as well as the letter of the respective sector; hence the second compound in Sector B is named Compound B2.

Excavations at Cerro la Cruz focused on two compounds (B3 and D3) as well as on a sample of noncompound areas that included two terraces, a ceramic workshop, and the spaces between the perimeter walls. In addition to identifying the various architectural elements of these areas and their functions, I paid attention to their locations within the layout of each compound, as well as within the overall spatial organization of the site. Ultimately, I used this data to interpret the site's spatial organization, sequence of construction, and room functions, as well as the meaning of the site's architecture.

Compound B3: Architectural Description

Compound B3 is the largest and most imposing compound at the site, with complex internal architecture (figure 5.1). It is located at the center of the five agglutinated compounds on the southern side of the hill (map 4.1). The large rock wall that separates Compound B3 from the adjacent compounds measures 97 m in length by 65 m in width, making Compound B3 nearly twice the size of Compound D3. The height of the compound wall varies but averages around 1 m, which is relatively tall compared to other compound exterior walls. The interior consists of thirty-two rooms built on terraces of varying heights and widths and is delimited from the adjacent compounds by a large rock wall on all four sides. As can be seen

Figure 5.1. Compound B3 (*circled*) viewed from the south. Photo by author.

in map 4.2, the compound is not strictly rectangular but has an irregular polygonal shape.

Most of the compounds are constructed entirely of uncut stone from the hillside. Compound B3, however, contains more adobe construction than any other structure at Cerro la Cruz, although in many walls the adobe rests on stone foundations. Most of the adobe is concentrated in the central section of the compound (map 4.2). The adobe-covered areas of this compound were virtually free of surface ceramic scatter in comparison to the rooms on either side. The lower portion of the compound contains a structure that bears resemblance to other small north coast burial platforms, except that rather than standing on relatively flat ground, it juts out from the hillside.

Silva (1992) suggested that Compound B3 was a public building, and I would propose that it may have had a ceremonial aspect as well. Given the size of Compound B3, it was neither practical nor necessary to excavate all the rooms. Instead, rooms were selected from each of the nine categories described in chapter 4 for a strategic sample (map 4.2). The first three units excavated were located in Rooms 3, 6, and 9—one room in each section of the tripartite division. These rooms are the largest and possibly most important in Compound B3. Units were also placed in Rooms 10, 18, 18a, and 30 of the First Section, Rooms 11, 12, 21, and 28 of the Second Section, and finally Rooms 22 and 26 of the Third Section. A total of seventeen units were excavated, one in each room except for Rooms 3, 6, 9, and 11, each of which had two units (map 4.2). Midden deposition was often not deep, and, therefore, excavations tended to be shallow, especially in the rooms farther upslope.[2]

Compound D3: Architectural Description

Compound D3 is sheltered within the U of the hillside, on the eastern slopes of the site (figure 5.2). It is the best-preserved and most complete compound in Sector D in terms of finished construction. In general, this side of the hill seems to have suffered more from the forces of ENSO events and earthquakes, and the structures on it are more eroded. Significantly smaller than Compound B3, Compound D3 measures 60 m long by 65 m wide and encloses seventeen rooms. The exterior compound wall is lower than that of Compound B3, varying considerably in height but averaging 0.5 m. The compounds on this side of the hill are not agglutinated as are Compounds B1 through B5; they do not share any exterior

Figure 5.2. Compound D3 (*outlined*) viewed from the north. Photo by author.

walls. However, the spaces between compounds are filled with terraces that may have supported a number of less permanent structures at some point. A wall runs along the front edge of a large terrace immediately below Compounds D2 and D3 (map 4.3), which permits easy passage between the two compounds. This prominent terrace may have been intended to demonstrate some connection between these two compounds or their occupants. One can only speculate on the nature of this connection, but perhaps these compounds were occupied by related families or closely associated officials.

Compound D3 exhibits the same uncut stone construction as Compound B3; however, the use of adobe to cover stone foundations is much less prevalent. Excavations were conducted in the same manner as in Compound B3. I selected eleven locations for excavation, sampling the same nine categories discussed in chapter 4 to test the tripartite spatial organization proposition. In the First Section, one unit each was placed in Rooms 2a, 3a, 6a, and 7a (map 4.3).[3] In the Second Section, two units were placed in Room 1 and one unit was placed in each of Rooms 4, 5, and 7, as well as in Corridor 3. In the Third Section, one unit was placed in Room 2 and one in Room 9. Fewer cultural materials were found in Compound D3 as compared to Compound B3.

Tripartite Division of Space in Compounds B3 and D3

The interior spatial organization of the compounds is complex and non-standardized, yet it does fit into a larger pattern. A quick comparison shows that niched rooms were found in both compounds at approximately the same place in the spatial organization: the upper half of the Second Section. Both compounds also have enclosed rock formations in their Third Sections. One of the ideas tested during excavations was whether the compounds exhibited a tripartite division of space, as shown in the interior maps of Compounds B3 and D3 (maps 4.2 and 4.3). This premise, based on differences in architectural and artifactual remains observed on the surface, suggested that the compounds could be divided into three sections, which served distinct functions. As demonstrated in table 5.1, the greatest sherd density was found in the First Sections of each compound, a lower density characterized the Second Sections, and the Third Sections showed a dramatic decrease in sherd density. This same re-

Table 5.1. Surface Ceramics by Section in Compounds B3 and D3

Compound	First Section rooms	Second Section rooms	Third Section rooms
B3	4,087 sherds	3,195 sherds	1,125 sherds
D3	1,318 sherds[a]	1,341 sherds	117 sherds

[a] Although the First Section in Compound D3 has slightly fewer ceramics than the Second Section, the First Section occupies less than half the surface area of either the Second or Third Sections. Therefore, the density of the distribution is highest in the First Section.

lationship of decreasing quantity by section was also found in the sample of excavated rim sherds.

As illustrated in map 4.2 (shaded dark gray), the First Section in Compound B3 contained rooms built from less formal stone construction and which held dense surface scatter of ceramics. This relatively high quantity of ceramic refuse, combined with the lower quality of the stone construction, suggests more domestic functions for the rooms in this section. The Second Section of Compound B3 (unshaded, map 4.2), consists of spacious rooms of adobe-covered stone that were left relatively clean, with little ceramic scatter. This section also included a room with three large niches (B3R28). The lower density of refuse and the predominance of adobe, a more expensive style of construction, indicate that these rooms may have been used for more public functions. The Third Section of Compound B3 (shaded light gray, map 4.2) contrasts markedly with the other two sections because it lacks terracing and room divisions. Instead, the hillside is left unmodified and a hefty boulder is enclosed within a large space. This section also contained the lowest densities of ceramic refuse.

The interior map of Compound D3 (map 4.3) shows a tripartite division of space similar to that of Compound B3, although the exact proportions and overall size of the compounds differ. The First Section (shaded dark gray, map 4.3) includes several small rooms of substandard construction compared to the rest of the compound. Again, I argue that this lower-quality construction, combined with a high density of surface ceramic refuse, is indicative of domestic activities. As in Compound B3, the Second Section of Compound D3 (unshaded, map 4.3) contains more adobe-covered stone construction as well as a niched room (D3R5). This section also includes architectural features, such as a front plaza complete with a small, ramped platform (D3R1), that are indicative of more public functions. Finally, the Third Section (shaded light gray, map 4.3) consists of an almost completely unmodified open space with deeply weathered granite left exposed. This area contained far less ceramic surface scatter than any other section. I suggest this lack of architecture was deliberate, perhaps even symbolic of the relationship between humans and the natural environment. The white color of the eroded granite (granodiorite) outcrop in this section may have been taken into consideration during the planning of Compound D3, especially since it was (and still is) visible from a significant distance.

My interpretation of these Third Sections of Compounds B3 and D3 is more difficult to substantiate, but I believe their meaning may be analogous to the later Inca practice of enclosing sacred rocks or rock outcrops (called *huacas*) within walled courtyards (Hyslop 1990:102). Some uncarved stones were venerated and received offerings, while others marked places important to the ritual system (Hyslop 1990:104–5). But the significance of certain stones did not originate with the Inca Empire. At least two examples on the north coast predate the Inca conquest. A sacred rock at the site of Túcume was so significant to the local people that it was made the central focus of a temple (Heyerdahl et al. 1996:113). Four adobe walls surround the unmodified stone, and post holes suggest that the area was roofed (Heyerdahl, Sandweiss, and Narvaez 1995:101–5, Figures 69–73; Heyerdahl et al. 1996:117, Figures 78–79). Numerous offerings were found, including *Spondylus* shells, miniature metal objects, figurines, clothing, and sacrificed llamas (Heyerdahl et al. 1996:118). This temple dates to approximately the same period as the occupation of Compound B3 (c. AD 900–1100) but is associated with the Lambayeque polity described in chapter 4. Evidence for the importance of certain stones on the north coast can be dated even earlier. At the site of Moche, an important Moche polity site, there is a rock outcropping enclosed within a courtyard of the temple Huaca de la Luna, associated with numerous sacrificial victims. Steve Bourget (2001) argued that this outcropping may have been viewed as symbolic of the mountain behind the temple, Cerro Blanco.

At Cerro la Cruz, the enclosure of boulders, rock outcrops, and "natural" space in the Third Sections of both Compounds B3 and D3 may have served as a symbol of the sacredness of the Andean landscape. Although the exact form of the enclosures is not the same, the Andean practice of planning architecture around important stones (e.g., Heyerdahl,

Sandweiss, and Narváez 1995:114–15; Hyslop 1990:102; McEwan 2006:170) may be analogous to the enclosure of boulders and rock outcrops at the site of Cerro la Cruz. Thus I have labeled the Third Sections of the compounds sacred spaces, probably reserved for ceremonial activities. In summary, the majority of residential activities would have taken place in the "domestic" First Section; the "public" Second Section would have been used for both administrative and ritual activities, since these were not entirely differentiated in early Andean polities; and the "natural" Third Section would have served ceremonial purposes.

Reception Areas

One room in each compound studied stood out as a likely area for receiving visitors: Room 6 in Compound B3 (B3R6) and Room 1 in Compound D3 (D3R1). B3R6 is a large open room divided into two halves by a low-walled corridor, Corridor 1 (map 4.2). A low bench was uncovered against the north wall, and underneath the front end of this bench was the burial of a child (figure 5.3). This was the only burial encountered in

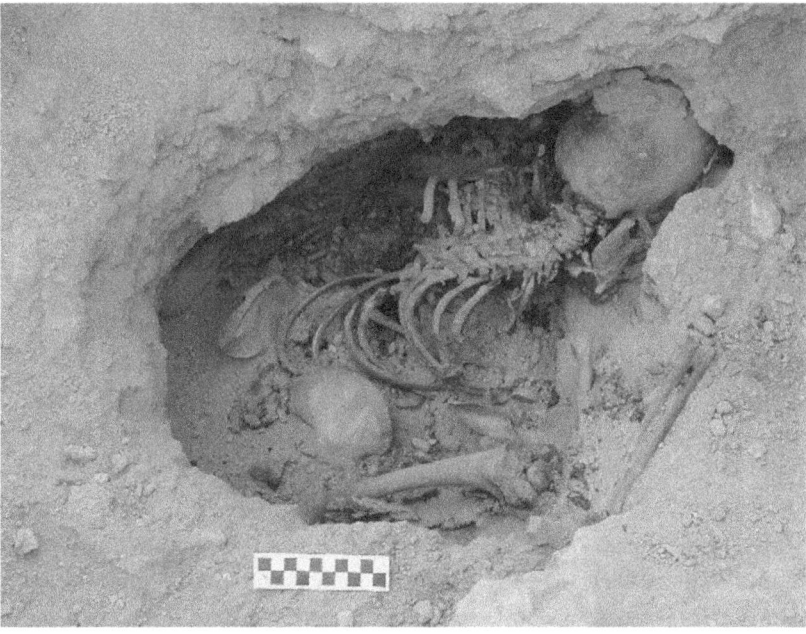

Figure 5.3. Close-up of Burial 1 in situ (B3R6U1). Photo by author.

these excavations. The small pit was barely large enough to fit the body and there were no associated grave goods, only a pendant made from a *mishpingo* seed. The results of the skeletal analysis are discussed later in this chapter.

Room 6 was the most interesting room in Compound B3, not only because of the unexpected burial (Burial 1) found beneath the bench but also for its well-preserved walls. Amazingly, the lower end of the North and East Walls of Room 6 Unit 1 retained some yellow paint, while the upper end of the East Wall appeared to have some white and red paint. In addition, pieces of adobe with cane imprints on one side and yellow paint on the other were found on top of the floor, along with a few pieces of cane. These remains come from a fallen roof, with cane supporting the painted plaster. There was only one floor in this unit, and it was topped by a thin layer of ash and burned material, a common feature in almost all units excavated. A second unit located in the northwest corner of the eastern half of B3R6 showed evidence of at least three phases of construction. Although this room appears to have been an area for receiving guests, it was quite clean, and no evidence for feasting was found.

In contrast, the central front room (D3R1) of Compound D3 exhibits an important, recognizable architectural layout (map 4.3). It consists of a small rectangular plaza with a low platform that runs along the back or West Wall of the room and a small ramp which leads up to the platform. This pattern of an enclosed plaza with a low ramped platform is common on the north coast as an area to receive visitors and conduct ceremonial activities (Moore 1996b:134–35). D3R1 contained the highest quantity of surface sherds in the entire compound, as well as food remains from a typical coastal meal, indicating that it may have been a venue for feasting.

Storage

Compound B3, Room 10 (B3R10) was interpreted as a storeroom on the basis of three criteria: its contents, its restricted access pattern, and an architectural feature known as a "step-over" doorway, which is associated with Chimú storerooms (Day 1982). First, this unit contained the highest quantity and variety of ceramics of all the excavated areas. Second, this room demonstrated a restricted access pattern (figure 5.4), consisting of a narrow doorway, only 0.75 m wide, and a U-shaped corridor that leads around an interior space, passing two storage areas. These storage areas

Figure 5.4. Compound B3, Room 10, Unit 1 (B3R10U1) showing restricted access pattern. Photo by author.

are equipped with the third criteria, "step-over" doorways. A "step-over" doorway has a high threshold, in this case the height of one adobe, which requires anyone entering to step over the adobes blocking the bottom of the door. Nearly all of B3R10 was excavated because it proved to be the only unambiguous storeroom in Compound B3.

It is rather strange that only one storage room was found in Compound B3 while none were found in Compound D3. This suggests that either new archaeological indicators for Casma storerooms are needed or, more likely, that the residents did not have many surplus goods to store. This may indicate that any surplus was being shipped somewhere else, such as to a capital city.

Niched Rooms

As mentioned above, there was a niched room in each of the excavated compounds. Compound B3, Room 28 (B3R28) consists of three large freestanding niches in the upper-central section of Compound B3. Of these three niches, only the two westernmost niches (Niches 1 and 2) were sufficiently preserved for excavation (figure 5.5). Each measured 1.25 m × 0.87 m. I interpreted the cane lying on the plastered floor of Niche 1 as the remains of a fallen roof. Two wooden poles were found at the base of the niches. These may have been used as supports for the roof. The construction of the niches consisted of a stone foundation covered by adobes and plaster.

Compound D3, Room 5 (D3R5) contained at least four niches, two on either side of what appears to be a small staircase or perhaps a collapsed fifth niche (figure 5.6). These niches were almost exactly the same size and shape as those found in B3R28. A poorly preserved plaster floor was uncovered in front of the niches. In D3R5U1, which measured 3 m × 2 m, only the two best preserved niches were excavated. Both measured 1.3 m × 1 m and were 0.75 m above the floor. Since the tops were eroded, it appeared that they were at least 0.52 m tall but may have been taller. Cane and pieces of adobe fragments with cane impressions were found lying on the floors of the niches, again indications of a fallen roof. A support pole similar to those found in the niched room (Room 28) of Compound B3 was also found on the floor in front of the niches. The construction of these niches, although similar in dimension and shape to those in B3R28, consisted mostly of rock covered in plaster and few adobes.

Silva (1992:42–43) also documented a structure on the hilltop (E1 on map 4.1) that includes a row of five niches similar in size to those found in Compounds B3 and D3. Unfortunately, these had been severely damaged

Figure 5.5. Compound B3, Room 28, Unit 1 (B3R28U1) with two niches and floor. Photo by author.

Figure 5.6. Compound D3, Room 5, Unit 1 (D3R5U1) showing two niches and Floor 1. Photo by author.

by looting by the time my project began, prohibiting further study. In addition, all of the niches in the two excavated compounds were found empty, as is often the case in Andean archaeological sites. However, based on ethnohistorical data and analogies to niches at other coastal sites, I suspect these were used to hold either sacred objects or perhaps even ancestor mummies (Conklin 1990:64–65; Isbell 1997:205).

Intrasite Access Patterns

Another aspect of spatial organization investigated in this project was the access system used in the compounds, the means by which people could move from room to room and terrace to terrace. This proved to be much more difficult to interpret than I had anticipated. Access points, such as doorways, stairs, and ramps, were few and difficult to find. I expected to find ramps leading from the lower platforms to higher levels in Compound B3 because ramps are commonly found in the architecture of both the Moche and Chimú polities. But with the one exception of the ramped platform in D3R1, ramps at Cerro la Cruz either never existed or have been so thoroughly eroded as to be unrecognizable. The few stairways, corridors, and one ramp that were found are shown in maps 4.2 and 4.3. In Compound B3, only two stairways were identified: one between Rooms 14 and 16 and one between Rooms 17 and 22. No *clearly* defined stairways were found in Compound D3. The only possible stairway may actually be a collapsed niche in Room 5 of Compound D3. Because the terraces are often too high to simply step up from level to level, ladders may have been used to traverse these divides. Ladders would restrict access even further since they can be easily removed to prevent ascension. This could serve defensive purposes in case of an attack. For lower terraces, it is also possible that there were stairways which have since collapsed and are now indistinguishable from other wall fall.

Corridors are the most common means for connecting rooms to one another at Cerro la Cruz. Compound B3 has at least five corridors (map 4.2), but not nearly enough corridors to explain how the occupants moved throughout the compound. Unfortunately, it is not always clear whether corridors connected rooms or were blind alleys. For example, Corridor 1 in Compound B3 runs down the middle of Room 6. It is unclear whether it connected Room 2 with Room 11 via ramps or stairways, but there was no indication of a door opening from the corridor into either side of B3R6.

With only a few exceptions, doorways in Compound B3 are often ambiguous because of collapsed walls. In those cases where doorways can be clearly identified, they are generally the only entrance into the room and tend to be narrow. For example, the only door into B3R10 measures a mere 0.75 m in width. Room 11 has only one doorway, and the entrance is "baffled," meaning one cannot walk directly into the room but must make two quick turns to reach the room from Corridor 2. In other rooms, doorways are speculated but cannot be confirmed because of the poor state of preservation. In addition, several rooms appear to have been left open without a fourth wall (Rooms 5, 8, 12, 19, 20, 24, and 28). Other rooms seem to have no obvious entrance at all, including Rooms 2, 4, 7, 18, 21, 22, 23, 27, and 30. Although the access points in Compound B3 were not fully recovered, access does not seem to follow a rigid pattern. In other words, there is no standard way to pass from room to room and from terrace to terrace. This lack of doors and stairways could be a product of the differential wall preservation; however, the pattern is so pervasive that I believe it was more likely part of the original architectural design.

In Compound D3, the corridors are more clearly defined than in Compound B3 (map 4.3). All eight corridors are located in the Second Section of the compound and show a relatively restricted access pattern. Corridor 1 stretches from the entrance to D3R1 along the compound's East Wall and turns right along the South Wall to connect with Corridor 3, which leads into D3R4. Corridor 6 connects D3R4 with Corridor 5, and these corridors are the only way to pass between Rooms 3 and 4, tightly controlling movement through the center of Compound D3. Corridor 8 appears to be another blind alley, which does not connect any rooms.

Access patterns in Compound D3 consist primarily of corridors between rooms, but there are a few doorways which should be mentioned. The most important is the entrance to D3R1, centrally located (in the Second Section) at the front of the compound. In contrast, neither of the two rooms in the Third Section have clear doorways. The First Section of Compound D3 seems almost divided into two room blocks, with easy access between Rooms 2a, 4a, 5a, and 7a, but no obvious connection to the rooms north. Similarly, Rooms 1a, 3a, 6a, 8a, and 9a are basically connected, and Room 1a may have an entrance to the outside. But this First Section does not have a clear entrance into the Second Section of the compound, which begs the question of whether one had to exit Room 1a and walk around to the front of the compound to enter Room 1. If my conclusion about the functions of the First (domestic) and Second (public) Sections is correct, this could mean that domestic and public activities were clearly segregated in the spatial organization of Compound D3.

In contrast to rooms within the compounds, rooms on outlying terraces have relatively easy access between them. In fact, often the only high wall in the room is the back wall, which forms the retaining wall for the next terrace above, and there is usually no wall higher than the surface of the terrace on the downslope side. In effect, the terrace walls may have functioned as the back walls of habitation structures. The side walls of these rooms are often quite low but may have served as a foundation for *quincha* architecture, the remains of which are often not preserved. *Quincha* is a type of architecture sometimes referred to as "wattle-and-daub" and commonly used for making temporary or fragile structures. The construction technique usually involves a small stone foundation supporting cane placed vertically into the ground, to which reed matting is attached and sometimes covered in mud. *Quincha* structures are generally thought to be the dwellings of the lower classes. In those cases where no side or front walls are found, the terraces may have been left open as patios or work areas. For example, the ceramic workshop area (Test3 and Test4) shows no signs of restricted access. This area consists of small terraces intended to level out the ground surface and perhaps delineate work areas, and it does not have side walls or doorways.

This difference in access patterns between rooms within compounds and those outside of compounds is surely linked to both social stratification and the function of the space, with persons of higher status wishing to segregate themselves spatially from others of lower status, restricting access to high-status spaces while protecting goods stored within their compounds. The higher walls of the compounds may also signify the wealth and status of the individual who occupied them. This practice shows long-term continuity in north coast architecture, with access becoming increasingly restricted over time (e.g., Moore 1996b, 2005; Pillsbury and Leonard 2004). During the period between the Moche and Chimú regimes, the development of restricted access accelerated, culminating in the royal compounds at the Chimú capital (the site of Chan Chan), which exemplify the extreme form of this pattern.

Construction: Labor-Saving Techniques

Several different construction techniques were required to produce the structures built at Cerro la Cruz. The builders of the site appear to have been frugal in their use of construction materials, minimizing the use of adobe and instead using the uncut stone readily available on the hillside or off the valley floor. This holds true for construction within and outside the compounds, as described below.

Terrace Construction

Terrace construction is a common practice in the Andes; however, terraces are rarely viable for agricultural functions when found on the coast. Since there is virtually no rainfall or other water source on the desert coast to support terraced agricultural fields, water would have to be hand carried up the slopes, demanding an inordinate amount of time and labor.

Instead, the construction of residences and activity areas on the terraced hillside allowed the inhabitants of the site to maximize their use of the arable land on the valley floor.

Building a settlement on the slopes and ridgetop of Cerro la Cruz required the construction of terraces, flat areas created to support habitation structures. On steep slopes there are two options for building terraces: either space terraces wider with higher walls and larger amounts of fill, or space them narrower with lower walls and higher amounts of fill. Both of these options are used at Cerro la Cruz, even within one compound. Because the slopes of the hillside are relatively steep, many of the terrace walls are quite high, but they range from 0.4 m at lower elevations to nearly 2 m at higher elevations of the site. Whenever a larger surface area was required, as in the case of Compound B3 Room 6, the terrace to support the surface was built higher and farther out from the hillside. Compound B3 incorporates the largest terraces into the construction of its lower levels, further distinguishing it from the adjacent compounds.

The terraces at Cerro la Cruz appear to have been used almost exclusively as platforms for habitation structures or activity areas. Some terraces may have also served as walkways, facilitating movement around the site. These terraces show no sign of irrigation canals or other evidence of agriculture, although the possibility of small gardens cannot be entirely ruled out. Terraces are constructed as simple stone walls to retain rock and earth fill. The cut-and-fill method described by Treacy and Denevan (1994) appears to be similar to that found at Cerro la Cruz. First, the topsoil is removed down to the bedrock and the wall base stones are placed. In a few cases, the bedrock actually forms the base of the wall, and then stones are stacked on top. Next, soil and rock are moved downslope or brought up from below to fill in behind the wall as the wall is built to the desired height to retain the soil. In some cases refuse may have been used as fill. This process is repeated to construct the next terrace upslope. Higher terraces require more labor to transport fill; thus it is not surprising that terraces within compounds tend to be taller than those outside of compounds. This interpretation is based on the assumption that the builders of the compounds (presumably elites) could exact more labor from workers than could the builders of outlying terraces (presumably commoners). This distinction in terrace height may have been deliberate as well, intended to show status differences between those who occupied the compounds and those who lived outside of them.

The differences between terrace walls consist mainly of the size of the stones used. Larger stones were used for the building of terraces within the compounds and also for the perimeter walls. There is some variation in the size of stones based on the tripartite division of space as well, with larger stones being used to construct the Second and Third Sections of the compounds more often than in the First Sections. Compared with the compound terraces, some of the outlying, noncompound terraces are built with small stones and are quite fragile.

Compound Construction

The vast majority of the construction at the site of Cerro la Cruz was completed with uncut stone collected from the hillside, stacked into rows to make walls. There is little evidence for the use of mortar between the stones and only a few examples of plastered stone walls, though the possibility remains that any mortar or plaster could have been washed away by rain. In a few cases, such as the terrace wall between Compound B3 Rooms 9 and 17, large river cobbles were brought up from the valley floor to use as building materials. River cobbles were easily gathered near the base of the hill and would not have required much labor for transport. This practice may have resulted from a scarcity of large stones for the building of compound walls but does not appear to be linked to the function of the room. Some of the compounds also used adobe construction, usually on stone foundations. Thus the base of a wall may be made of stacked stones, but with adobes stacked on top to form a second layer. There are also some walls built entirely of adobe, as in B3R10. Compound B3 contains, by far, the largest area of adobe construction at Cerro la Cruz, indicating a significant labor investment in this particular building.

When adobes were used, they were surprisingly similar in dimension, despite the passage of a millennium since their construction. Lengths ranged from 30 to 40 cm, widths averaged close to 20 cm, and heights were all between 10 cm and 12 cm. There were no maker's marks on the adobes, which suggests that they were made locally as opposed to by the type of tribute labor evidenced by the marked adobes found at other north coast sites (e.g., Mackey and Klymyshyn 1981; Shimada 1990).

The low level of discharge in the Chao River has an unintended side effect—a lack of alluvial soil deposits along the riverbanks. Thus high-quality clay would have been scarce, requiring the builders of Cerro la

Cruz to economize their use of preferred soils (Brett 2002:31). Adobe construction in the Chao Valley involved a higher economic investment than in valleys whose rivers had greater annual discharge. The builders maximized the economic efficiency and structural integrity of the adobe construction by using the type of adobe most appropriate for the task, whether that was internal wall construction, external wall construction, or roofing.

Although the architecture is generally well designed and impressive from a distance, on closer inspection, one can see that most construction was completed quickly and cheaply. The use of uncut stone for foundations is easy and inexpensive, and it saves on the number of adobes that are then required to cover the stone and present a more "expensive" appearance. Adobes are considered more expensive because of the minimal water resources available in the Chao Valley and because they require time and labor to make them. In addition, Shimada points out that "adobe architecture, particularly structures with elaborate vertical differentiation (such as *huacas* and nested terraces), denoted political and religious power and prestige" (Shimada 1994:247). This prestige may be the reason for creating the appearance of adobe construction without using many adobes. In some cases, plaster was simply applied directly over the rocks, negating the need for adobes at all. This technique was used on the rock wall that formed the base of the niches in D3R5, duplicating the appearance of the plastered adobe wall used to form the base of the niches in B3R28 without the expense.

Similarly, the case-and-fill construction (sometimes called chamber-and-fill) used for most of the perimeter walls is also a labor-saving technique. At Cerro la Cruz, case-and-fill construction can take two different forms. Two walls may be spaced closely together and the space between filled with soil or sand or rubble. Alternately, four walls may enclose a rectangular space filled with soil or sand or rubble. The encasing walls may be made of stone or adobe. This technique requires fewer rocks since they are only needed to encase the soil and rubble fill, which is readily available on the surface. The chamber-and-fill construction technique appeared for the first time on the north coast during Moche Phase V (ca. AD 550–700) and was used for nearly one thousand years thereafter (Shimada 1994:266 n.48). However, on the central coast this technique was used earlier, in mounds built by the Maranga culture of the Rimac Valley during the Early Intermediate period (Shimada 1994:160).

Sequence of Construction and Modification

Radiocarbon samples recovered during excavations greatly enhanced my interpretations by giving the events at the site of Cerro la Cruz absolute dates (table 2.2), thereby linking them with the regional culture history.[4] Carbon samples were chosen strategically for analysis based on their provenience beneath unambiguous floors and their distribution throughout the tripartite division of the compounds. These dates, in conjunction with superimposition of architectural features, analysis of ceramic styles, presence of fortifications, and patterns of artifact deposition, provided multiple lines of evidence for the following synopsis of the construction sequence for Compounds B3 and D3.

In addition to its larger size, numerous levels of occupation, and overall importance, the results of radiocarbon dating demonstrated that Compound B3 was built earlier and used longer than Compound D3. Using superimposition of floors and radiocarbon dates, I identified at least three phases of construction in Compound B3 and two possible phases for Compound D3, which are outlined in table 5.2.

In Compound B3, Phase 1 corresponds to the construction of the lowest terraces and floor levels found in Rooms 3, 6, 9, and 11. These are the three earliest radiocarbon dates in the sample, placing Phase 1 at approximately AD 900–1000. During Phase 2 the compound took shape, ca. AD 1000–1150. Because the rooms farther upslope showed a maximum of two floor levels, and the uppermost rooms of the compound showed only one level of occupation (Rooms 22, 26, 28, and 30), it is difficult to determine whether these rooms were built during the second or third phase. Floors in Rooms 3 and 9 were replaced most often during Phase 2, which may indicate frequent use of these areas. Only slightly later in time, the platform in B3R6 was built over the earlier wall and a child

Table 5.2. Phases of Compound Construction

Compound	Phase	Approximate dates
B3	1	AD 900–1000
B3	2	AD 1000–1150
B3	3	AD 1200–1290
D3	1	AD 1150–1250
D3	2	AD 1250–90

buried in B3R6U1, probably as a dedication.⁵ Phase 3 construction is the most obvious because that is what remains on the surface today. This last phase shows a significant enlargement of some rooms (as suggested by the new terrace walls that expand the size of B3R9 and B3R18) but less drastic modifications in other rooms. These highest floors show much evidence for burning, and possibly the deliberate filling of storage areas in Rooms 10 and 11. All of these changes probably occurred during the closing of the site, when it was abandoned (as described below).

In Compound D3, which appears to have been occupied for significantly less time, I identified only one phase of new construction (ca. AD 1150–1250) followed by some remodeling during Phase 2 (ca. AD 1250–1290). It appears that the entire compound was built in one phase, and the few cases of higher floors represent repair and remodeling of existing structures. But the overall shape and composition of the compound remained the same. The radiocarbon assays from Compound D3 date its construction to around AD 1200, shortly before the site's abandonment. In fact, the entire eastern side of the site seems to have been developed later than the southern side. Compound D1 may not have been finished at the time the site was abandoned since it lacks much of the interior architecture found in the other compounds. There may also have been a fourth compound under construction north of D3 on this side; however, the perimeter walls either were never completed or are badly eroded, so it was not included in this sample as a compound.

Functions and Significance of Compounds

The fact that walled compounds are the most common and visible architectural form at the site of Cerro la Cruz is highly significant because these compounds date to a period between the reigns of the Moche and Chimú polities and thereby demonstrate a transitional form in the long-term development of north coast architecture. Five of the six compounds in Sector B are agglutinated, while the three in Sector D are spaced slightly apart (map 4.1). There are no compounds in Sectors A and C, and the structures on the ridgetop (Sector E) each have their own unique form. The concept of a walled compound is consistent with other north coast architectural traditions and could be considered a form of cultural continuity. Based on examples from earlier Moche sites (e.g., Moche/Cerro

Blanco, Galindo) and later Chimú sites (e.g., Chan Chan, Farfán), walled compounds tended to be residences for the elite and locations for administrative and ritual activities as well as storage (e.g., Bawden 1982, 1990; Chapdelaine 1998; Chapdelaine et al. 1997; Day 1982; Moore 2005). While some scholars have associated this architectural form with the Wari state and the rise of urbanism (e.g., Lanning 1967; Lumbreras 1974; McEwan 1990; Nash and Williams 2005; Schaedel 1951; Topic 1991), many others have asserted that there is "an unbroken line of architectural descent" between the compounds at the site of Galindo, which Bawden (1977, 1982) refers to as *cercaduras*, and the compounds at the site of Chan Chan, commonly known as *ciudadelas* (e.g., Conrad 1974; Day 1972; Moore 1996b:63, 2005:189–211; Pillsbury and Leonard 2004).[6]

McEwan (1990) listed eight formal characteristics that he believes to be shared between the Chimú and Wari architectural styles, which I found useful for comparison with the compounds at the site of Cerro la Cruz.[7] These eight characteristics are as follows: (1) large, high-walled rectangular enclosures, (2) north-south orientation of these enclosures, (3) tripartite division of the internal space into sectors, (4) the presence of annexes, (5) a long, torturous entryway, (6) the presence of small, conjoined rooms with high thresholds and gabled roofs, (7) sectional wall construction, and (8) double-walled passageways surrounding large portions of the compound perimeter (McEwan 1990:107–8). Comparison of these criteria with Compound B3 and D3 at Cerro la Cruz reveals the following: (1) the compounds at Cerro la Cruz are only vaguely rectangular, but they are large and high-walled; (2) Compound B3 is basically oriented north-south, but Compound D3 is generally oriented east-west; (3) the tripartite division of internal space I have proposed for the two compounds is quite different from that of the Chimú and Wari styles in that those run the length of the compound,[8] while my version runs the breadth; however, they are similar in that one sector is left largely empty; (4) while Compound B3 does not have an annex, the First Section of D3 could be viewed as an annex; (5) neither compound has a torturous entryway, but both show some restricted access; (6) Compound B3 has one storeroom with a high threshold but no conjoining rooms, and there is no way to determine whether the few roofed areas were gabled; (7) there is no evidence for sectional construction of walls; and (8) both compounds have walled corridors, but they are different in form from those described by McEwan.

This comparison does not show that the compounds at Cerro la Cruz constitute a clear intermediate step between either the Moche or Wari architectural styles and the subsequent Chimú architectural style. However, it does demonstrate that many of the concepts common to both Wari and Chimú compounds were present in a modified form at the site of Cerro la Cruz. This form may be the version characteristic of the Casma polity; however, further investigation of other Casma sites is required to test this proposition. The two possibilities described above—Wari stylistic influence versus coastal continuity in the development of walled compounds—need not be mutually exclusive, as long as Wari influence is seen as indirect and not as the result of conquest. Several north coast valleys show ceramic evidence for interaction and exchange with the Wari state but not necessarily for military conquest. Moore (2005:191) points out that, while walled compounds existed on the north coast prior to Moche V, it is only during that phase that they became a "principal focus of political activity." Thus the development of walled compounds as a north coast architectural form may have been influenced by Wari style without being directly under the control of the Wari state, or north coast residents could have developed this form more or less independently.

The compounds at Cerro la Cruz are clearly multifunctional, and yet their internal organization remains distinct from those of both the Moche and Chimú traditions.[9] This is most likely due not only to differences in Casma architectural style but also to the site's location on the frontier, and it may reflect some degree of autonomy enjoyed by the local elites. Compound B3 is clearly more focused on public activities and appearances, as the largest and most impressive of the compounds at the site. Compound D3, on the other hand, is located in a more private position on the hillside, encompasses only half the area of Compound B3 and was occupied for a shorter period of time. It represents a smaller labor output not only in size but also in quality of building materials (more rock than adobe). Yet the basic organization of the space remains the same and probably served similar functions, on a less grandiose scale.

The relationship between the compounds and the other architecture at the site is most likely indicative of the social hierarchy of the inhabitants. High compound walls, plastered floors, baffled entryways, and plastered roofs tend to be associated with elites rather than commoners. Therefore higher-status families would have resided in the compounds, while lower-status families would have made their residences on the outlying terraces.

Just as the compounds contained areas for various functions (e.g., domestic, administrative, ritual), so the outlying terraces may have served varied purposes such as areas for sleeping, workshops (including the ceramic workshop in Sector D), and activity areas for the production of textiles, tools, and foodstuffs. The placement of the ceramic workshop at the base of the compounds in Sector D may indicate that this industry was under the control of the elites, who could have easily supervised the work from uphill. Or certain aspects of ceramic production, such as the burning of hot, open-pit fires, may have been considered inappropriate inside a compound, and were preferably accomplished in an open, flatter area. Regardless, a clear distinction appears to have been made between activities that took place inside and those that took place outside compounds.

Ceramics: Casma Incised and Casma Molded

The ceramics found at Cerro la Cruz played a major role in determining the site's cultural affiliation and the interpretation of room functions. In addition, I used the ceramic data to further define what constitutes the Casma style. In the past, the presence of blackware sherds on the surface and the division of architectural space into large compounds prompted several scholars to suggest that the site of Cerro la Cruz was an Early Chimú occupation. But the evidence recovered in this study showed that Cerro la Cruz was actually established by people from the Casma polity. The preponderance of sherds belong to the Casma Incised and Casma Molded styles. Collier (1962) described Casma-style pottery as redware, primarily ollas[10] decorated with incision, punctation, stamped designs such as circles and dots, and various appliquéd bumps, serpents, and zoomorphic adornos such as the common "rope design" around the neck (figures 2.2–2.6). To his description, I add the type Serpentine Appliqué described by Daggett (1983), in which designs consist of appliqués in a crescent or S-shape on which small circles are incised, giving a spotted serpent appearance (figures 2.4 and 2.5).

Fine versus Utilitarian Ceramics

Ceramics are generally distinguished into two basic categories based on function and quality: fineware and utilitarian ware. Fineware is considered to be of higher quality and includes vessels used for serving food and drink, in ceremonial activities, and as funerary objects, and are generally associated with higher-status individuals. On the north coast, vessel forms such as stirrup-spout bottles,[11] plates, bowls, floreros,[12] and keros[13] are generally considered to be fineware. Utilitarian wares are thought to have been used for cooking and storage; they are considered to be of lower quality. Utilitarian vessel forms include ollas, tinajas,[14] and graters.[15] Jars[16] may be either fine or utilitarian, depending on their quality.

Various authors (Collier 1962; Daggett 1983; Fung and Williams 1977) have described Casma Incised pottery as a utilitarian ware, which then begs the question of what fineware, if any, was used by the Casma polity. Ongoing research at the Casma capital city, El Purgatorio, has shown that some Casma Incised and Casma Molded vessels could be considered fineware, especially those that are also blackware (Vogel 2011). Certainly the face-neck jars and a few other molded and blackware sherds found at Cerro la Cruz came from fineware vessels. At El Purgatorio, fineware vessels are frequently found in burials, and many of these are Black-White-Red painted wares, a style not found at Cerro la Cruz. Since the modern town of Buenavista is apparently built on top of the cemetery that served the site of Cerro la Cruz, ceramics found in living spaces could not be compared with those found in mortuary contexts. Moreover, the one burial found in B3R6U1 contained no grave goods. Therefore it is entirely possible that the lack of ceramics from mortuary contexts has biased the Cerro la Cruz sample in favor of utilitarian wares. If it had been possible to excavate in mortuary contexts, there might have been more examples of Casma fineware from Cerro la Cruz. But I suspect that as a remote frontier outpost, the residents of Cerro la Cruz simply did not have access to as many fineware vessels as did the residents of the Casma capital.

Surface Sherds

Surface collections from Compounds B3 and D3 showed that the majority of body sherds were redware: 61 percent of sherds in Compound B3 and 54 percent of sherds in Compound D3. In an attempt to approximate the storage capacity of the compounds, tinaja sherds were tallied separately and accounted for 22 percent of sherds in both Compounds B3 and D3. Blackware constituted the remaining 17 percent of sherds in Compound B3 and 24 percent of sherds in Compound D3.[17] As explained above in the spatial organization section, the distribution of surface ceramics by room (table 5.1) also contributed to my tripartite spatial division interpretation. In Compound B3, 49 percent of surface sherds were found in the First Section, 38 percent in the Second Section, and 13 percent in the Third Section. This pattern was nearly repeated in Compound D3, where 47 percent of surface sherds were found in the First Section, which covers less than half of the surface area of either the Second or Third Sections. The Second Section contained 48 percent of surface sherds, while the Third Section held 4 percent. In other words, the highest number of surface sherds was found in the domestic area (First Section), and the lowest quantity was found in the ceremonial area (Third Section), with an intermediate amount found in the public area (Second Section).

Vessel Forms

The rims of ceramic vessels are especially useful for analysis because they can often be used to determine vessel form. Body sherds, on the other hand, can be analyzed for paste color, thickness, inclusions, finish, and decoration but generally cannot convey vessel form. The predominant vessel forms at Cerro la Cruz include ollas, jars, bowls, stirrup-spout bottles, tinajas, and graters (table 5.3). The quantity and variety of vessels suggests that the compounds included areas for the storage, preparation, and consumption of foodstuffs. It is possible that many of the vessels were produced locally, considering the small ceramic workshop in Sector D. Some vessels show typical coastal designs and themes, such as birds and fish (Mackey 2001:134). But most are utilitarian vessels without ornamentation or showing only the simple designs of the Casma Incised or

Table 5.3. Percentage of Each Vessel Form Based on Number of Rim Fragments

Vessel form	No. of rims	% of total
Jar/*cantaro*	44	12.15
Bowl/*cuenco*	51	14.09
Olla	206	56.91
Tinaja	57	15.75
Other (mold, grater)	4	1.1
Total	362	100

Figure 5.7. Face-neck jar showing Transitional style (B3R6T1-1,2,4). Photo by author.

Casma Molded styles. There are no Moche-style ceramics, but there are a few sherds showing characteristics of the transitional period between the Moche and Lambayeque styles (figure 5.7). There are also no flat-bottomed plates, a common Chimú vessel form.

By far the most common vessel form found at Cerro la Cruz is the redware olla, just as Collier described (1962). These were produced in a range of sizes and designs.[18] Ollas are frequently decorated around the shoulder, the most common designs being the incised circle-and-dot motif (figure 2.2) and the molded stipples within raised lines (figure 2.3).

Another major vessel form is the large blackware jar, often with human faces molded or incised on the jar neck (figures 5.7–5.9). As mentioned

Figure 5.8. Face-neck jar resembling the Moche style. Photo by author.

above, some of these jars may be of sufficient quality to be considered fineware. Face-neck jars are common to the Middle Horizon ceramic styles such as Late Moche, Transitional, and Wari, and are thought to reflect Wari stylistic influence on coastal styles. In particular, face-neck jars on which incised lines depict hair are considered typical of the Transitional ceramic style. The face-neck jars found at Cerro la Cruz are remarkable for the wide variety of styles represented in the faces—no two are exactly the same. Some resemble the Moche style (figure 5.8), others the Transitional style (figure 5.7), and still others may show a Wari stylistic influence (figure 5.9).

Figure 5.9. Face-neck jar with possible Wari stylistic influence. Photo by author.

Ceramic Decoration

Two of the most popular designs on the ceramics at Cerro la Cruz are those of the serpent (figure 2.4) and the lizard (figure 5.10). Serpents are generally shown forming an undulating S shape or coiled into a circle on the body of a vessel, while lizards are usually splayed out over the shoulder of the vessel (figure 2.5). These appliqués are found more frequently, but not exclusively, on blackware vessels. The local Casma style does appear to have incorporated some elements of Chimú iconography, such as the front-facing god shown on a typical Casma-style rope-necked

Figure 5.10. Sherd showing part of a lizard with incised circle-and-dot motif. Photo by author.

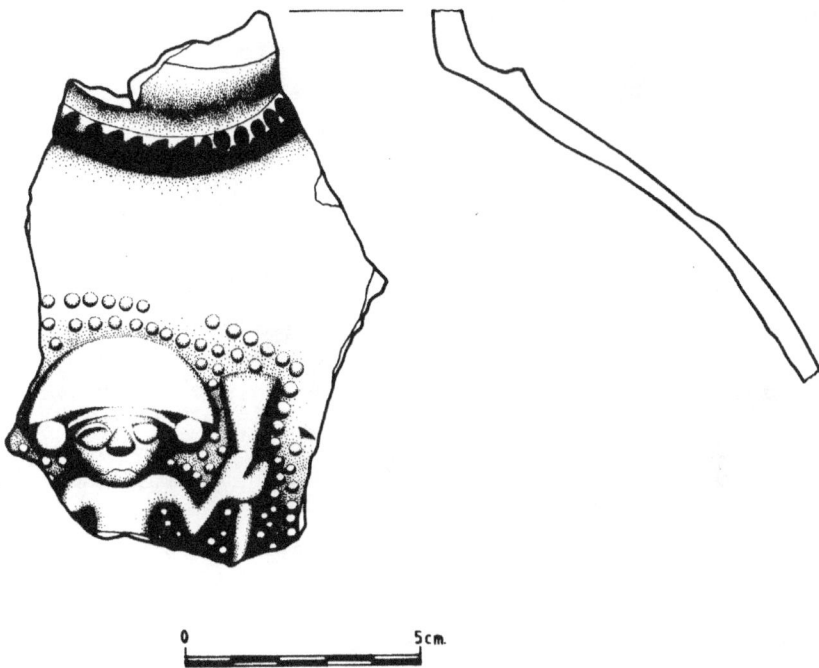

Figure 5.11. Drawing of a sherd with both Casma-style rope design and Chimú-style front-facing god (SA01-1). Drawn by Jorge Gamboa.

jar (figure 5.11). There are also some blackware vessels with tiny stipples similar to those in the Early Chimú style. But the potters at Cerro la Cruz were producing their own version of subjects that had a long continuity in coastal styles (Mackey 2001:134), such as birds (especially pelicans), fish, serpents, and *Spondylus* shells (figure 5.12). These designs are not as naturalistic as those of the Moche style, but also not as standardized as those of the Chimú Imperial style.

There are also some variations in vessel forms. One ceramic kero was found (figure 5.13), along with a few decorated tinajas (figure 5.14) and several grater bowls (figure 5.15). Thus the inhabitants of Cerro la Cruz seem to have been incorporating stylistic elements from various coastal and highland traditions, such as the Chimú and Wari styles, into their ceramics. This influence may be the result of the trade facilitated by the Chao Valley's strategic location or due to political alliances with these states.

Figure 5.12. Fragment with appliquéd *Spondylus* design. Photo by author.

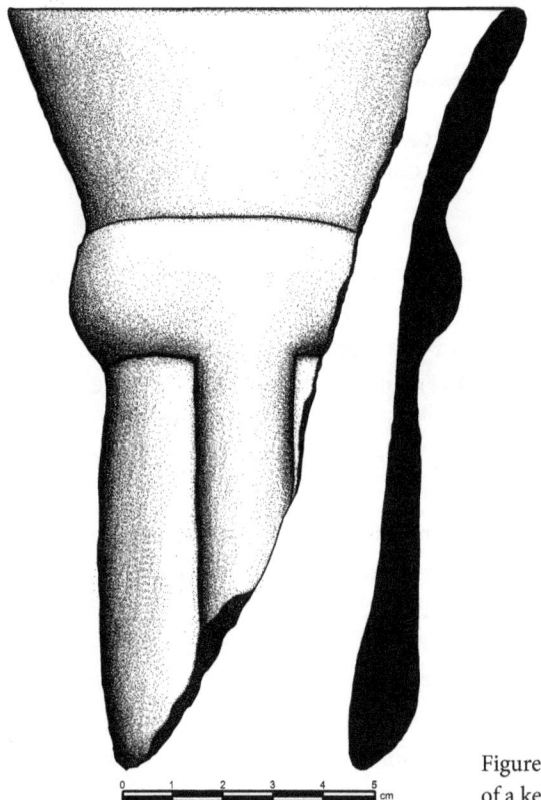

Figure 5.13. Drawing of a fragment of a kero. Figure drawn by author.

Figure 5.14. Tinaja rim with appliquéd dotted swirl (possibly spotted serpent or other animal tail). Photo by author.

Figure 5.15. Fragment of a grater. Photo by author.

Ceramic Workshop

Excavations in a small ceramic workshop located at the foot of the eastern slope (figure 4.2) inside of Wall 3 were especially useful for understanding ceramic production at Cerro la Cruz. In two units, Test3 and Test4, I encountered four firing pits and at least seven ceramic molds, as well as polishing stones, wasters,[19] and sherds representing a wide variety of vessel forms. The two firing pits in Test3 measured approximately 1 m × 0.65 m (figure 5.16). Both firing pits found in Test4 were near the northeast corner of the unit. The first pit was 0.66 m × 0.33 m and the second was 0.92 m × 0.56 m. Only one mold for a stirrup-spout was found (figure 5.17); all other molds found would have produced ollas or jars of various sizes (figures 5.18–5.22). These molds clearly demonstrate that Casma-style vessels were being produced at Cerro la Cruz. Although the potters seem to be introducing a few Chimú stylistic elements into their designs, they were not producing Chimú state pottery.

Left: Figure 5.16. Test3U1 in ceramic workshop showing two firing pits. Photo by author.

Below: Figure 5.17. Fragment of a stirrup-spout mold found in ceramic workshop (SA01-18). Photo by author.

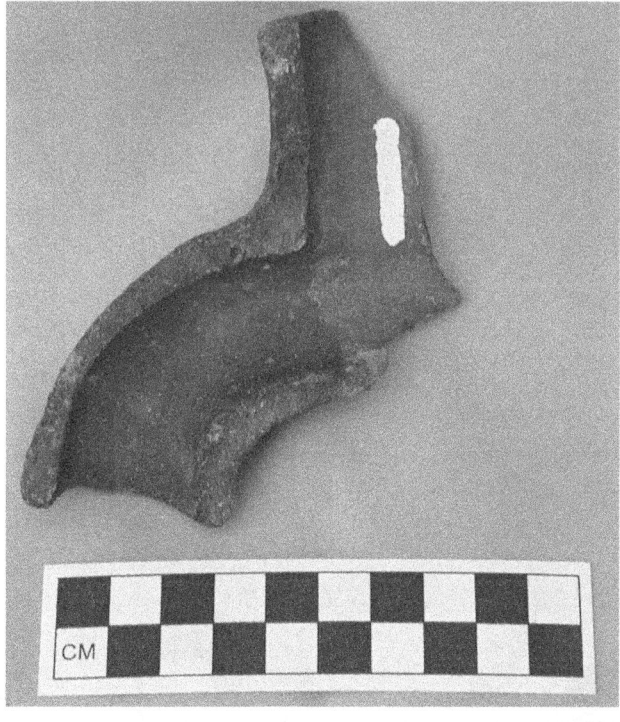

Figure 5.18. Fragments of mold found in ceramic workshop (SA01-20). Photo by author.

Figure 5.19. Fragment of mold found outside Wall 2 near ceramic workshop. Photo by author.

Figure 5.20. Exterior of decorated mold found in ceramic workshop (SA01-9). Photo by author.

Figure 5.21. Interior of decorated mold found in ceramic workshop (SA01-9). Photo by author.

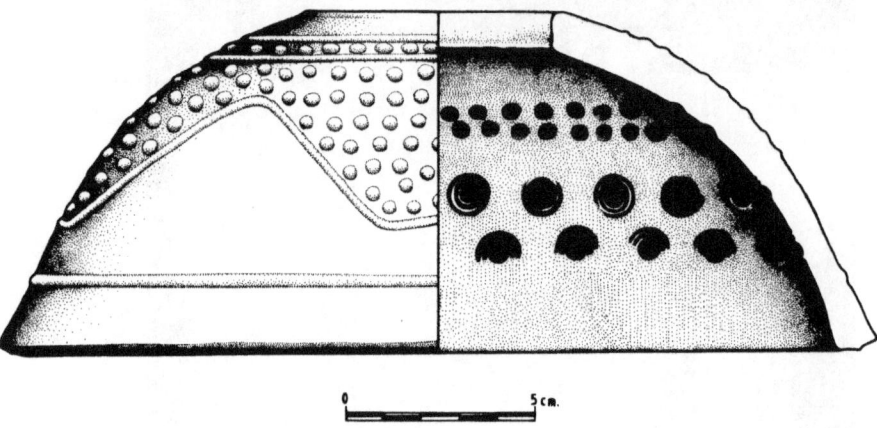

Figure 5.22. Drawing of decorated mold found in ceramic workshop (SA01-9). Drawn by Jorge Gamboa.

Ceramic Molds

One interesting aspect of the Casma-style molds found in this workshop is that nearly half of them (three out of seven) are decorated on their exterior (figures 5.20–5.22). It is generally considered unnecessary for molds to be decorated since their purpose of manufacturing new pots is fulfilled by the incisions on their interiors. Molding clay to the outside of a decorated mold would produce concave designs on the inside of a vessel, which would presumably never be seen. Margaret Jackson (2000) has argued that exterior decoration on molds from the Moche polity site of Cerro Mayal indicate a system of visual notation used by ceramic specialists. However, all of the molds in her sample have *incised* exterior markings, while the decorated molds from Cerro la Cruz show *press-molded* exterior decoration. Also, several of Jackson's molds simply duplicate some aspect of the interior design. None of the molds from Cerro la Cruz have the same design on both the interior and exterior. Interestingly, I have recovered a few more decorated molds in my excavations at the Casma capital, El Purgatorio. Once I have a larger sample and the analysis is complete, systematic comparison may yield some sort of explanation for the external decoration.

Maker's Marks

The ceramic workshop located below Compound D3 is rather small to have produced the large quantities of pottery found at the site (figure 4.2). However, several examples of maker's marks have been found on sherds at Cerro la Cruz. Some resemble a letter V, others are parallel lines, and some look like a squiggle or hook (figures 5.23–5.24). Most of these maker's marks are found on the interior of rims, but they may also be found on the interior of the body or possibly on the exterior of the base. This is how maker's marks are distinguished from decoration, which is found on the exterior of the vessel.[20] Maker's marks may provide evidence for off-site production by tributary groups to the site of Cerro la Cruz (Bawden 1996:100–101; Donnan 1973:93–95). None of the sherds with maker's marks were found within the workshop area. This could mean that ceramics made in the workshop stayed at the site, while those with maker's marks were brought in from other sites. The presence of maker's marks also implies that elites at Cerro la Cruz may have used ceramics as a form of taxation or were able to control others' labor. These marks could also be evidence for provisioning of this frontier outpost by elites at the core.

The ceramic analysis from these select contexts at Cerro la Cruz is intended to broaden and enrich our understanding of what constitutes the

Figure 5.23. Maker's mark on fragment from D3R1 (D3R1U2-57). Photo by author.

Figure 5.24. Maker's mark on rim from B3R10 (B3R10U1-172, 221). Photo by author.

Casma Incised and Casma Molded ceramic styles. However, the remains from any one site cannot encompass all the elements of Casma style. The ceramics from Cerro la Cruz probably include variations local to the valley, in addition to reflecting multiple cultural influences. Further research at other Casma polity sites, such as El Purgatorio, is helping to determine the nature and degree of variation from valley to valley.

Human Skeletal Remains

Conversations with the townspeople of Buenavista suggest that the cemetery for the site of Cerro la Cruz is located underneath the school and houses of the modern town. When the school was expanded in September 1999 two graves were found, and residents admit to having unearthed burials when digging the foundations of their houses. The location of the cemetery under the town prevented an investigation of the mortuary practices at Cerro la Cruz but shows that the area used by the site's occupants extended beyond the perimeter walls.

Despite this lack of access to a cemetery, the remains of one human skeleton were recovered in these excavations.[21] It was found in a small burial pit beneath the bench in the northwest corner of Compound B3, Room 6, Unit 1 and given the feature label of Burial 1. The burial contained no grave goods (figure 5.3), and the body was wrapped in a cotton shroud that had almost completely deteriorated. The remnants clinging to the skull showed a red color, and the bodily fluids released during decomposition likely darkened the blackened bits of textile stuck to the walls of the pit. Preservation of the bones was relatively good, with a few strands of hair, bits of skin, and fingernails remaining. The only item of personal adornment found in association with the body was a small *mishpingo* seed (*Nectandra* sp.), pierced with a hole and probably used as a pendant. The lack of grave goods is somewhat surprising for a dedicatory burial but perhaps in accordance with the overall level of prosperity (or lack thereof) expressed by the elites at Cerro la Cruz.

The project osteologist, Susan Haun Mowery, determined the age at death to be 11 years (±30 months). Because of the age of the individual, sex could not be determined. Mowery noted that, with one exception, all pathologies could be classified as indicators of generalized stress, such as inadequate nutrition, parasites, or disease. The one exception refers to healed porotic hyperostosis on the cranium, which is probably a localized response to cranial modification. This fronto-occipital modification proved to be the most significant finding of the skeletal analysis. The reshaping is slightly asymmetric, showing greater deformation on the left side. Cranial modification was a common practice in the Andes, often used to convey either ethnic identity, elite status, or both (e.g., Imbelloni 1925; Moseley 2001; Munizaga 1976; Newman 1947). Whether the type of cranial modification indicates a particular ethnicity cannot be determined at this time. As further comparative analyses are completed on the north coast, these could be used to determine isotopic signatures of local populations and possibly indicate ethnicity. Unfortunately, I found no other burials at Cerro la Cruz for comparison.

The cause of death could not be determined, so I cannot be sure that the child was deliberately killed. But the lack of any other burials within the compounds investigated suggests that the architecture at Cerro la Cruz was *not* a common place for burial. In addition, the isolated location of the child's body under a bench, in the most public room (B3R6) of the most important compound at Cerro la Cruz, implies special significance for this burial. I believe that it was dedicatory, commemorating the second phase of construction when the bench above it was installed. The sacrifice of a child, who may or may not have been a member of the local population, would have been a significant offering.

Subsistence: Floral and Faunal Remains

The floral and faunal remains recovered at Cerro la Cruz clearly indicate a coastal subsistence base. The residents of the site were depending in large part on marine resources such as fish and shellfish. In fact, thirteen species of shellfish were recovered, including crab (*Arthropoda* sp.), sea urchin (*Tetrapygus niger*), chiton (*Acanthopleura echinata*), and other mollusks (*Enoplochiton niger, Thais chocolate, Choromytilus chorus, Concholepas concholepas, Perumytilus purpuratus, Semimytilus algosus, Spisula adamsi, Donax obesulus,* and *Semele corrugata*), as well as fish bones from the class Osteichthyes that were too small to be identified by species. One marine fish, the sardine, was recovered, as well as two species of freshwater fish. Other faunal remains included terrestrial snails (*Pupoides* sp.), which are common in the hills of north coastal Peru, and bird bones. There were also mammal bones from rodents (common in domestic refuse), camelid teeth, and coprolites. A tuft of fur found in the fill of B3R10 (the storeroom) was tested and determined to have come from a domesticated dog.

Ten species of plants were identified from seeds and leaves, five domestic and five wild. The domesticated species include gourd, maize, squash, chili pepper, and cotton, all typical indigenous South American crops. The five wild species include amaranth (*Amaranthus* sp.); algarrobo (*Prosopis pallida*), a thorn tree common on the north coast; and three species of weeds (*Pseudelephantopus spiralis, Neptunia* sp., and *Echinochloa* sp.). The site's residents were probably growing maize (*Zea mays*), since the remains of three different varieties were found: 8-, 10-, and 12-row. A wide variety of indigenous fruits and vegetables were also represented in this sample, including avocado (*Persea americana*), chili (*Capsicum frutescens*), squash (*Cucurbita maxima*), gourd (*Lagenaria siceraria*), lúcuma (*Lucuma obovata*), pacae (*Inga feuillei*), "guayaba" or guava (*Psidium guajava*), and guanabana (*Annona muricata*). The presence of guanabana is important since it has been argued to be a temporal marker of the Late

Intermediate period (post–AD 1000) (Pozorski and Pozorski 1997). Industrial materials such as cotton (*Gossypium barbadense*) and two kinds of cane (*Phragmites communis* and *Gynerium sagittatum*) were found as well. Cane was primarily associated with the roof remains.

The largest quantity and variety of species were found in Room D3R1, including remains of maize, chili pepper, squash, guayaba, gourd, wild greens, and algarrobo. These plants form a complete meal, typical of the Peruvian coast, supporting the idea that this plaza was used for feasting. The co-occurrence of maize and chili pepper suggests that the maize was consumed with chili as a condiment, as it is still consumed by Peruvians today. The gourds may have been used as containers to serve food or drink. Two other species, flor de arena (*Tiquilia paronychioides*) and grama (*Paspalum peruvianum*), are known for their medicinal purposes as diuretics. The cotton, agave, and ciperácea species also found in this room are used to produce textiles, baskets, and ropes, respectively.

The various floral and faunal species found at Cerro la Cruz provide a wealth of information regarding subsistence, production, and consumption. Maize is used primarily as a human food in the Andes, although stalks and leaves may be used as livestock fodder and cobs burned as fuel (Hough 1999). The most important product made from maize is *chicha*, a beer, but it can also be toasted or popped to make *cancha*, boiled for *mote*, or used in a number of other traditional dishes (Grobman et al. 1961:35–37). Gourds served as containers, while chili peppers were used for seasoning food. Squash and fruits such as avocado, lúcuma, guanabana, guava, and pacae were eaten as food. Cane was used both as roofing material and in *quincha* architecture.

The presence of both domesticated and wild plant species is especially important for understanding the magnitude of agricultural activity undertaken at Cerro la Cruz. The domesticated species indicate that the site's residents were growing typical Andean crops. In addition, the weed species mentioned above (*Pseudelephantopus spiralis*, *Neptunia* sp., and *Echinochloa* sp.) are plants that commonly invade agricultural fields. The fact that these weeds were gathered and brought to the site together with the cultivated species could mean that they were used for such purposes as guinea pig[22] and llama fodder (Fernández 2002).

The presence of faunal remains makes it possible to infer a number of other activities. For example, the abundance of marine resources found at Cerro la Cruz indicates that either the site's inhabitants were traveling regularly to the shore to fish or they were trading frequently with fishermen. The presence of sea urchin spines indicates that these animals were arriving at the site whole for later processing. Small mussels such as donax are frequently used to make soups. One larger mussel (*Concholepas concholepas*) also produces a purple liquid that can be used to dye textiles. The tiny fish bones, which could not be speciated, may come from anchovies, used commonly as food and fertilizer in the Andes. Small fish could be dried and stored whole or ground into meal for storage (e.g., Moseley 2001:41).

In terms of domesticated animals, camelid bones, teeth, and coprolites were recovered at the site, suggesting that llamas were either raised there or passed through with trade caravans. Prior to 1942, the middle Chao Valley contained an extensive forest of algarrobo (*Prosopis pallida*) and huarango (*Acacia macracantha*) trees, from which camelids often forage. Fernández (2002) found algarrobo remains in a camelid coprolite, which he believes confirms the raising of llamas in the Chao Valley. Rosales and Kent (2000) have confirmed the raising of camelids up valley at the site of Santa Rita B, where there are three large corrals and numerous camelid bones and coprolites. Therefore any camelid remains found at Cerro la Cruz may have come from the site of Santa Rita B. Camelid dung may have been used as fuel while camelid meat may have been eaten or used for sacrifices. The only other clear evidence for domesticated animals is the dog fur (*Canis familiaris*) found in B3R10; the breed of dog could not be determined.

In addition to the various species discussed above, one seed was found in the pit with the juvenile burial, the only item associated with the body. This seed was identified as a *mishpingo* (*Nectandra* sp.) and appeared to have a perforation through the middle. *Mishpingo* seeds have been found perforated for stringing at the site of Chan Chan, presumably so that large quantities could be easily transported (Pozorski 1982:184). They are also found in burials, strung together in necklaces (Soukup 1970:228). Thus it seems likely that the *mishpingo* seed found in the juvenile burial had served as a pendant. The seeds can also be used for medicinal purposes. The plants grow only in tropical areas of Peru, such as in the tropical forests of the Zaña Valley (Pozorski 1976:161), so this one seed provides further evidence for trade between the far north coast and the residents of Cerro la Cruz.

Textiles: Style and Technology

Although only sixteen of the textile fragments recovered were sufficiently preserved for analysis, they still provided important pieces of information about the residents of Cerro la Cruz (table 5.4).[23] All but one consisted entirely of cotton, as is common for coastal textiles in Peru. The one important exception (B3R11U1-17) is made entirely of camelid wool. The wool is yellow-orange in color, with only one small, dark green thread to suggest any type of decoration. Pure wool textiles are more likely to have been traded from the highlands. Cotton and wool blend textiles were produced on the coast, but pure wool textiles are rare (Rowe 1980).

Table 5.4. Textiles Analyzed and Their Contexts

Compound/ room/unit	Context	Results	Associations
B3R3U2	Between Floor 1 and fallen roof	Cotton, folded, possible offering	Burned maize, burned plaster, ash
B3R6U1	Burial 1	Cotton, fine threads, burial shroud	Insect larvae
B3R11U1	Level 2	All wool, yellow-orange with green	Lots of string
B3R18U1	Level 1 (in fill)	Cotton, several fragments	Maize, shells
B3R21U1	Level 3 (below Floor 2)	Cotton, high quality, fringed bag, burned	Incised gourd, beads, burned shell
B3R28U1	Level 1 (in Niche 2)	Vegetable material, woven mat	Gourd, avocado, maize, fish bone
D3R1U2	Level 2	Cotton, possible offering	Raw cotton, human hair, knotted rope, other food remains
D3R9	Level 1 (in fill)	Cotton, several fragments	Rope, string made from human hair, maize, shell
E4	Surface	Cotton, knotted, possible offering	Raw cotton and maize, rope
SA01–4	Surface	Cotton, blue yarn decoration	None

Most of the colors are natural (e.g., white, beige, brown); however, one of the textiles shows a simple decoration and blue dye. Relatives of the *Inga* genus, such as indigo, were used as textile dyes (Hough 1999:58). Since pacae seeds (*Inga feuillei*) were found at the site of Cerro la Cruz, the blue dye could have been made locally. A few textile fragments were tied in knots and may have been used to contain substances.

Our textile analyst, Dr. María Jesús Jiménez Díaz, found that the patterns of the weave are typical of the north coast during the Late Intermediate period, mostly two by one, meaning two warp strands cross one weft strand in every pass (e.g., Emery 1966; Rowe 1980). The two-by-one pattern is typical of Lambayeque- and Chimú-style textiles but not of the Moche style, again suggesting the fragments are northern and late, which is consistent with the location and dating of Cerro la Cruz. Jiménez considered the weave pattern to be similar to textiles she has analyzed from the Lambayeque site of Cabúr and the Chimú site of Farfán. The textile fragments from the burial pit contain insect larvae, suggesting that the fragments probably came from the body's shroud.

The torsion of the yarn, which includes the direction and tightness of the twist, is also northern in style. All of the cotton textiles show warp and weft threads with S (one-thread) torsion, while the thread for fringe, seams, and cords tends to have S2Z (two-thread) torsion. Variation in fringe torsion includes S2Z4S (four-thread), Z, Z2S, or Z2S4Z (four-thread) torsion. S torsion is typical of the north coast of Peru from Moche through Chimú-Inca times (Early Intermediate period through the Late Horizon, approximately 100 BC–AD 1500). High torsion also indicates good-quality thread. The Z2S torsion of the wool textile fragment is typical of highland textiles throughout the Andes, both in prehispanic and modern times.

Due to their poor preservation, Jiménez was unable to analyze the technique of most of the excavated textile fragments. At least twelve of the sixteen fragments analyzed utilized a simple technique. But in one case (B3R21U1X-20), an elaborate fringe had been sewn onto the edges of the plain cloth. This was the highest quality textile fragment, made of a fine weave with a fringe, and it is burned. Jiménez suggests that this fragment is from a "cloth container" similar to those found at the sites of Cabúr and Farfán in the Jequetepeque Valley and in the collections of the Museo de América in Madrid. In these cases the fringe is sewn onto all four sides of a rectangular bag. Since the fragment from Cerro la Cruz is incomplete, a similar form can only be inferred. But this technique is typical of the cloth bags documented during the Late Intermediate period and Late Horizon on the north coast (María Jesús Jiménez Díaz, personal communication 2002). These bags are thought to have been for ritual use during ceremonial events, rather than in daily life. Fringed bags are still used by Andean people to hold coca leaves, and they are often worn during rituals or festivals. The placement of this burned textile under the floor in Room 21 suggests that it may have been burned as an offering, a common practice in the Andes (e.g., Moseley 2001). Or it may simply have been accidentally burned, thrown in the trash, and thereby included in the construction fill. There were various shells, pieces of incised gourd, broken beads, and sherds in the same fill, but only the textile, a crab claw, and some charcoal were found burned.

Fragments of cord and rope made of an indeterminate plant fiber were also recovered, but they were too small to analyze for type or function. A few small pieces of string were unearthed, made from hair which may be either human or camelid. And a piece of mat woven from plant fibers was found in remarkably good condition in the fill of B3R28. Ultimately the poor state of preservation of the textiles precludes a definitive characterization of their stylistic and chronological affiliation or function. However, when they are compared to other examples, the textiles from Cerro la Cruz appear to be typical of the north coast during the Late Intermediate period.

Special Artifacts

In addition to the more common artifact classes mentioned above, I was fortunate to recover a number of special artifacts as well. These were classified as "special" due to the rarity of their presence at most archaeological sites, usually because they are made of a material that does not preserve well, such as wood. In fact, several wooden artifacts were recovered, aside from the poles used to support the roofs of the niches in B3R28 and D3R5. The most remarkable of these is a wooden harpoon with an unidentified shape carved into its shaft, perhaps a human profile (figure 5.25). Microbiotic analysis by Alejandro M. Fernández Honores at the University of Trujillo showed the wood to have come from the zapote bush (*Capparis angulata*), a pliable material but not a hard wood. In addition, Fernández (2002) found microscopic traces of a brilliant metallic pigment on the

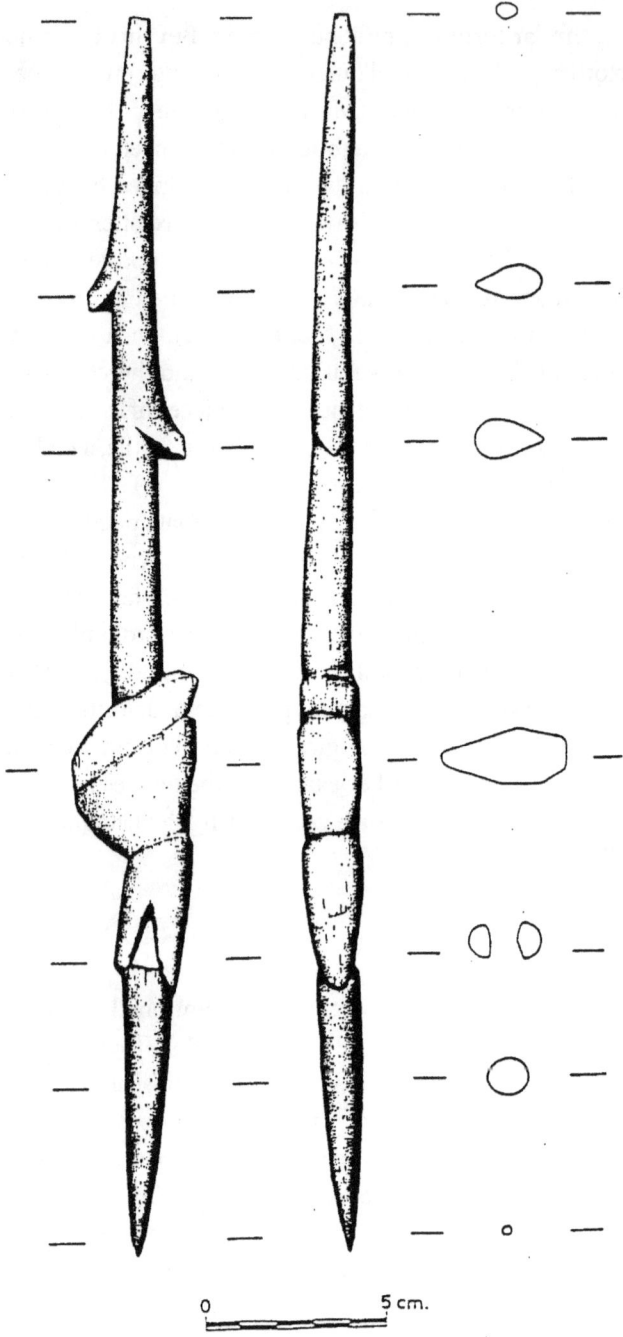

Figure 5.25. Drawing of a wooden harpoon found in Test3U1. Drawn by Jorge Gamboa.

harpoon's surface, demonstrating that it had been brightly painted. Thus the harpoon was more likely ceremonial in nature rather than viable for use in hunting. Other wooden artifacts included a *tapa*, or stopper for a jar; a possible small weaving sword used in textile production; and a small implement of unknown function that was shaped like a lightning bolt. Metal can also be difficult to recover, yet three copper needles were found: two complete and one broken.

The most extraordinary find was a small stone jaguar pendant with inlaid turquoise eyes and spots (figure 5.26). The style of this jaguar, with its tongue extended upwards, is reminiscent of the Lambayeque style from much farther north. In the Lambayeque style, felines are frequently depicted with outstretched tongues that curl back toward the nose. This is the only pendant of its kind that was found at the site.

Only two spindle whorls were found at Cerro la Cruz. This may be because spindle whorls were either in use or buried with their owners and were rarely discarded. These round objects function as weights on thin wooden spindles used to spin yarn. But there is an important difference between the two, which were found in B3R3 and Test2. The example found in B3R3 was located in the largest and most impressive compound at the site. It bears elaborately incised decoration on one side, and the surface on both sides is burnished (figure 5.27). In contrast, the whorl found

Figure 5.26. Stone pendant of spotted feline with protruding tongue found in Sector D. Photo by author.

Figure 5.27. Decorated spindle whorl (SA01-2). Photo by author.

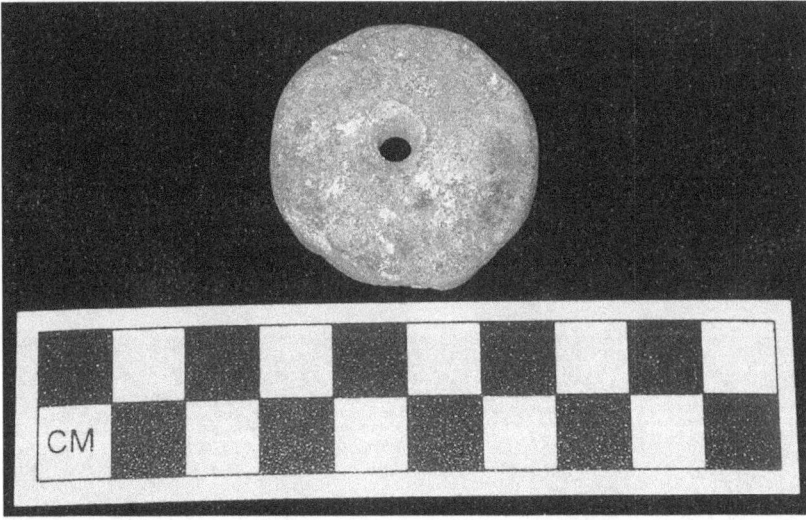

Figure 5.28. Plain spindle whorl found in Test2U1. Photo by author.

in Test2 is made of plain clay and undecorated (figure 5.28). Since Test2 was located on a terrace outside the compounds near the limits of Sector B, the differences in these whorls reinforce the idea that the occupants of the compounds were of higher status than those of the outlying terraces. The fancy whorl was found in the compound, a higher-status location, while the plain whorl was found in an area that was probably inhabited by commoners.

Ritual at Cerro la Cruz

Ritual activities occurred on three spatial and social levels at the site of Cerro la Cruz. At the first level (within the compounds), rituals were probably conducted by elites and for elites, although commoners may have been invited to some feasts. At the second level, along the ridgetop, ceremonial activities would have been performed on behalf of the community, most likely by ritual specialists. The third level consists of forms of individual or household ritual, such as offerings of maize and cotton, which could have been performed by individuals at any social level.

The evidence for ritual at the site of Cerro la Cruz tends to be indirect, primarily in the form of architectural features. These features, mostly niches, have been linked to ritual purposes in the Andes as documented in ethnohistorical sources (Moore 1996b:134–35). Formal niches in Moche and Chimú structures are thought to have housed sacred objects such as idols or ancestor mummies (Moseley 2001; Protzen 1993:223). Scholars have argued that niches at the sites of Marcahuamachuco and Ventanillas de Otusco in the northern highlands were tombs for mummies, but they had been so heavily looted that no human remains were found (Isbell 1997:205–6). In fact, niches are nearly always found empty, so these arguments are difficult to confirm. Still, the niched rooms in Compounds B3 and D3 (B3R28 and D3R5) suggest that some aspects of ritual took place within the compounds, or at least that sacred objects were stored within the compound niches. In addition, the evidence for feasting in Compound D3 Room 1 indicates ritual consumption of food and drink. These compound rituals constitute the first level of ritual mentioned above.

At the site of Cerro la Cruz, niches are also found in areas dedicated to community level activities, the second level of ritual. I believe that all the structures along the ridgetop of the site of Cerro la Cruz were intended primarily for ritual purposes, although it is certainly feasible that this area was useful for keeping watch over the surrounding valley. One such structure (E1), which Silva (1992) referred to as a temple (and which he labeled "recinto 2"), has garnered the most attention of all the structures in Sector E (map 4.1). I chose not to excavate here because of the previous research conducted here and the many looters' holes that have largely destroyed it. Structure E1 consists of three low platforms, each slightly higher than the preceding level, culminating in a room with five niches (although only four niches were still visible at the time of my project). The temple is made almost entirely of adobe with stone foundations. The expense of this material testifies to the importance of the structure.

Sector E also contains four other structures whose spatial organization is unique to the site of Cerro la Cruz. These structures are built mostly of stone, but two use some adobe in their construction (Structures E1 and E3). Structure E2 consists of four contiguous rooms whose organization does not conform to any of the patterns seen in Compounds B3 and D3. The first and second rooms each contain square enclosures without doorways, and the fourth room includes three narrow rectangular enclosures without doorways. The function of these spaces is unknown, but their unique layout and location on the ridgetop near a niched structure imply a special purpose, probably ritualistic in nature.

Ancient Andean societies did not fully distinguish ritual activities from administrative or governmental activities, and many ceremonial events served multiple functions. Despite references to the "secularization" of the state in late Andean prehistory (Bawden 1982; Fung and Williams 1977; Isbell 1988), ethnohistorical evidence shows that the sacred and secular aspects of the Inca state overlapped in many ways (D'Altroy 2002; Hyslop 1990). In a similar manner, administrative activities which took place within the compounds at Cerro la Cruz, such as receiving visitors and tribute in spaces like B3R6, may have included some form of ritual. Similarly, the feasting that took place in D3R1 may have had religious, political, and social elements.

The third level of ritual at the site of Cerro la Cruz involves the placement of what appear to be small offerings. At least three textile fragments were found (in B3R3U2, D3R1U2, and E4) in close association with raw cotton and various botanical remains, usually maize cobs, and in one instance with human hair (table 5.4). The textiles were often found near rope, which may have been used to tie the cloth together into a packet. While some of the textiles may be fragments of bags like B3R21U1X-20, others are folded in a manner that is used for offerings (known in the Andes as *pagos*)[24] or in funerary contexts (Ackerman 1991). These offerings may have served one of several purposes: small sacrifices to have prayers answered, tributes to appease the spirits or deities, or as part of the closing ritual of the site. Unlike large caches or dedicatory burials, these packets of everyday materials probably reflect individual or household ritual rather than community level or elite ritual practices. One fragment

Figure 5.29. Packet of hair found in Compound B3, Room 12, Unit 1 (B3R12U1). Photo by author.

(B3R3U2–40) found among ash and burned remains between a floor and a fallen roof was rolled up, similar to examples documented in Chimú and Chimú-Inca contexts (Rowe 1984:101, Figure 85). Of course, there is a chance that these packets were simply leftover trash from the last days of the occupation, but the similar contents of the different bundles suggest otherwise.

In contrast to these offerings, the packets of human hair found in B3R12 and B3R21 probably relate to Andean superstitions about witchcraft (Ackerman 1991; Frazer 1979). One packet of hair was tied in a bow (figure 5.29), and microscopic analysis confirmed that the hair was human. These packets may be evidence for the common Andean practice of saving or hiding hair and nail clippings, so that they cannot be acquired by witches and used against an individual in a form of contagious magic (e.g., Ackerman 1991; Frazer 1979). According to these beliefs, if a witch obtains some part of a person's body, such as a lock of hair or fingernail clippings, he or she can work powerful magic against that person. So these items must be carefully guarded, especially among higher-status people who presumably have more to lose in terms of wealth or status. Since B3R12 showed evidence for having been used as a hearth of some kind, the deposition of the hair may have come from an attempt to burn the strands and thereby keep them safe from sorcery. Again, these packets could simply be trash, but the careful arrangement of the hair in B3R12 seems excessive for trash (figure 5.29).

As demonstrated by the evidence discussed above, ritual took place at the site of Cerro la Cruz at the household, compound, and community levels. These rituals were likely an integral part of daily life, as were the productive and consumptive activities discussed in the following sections.

Production at Cerro la Cruz

There is abundant evidence for a variety of productive activities at Cerro la Cruz, including the manufacture of ceramics, textiles, and adobes, as well as subsistence activities such as agriculture and the making of maize beer. However, the degree to which specialists performed this production remains unclear, as is the degree to which the local elites controlled these processes. One specialization that does appear to have fallen under elite control to some degree is ceramic production, as observed in the ceramic workshop excavated in Sector D. The elites of Cerro la Cruz may have deliberately located the ceramic workshop at the base of the site's eastern slope for supervisory purposes, since the people in the compounds above could have easily overseen it.

The makers' marks incised on seven ceramic sherds found in both compounds (figures 5.23–5.24) also indicate the use of pottery made elsewhere or in home industries and given as tribute or taxation to the rulers of Cerro la Cruz. Maker's marks have been found on various types of material culture on the north coast, including ceramics and adobes, and are thought to show an individual's or group's contribution to community projects, such as the building of platform mounds. Donnan (1973:94–95) has also pointed out that modern potters are known to use such marks when firing pots communally, so that individual potters can distinguish their vessels from those of others. Maker's marks would not be necessary if all ceramic production was local or conducted at the household level (Bawden 1996:100–101; Donnan 1973:93–95).

The degree to which textile production may have been controlled or sponsored by local elites is unknown, but the spindle whorls, raw cotton, threads, needles, and possible weaving sword provide clear evidence for the production of textiles at the site. A shell (*Concholepas concholepas*) with remains of purple dye inside may also indicate the dyeing of cloth produced on site. Since the artifacts of textile production were found in both compounds and in a test unit, textiles were likely produced at the level of the household.

Adobe analysis suggests that the adobe bricks used in construction at the site of Cerro la Cruz were produced locally as well. I did not find makers' marks on the adobes, suggesting that adobes were made by local laborers, as opposed to the type of tribute labor suggested by adobe markings found at other north coast sites (e.g., Mackey and Klymyshyn 1981; Shimada 1990). Although it was not possible to source the clay, it seems unlikely that clay would have been brought at great expense from another valley to make bricks for the site of Cerro la Cruz. If the bricks themselves had come from another valley or even from other localities within the Chao Valley, one might expect to see maker's marks or at least a higher quantity of adobe construction. Instead, the discriminate use of the various soil qualities for different types of bricks and the economizing of adobe construction at the site in general suggest that the residents were relying on a local clay source and local production of adobes to build their compounds.

The site of Cerro la Cruz shows clear evidence for local agricultural production and the harvesting of marine resources. Whether the fish and shellfish consumed at Cerro la Cruz resulted from the work of local residents or from trade with fisher folk living at the shores is difficult to discern, but clearly regular contact occurred between the residents of Cerro la Cruz and fishermen on the ocean, as was common on the Peruvian coast (e.g., Rostworowski 1977). It also seems probable that llamas were herded in the vicinity of Cerro la Cruz, as supported by the evidence for algorrobo in the flotation samples and in a llama coprolite recovered at the site. However, the relative paucity of evidence for a strong camelid presence at the site suggests that these llamas were only traveling through with trade caravans, stopping to eat the local fodder along the way.

Although more indirect, there is some evidence for the production of maize beer in the form of maize cobs, a kero, and large tinajas or storage vessels. Maize beer has a long history throughout the Andes as an important ceremonial beverage, necessary for many ritual activities and feasting (Moore 1989). The large tinajas were used to brew and store maize beer, among other foodstuffs. Two examples of tinajas decorated with appliquéd Casma-style snake designs were recovered (e.g., figure 5.14). The extra effort involved in decorating them may indicate that they were used for serving during feasts or ceremonial events, as well as for storage.

However, the excavations produced no evidence for metallurgy or featherwork. Although one pendant and a few shell beads were found

Figure 5.30. Compound B3, Room 9, Unit 1 (B3R9U1) showing wall of Terrace 2 with floor. Photo by author.

at the site, there is no evidence to suggest that raw materials were converted into jewelry locally. Instead these pieces, along with the copper needles, were probably gained in exchange with other groups. This may indicate that the inhabitants of Cerro la Cruz were shipping raw materials to another (perhaps more central) location for processing. In addition, all stone used in construction appears to be uncut (figure 5.30), suggesting that stone cutting was not a part of production at Cerro la Cruz.

Consumption at Cerro la Cruz

Evidence for consumption of resources and goods comes primarily from the botanical and faunal analyses, but also includes ceramics and textiles. As discussed above, the subsistence base at the site was heavily dependent on marine resources, including various species of fish and shellfish. Therefore either some residents of Cerro la Cruz specialized in fishing and gathering mollusks or they had established a consistent trade with fisherman living at the shore. One can walk from Cerro la Cruz to the coast and back in a day if necessary. However they may have obtained it, the inhabitants of Cerro la Cruz enjoyed a wide variety of seafood, especially within the compounds.

There is also evidence for the consumption of typical Andean agricultural products such as maize, chili peppers, squash, cotton, gourd, and avocado. As mentioned above, feast remains in D3R1 consisted of a typical and complete Andean meal, with chili to season the maize cobs, squash, guayaba, wild greens, algarrobo, and fragments of gourd containers. Feasting is an important ceremonial activity in the Andes; it promotes social cohesion and group identity. The location of these food remains in a public space, the front plaza of Compound D3, suggests that this was more than a casual family meal.

A number of trade goods, including jewelry and copper needles, were consumed by the residents of Cerro la Cruz but not produced locally. The wool textile found in B3R11 was likely the result of trade with the highlands. Similarly, the presence of maker's marks on the rims of some ceramics suggests that a portion of the pottery used at Cerro la Cruz was made elsewhere and brought to the site as tribute, taxation, or through trade. The *mishpingo* seed found as a pendant in Burial 1 may be evidence of trade with more tropical areas. The strategic location of the site for trade combined with the lack of abundant water resources, especially during the great drought that began in AD 1100, could point to an increased reliance on trade in later years. However, the scarcity of onsite storage facilities may indicate shipment of at least some goods to the Casma capital. If a large number of goods had been stored at the site of Cerro la Cruz, I would expect a greater number of storage rooms.

Ritual Termination Event

The occupation of Cerro la Cruz officially ended with the execution of a termination event to ritually close the site (or at least aspects of the site) at the time of its abandonment. This type of ritual closing may be distinguished from the destruction caused by invading forces and is a practice known from several other relatively contemporaneous Andean sites, such as Tiwanaku[25] (Janusek 2004:111–12), Cerro Baúl (Williams 2001:72, 78–79), Túcume (Heyerdahl et al. 1996:110), and Pampa Grande (Shimada 1994). McEwan (1991) has also identified intentional burning associated with the abandonment of the Wari site Pikillacta. The evidence at Cerro la Cruz somewhat resembles that described by Shimada (1994:247–48) at Pampa Grande, in the sense that at both sites there was selective, patterned burning; no evidence for hiatus or reoccupation; and the burnt structures were still found in good condition, suggesting a hasty and superficial burning event. However, the two sites differ in that Shimada argued for an internal revolt of Pampa Grande's residents, an idea for which there is no evidence at Cerro la Cruz. While some form of hostile activity cannot be completely ruled out, I propose that the ritual closing or termination event at Cerro la Cruz was probably intended to protect the former inhabitants from witchcraft and prevent the desecration of their homes and sacred areas. I believe that this event was conducted by the local elites, the ritual specialists in particular, on behalf of the entire community.

The primary support for the performance of some kind of termination event at Cerro la Cruz lies in the presence of ash and burn marks on the top surface of nearly every floor that was uncovered. Compound B3, Room 21 was especially fire damaged, with large orange scorch marks on the north wall and floor as well as ash on the floor near the burned wall. This was not a pattern repeated during the various construction phases, for indications of this practice were not found between each floor level.[26] However, the lack of proof for burning in some rooms does appear to be linked to differential preservation, since the better-preserved rooms are more likely to show an ashy burn layer.[27] The following sections describe the evidence for this event in each compound excavated.

Compound B3: Termination Evidence

The fill above the first floor in B3R3U1 contained charcoal and burned maize, although the floor itself was not scorched. However, B3R3U2 consisted of a burn layer with ash, charcoal, burned adobe, and burned maize, all sandwiched between the floor and a fallen roof. B3R6U1 contained a thin layer of ash and burned bits of roof above the uppermost floor, which bore burn marks. Possibly related to this event, a human maxilla was found in the adobe melt above this floor. Oddly, B3R6U2 did not contain an ashy layer, but this side of the room suffered more damage from the forces of erosion, which may have washed away the ash. B3R9U1 contained reddish, possibly burnt soil and charcoal in the fill above the uppermost floor. B3R9U2 did not contain ash but it also had no floor and was fully exposed to erosive forces in the middle of the steep, unmodified slope.

B3R10U1 showed a different kind of closure. It appeared to have been deliberately filled in with the remains of many broken vessels and contained the highest quantity of ceramics of all areas excavated. This may indicate that the vessels in this storeroom were smashed in situ as part of the room's closure (e.g., Nash 2009:243). The fact that some sherds can be refitted together suggests that at least those vessels had been smashed in the room. B3R11U1 contained an ash and charcoal layer above the uppermost floor and beneath the fallen roof, which was in turn covered by adobe melted from the side walls. This same pattern was found in the deposition of B3R11U2, except that here, there was no roof. B3R12U1 was more difficult to explain, since the area seems to have been used as a hearth. However, a layer of ash and burned materials was found immediately beneath the surface, above the adobes that partially define the hearth. The stratum corresponding to the adobes was associated with ash and burned remains. Indeed, the fact that this hearth was not clearly defined may imply that it was used only briefly, perhaps specifically during the termination event.

B3R18U1 contained a high quantity of carbon immediately beneath the surface, although this room had no floor. Similarly, B3R18aU1 had a sandy layer with charcoal near the surface but no floor. B3R21U1 showed more substantial fire damage. This room had a well-preserved floor and plastered wall with obvious scorch marks (large orange stains on the wall and floor) as well as some ash on the floor near the burned wall. B3R22U1 contained an ash layer with abundant charcoal above the hard-packed soil layer that served as its floor. Directly above B3R22U1, in B3R26U1, the only remains found were of a multicolored layer of ash immediately below the surface, but no floor. The location of this room in the middle of the highest portion of the Third or "natural" Section of Compound B3 and the lack of any flammable architecture or roof support the idea that the burning was a deliberate act. Someone would have had to bring combustible materials into that room to produce such rainbow-colored ash in such high quantity.

Interestingly, the niched room (B3R28U1) showed neither an ash layer on the floor nor any burn marks. Since this room contained wooden poles and a fallen roof, the evidence here also argues against a random burning by the site's attackers, or else the wooden poles probably would have burned. It may be that this room's special function called for differential treatment during the closing. Finally, excavations in room B3R30, at the highest point in the compound, showed no ash layer and no floor. This again may be due to poor preservation, since this room was essentially barren.

Neither Trench 1 nor any of the test units showed significant evidence for burning, suggesting that this practice may have been reserved for the more elite and ritually oriented structures at Cerro la Cruz. Nevertheless, evidence for burning was found in at least one unusual area. A piece of plastered floor found in Trench 2 was surprising not only for its location but also for the ash layer on it.

Compound D3: Termination Evidence

There was further evidence for burning in Compound D3, albeit in smaller quantities. This may be related, in part, to the lower preservation in this compound compared to Compound B3, or it may be due only to differential status between the compounds. D3R1U1 contained charcoal and a small ash lens but no floor, while D3R2U1 only showed an ash lens associated with food remains and probably related to the feast that took place there. D3R2U1, D3R4U1, and D3R9U1 all lacked floors or ash layers. Similar to the niched room in Compound B3, the niched room in Compound D3 (D3R5U1) had a floor and wooden poles but no ash layer. This again may be related to the room's specialized function. However, a thin layer of ash was found on the floor in D3R7U1, as well as a burn layer between the floor and the fallen roof in D3C3U1. In the domestic or First Section, the evidence for burning is more inconsistent. D3R2aU1 had a floor but no ash, while D3R3aU1 contained ash immediately below the surface but no true floor. Both D3R6aU1 and D3R7aU1 showed only hard-packed soil floors and no ash layer.

Although it is possible that the invading forces of the Chimú state simply burned the site, there are many areas with evidence for burning that did not originally include combustible materials as part of their construction. Again, this lack of any flammable architecture or roofing material supports the idea that the burning was a deliberate act. I find it unlikely that an outside group would trouble themselves with moving combustible materials in order to set fires in all these areas. It seems even more unlikely that the ash and charcoal could have blown onto the site from the burning of fields at some point in the last several hundred years, given the presence of actual scorch marks on some floors and walls. These floors and walls would have been covered by adobe melt after the site's abandonment, preserving the scorch marks and ash layer. Also, in the case of rooms higher up the slope, there was no evidence for vegetation taking root even during El Niño years to provide fuel that later burned. This last explanation remains a possibility for the lower-lying areas, where occasionally enough water might collect to support the growth of vegetation, which then could have burned after the site's abandonment. However, no evidence for the growth and subsequent burning of such vegetation was found.

The Site of Cerro la Cruz as Both Stronghold and Showplace

In addition to seeking to understand how the site was built, this study addressed the question of why or for what purpose it was established. I concluded that the location and fortifications of the site of Cerro la Cruz served to create both a stronghold and a showplace while making the most efficient use of space and resources possible. This section addresses the functions of the site of Cerro la Cruz, relating the four reasons for the site's location described in chapter 4 (control, protection, visibility, and subsistence) to previous explanations about the site. In addition, other aspects of daily life on the frontier such as ritual, production, and consumption, are explored.

The Fortification Premise

The defensive aspects of Cerro la Cruz are obvious. The location of the site on an isolated hill in the middle of the Chao Valley allowed approaching armies or travelers to be seen from quite a distance. Similarly, the three perimeter walls served to prevent an easy entrance onto the site proper, protecting the goods and people within, at least to the extent that the walls present a barrier which must be surmounted. The walkways or parapets that run along the inside of some wall segments could have been used for keeping watch and certainly made for easier passage across unterraced portions of the hillside. And the scatters of fist-sized stones found on top of the portions of Wall 2 and between Walls 1 and 2 on the east side of the hill may have been stockpiled for slinging. If indeed the Chao Valley was the northern extent of the Casma polity, established just as the Chimú state was developing in the Moche Valley, it seems logical that the site of Cerro la Cruz would have been fortified. Settlements along the frontier or in border zones would be more likely to encounter conflict and need to defend themselves, so far from the shelter of the polity's core area.

However, the establishment of Cerro la Cruz served not only defensive or militaristic purposes but also presented an impressive appearance using a minimum amount of effort. The hillside itself can be seen from miles away, as can the larger structures such as Compound B3. These buildings would have stood out quite plainly from the surrounding landscape, especially when the adobe surfaces bore fresh plaster and paint. Using the steep slopes to their advantage, the designers of the site could create the illusion of a large complex similar to the pyramidal mounds of earlier groups like the Moche polity with a fraction of the labor investment. Similarly, mountains and hills occupy an important position within Andean conceptions of the sacred landscape, as the dwelling places of spirits, or *apus*,[28] and as landmarks. The benefit of capitalizing on this ideology may have been one reason the builders of Cerro la Cruz chose the hillside for their town.

Finally, on a more practical level, the perimeter walls and various other wall segments in the *quebradas* (ravines) of the hillside would have served to retain earth and slow the flow of water down the slopes and around the hill's base during ENSO events. In a desert as dry as that of coastal Peru, a brief hard rain can have disastrous effects on the landscape. Even the modern inhabitants of the area repaired a few wall segments to protect their crops from flooding during the 1998 El Niño rains. Thus the location and fortifications of Cerro la Cruz create an impressive appearance in a defensive position, while making the most efficient use of space and resources possible.

The Strategic Location Premise

Silva (1992) has argued that the site of Cerro la Cruz is located in a strategic position for trade, at the intersection of two routes running north-south and east-west. Topic and Topic (1987) also remarked on the strategic location of the site, but for defensive purposes. I suggest that the site is strategically located for subsistence reasons as well. First of all, the site's founders chose the hill nearest the confluence of the three tributaries that form the Chao River, which provided water and clay resources.

Second, restricting the construction of compounds to an area unsuitable for farming was an astute decision on the part of the founders. Had the compounds been built on the valley floor, Compound B3 alone would have occupied 6,305 m^2 of arable land, a wasteful position for a valley with scant water and land resources. Thus the site of Cerro la Cruz is strategically located in several ways.

Identifying the Chao Valley as the Casma Polity Periphery

The Chao Valley appears to have been a frontier for the Casma polity that later became a border zone (ca. AD 1000) between the Casma polity and the emerging Chimú state. This short, narrow valley lies at a pivotal juncture between the heartland of the Chimú state to the north and the agricultural wealth of the Santa Valley to the south. At least four hillside sites, tentatively identified as belonging to the Casma polity and located strategically along the course of the valley, appear to have served as a border zone, controlling access both from north to south and from the coast into the highlands (map 1.2).[29] These hillside sites could also have served as control points for the traders and travelers seeking passage through the Chao Valley and as centers of habitation, ritual, or military activity.

As might be expected in a frontier or border zone, the Casma polity's presence in the Chao Valley (in terms of population density) is sparse compared to their heartland in the Casma Valley. However, the Chao is so small that the placement of four sites in the lower valley is actually significant, especially considering their tight distribution. In addition, artifacts and architecture at the frontier site of Cerro la Cruz reflect a variety of cultural influences, indicative of the cross-cutting social networks described by Lightfoot and Martinez (1995). Although I argue that the high percentage of Casma-style pottery and certain architectural features link the establishment of the site to the Casma polity, it is possible that the site of Cerro la Cruz was semiautonomous from both the Casma and Chimú polities. In this case, the artifact assemblage might not look all that different from that of a Casma polity frontier site because of its proximity to their territory. However, if the site of Cerro la Cruz were completely autonomous, excavations would be expected to reveal a lower concentration of Casma-style pottery and instead a higher concentration of unique local styles in pottery, architecture, and textile remains. These ideas about the position of Cerro la Cruz and the Chao Valley relative to the region and the organization of the Casma polity are discussed further in the next chapter.

Summary

The artifacts recovered from the site of Cerro la Cruz paint a picture of life on the frontier of the Casma polity, revealing the cultural intersections and influences that shaped the lives and identities of the site's inhabitants. In answer to the questions posed at the beginning of this chapter, there is abundant evidence for numerous daily activities in the lives of the site of Cerro la Cruz residents. There is direct evidence for spinning, weaving, pottery making, fishing, farming, small-scale ritual in the form of offerings, and the preparation, consumption, and storage of various foodstuffs. The function and meaning of the site's compounds were interpreted, including the evidence for an internal tripartite division of space. Evidence was presented which argues that the site of Cerro la Cruz was built by the Casma polity over the course of four hundred years using the construction techniques and phases described above. On a larger scale, the data indicate interregional exchange, architectural renovations, and the potential need for defense.

Although the defensive aspects of the site are obvious and typical of a frontier zone, the labels "fortification" or "fortress" may imply to some that the site was merely a military outpost populated by soldiers or warriors. As the results of this investigation show, the site of Cerro la Cruz served multiple functions. In addition to defensive or border-patrolling functions, this site provides evidence for production of local goods, consumption of both local and nonlocal goods, both intercoastal and coastal-highland exchange, ritual events, and administrative activities. In chapter 6, the site of Cerro la Cruz and the Chao Valley will be placed in the larger regional context of the five valleys that are thought to have comprised the Casma polity's territory. The evidence for a Casma occupation of these valleys is explored, as well as the implications for understanding the geopolitical landscape of the north coast in late prehistory.

6

The Geopolitical Landscape of the Peruvian Coast in Late Prehistory

The archaeological remains recovered at Cerro la Cruz may paint a picture of life in a frontier town, but how do we determine the relationship of this site to the rest of the Casma polity? One cannot examine core/periphery relationships without establishing the extent of a given polity's territory and placing a site in its proper geopolitical context. This chapter synthesizes our current knowledge of the geopolitical landscape of Peru's north coast during the Middle Horizon–Late Intermediate period transition. As I examine several north coast valleys for evidence of interaction with the Casma polity, one must keep in mind the incomplete state of our knowledge regarding the Casma polity and the events that shaped sociopolitical change on the north coast after the collapse of the Moche polity.

Investigating the valleys closest to the Chao Valley is especially necessary to elicit supplementary evidence of the valley's potential as a periphery during the late Middle Horizon (ca. AD 900–1000) and first half of the Late Intermediate period (ca. AD 1000–1250). Therefore, I will begin by focusing on the valleys immediately north and south of the Chao Valley, the Virú Valley and the Santa Valley, respectively. Fortunately, both valleys have been well-documented archaeologically, and the data on ceramic sequences and settlement patterns provide evidence regarding the influence of the Casma polity in these valleys. Following these somewhat detailed sections, I will discuss other north coast valleys and their relationship (or lack thereof) to the Casma polity. Next I will use the perspective of frontier dynamics to interpret the region encompassed by the five valleys from Virú to Casma. Finally, I will discuss the relationship between the Casma polity and its closest contemporaries, the Wari and Chimú polities, tracing the dynamic movements of geopolitical boundaries as the Chao Valley became first a Casma polity frontier, then a border zone, and eventually part of the Chimú Empire.

My research utilized ceramic style, architectural style, and settlement patterns as indicators of a Casma polity presence. I selected five common characteristics of the Casma Incised and Molded ceramic styles to gauge the relative variation between valleys: the incised circle-and-dot motif, appliquéd serpents, press-molded geometric designs, the rope design, and face-neck jars. Table 6.1 presents a preliminary comparison of regional ceramic styles from the five valleys discussed here: the Virú, Chao, Santa, Nepeña, and Casma. Casma architectural style consisted primarily of rectangular stone compounds with enclosed patios and small platforms. Occasionally the Casma used adobe bricks atop stone foundations instead of the more common uncut stone construction. While we do not yet fully understand their settlement patterns, we do know that they tended to include defensively located and fortified sites, and that they were often situated on terraced hillsides. In the sections that follow, I will compare these indicators with the ceramics, architecture, and settlement patterns found in the Virú, Chao, Santa, Nepeña, and Casma valleys to interpret the possibility of interaction with or occupation by the Casma polity.

The Virú Valley in Regional Context, AD 800–1350

The Virú Valley is relatively well known in archaeological literature as the location of the first large-scale interdisciplinary settlement pattern study, the Virú Valley Project, which was led by Gordon Willey in the late 1940s (Willey 1953). The work of his colleague Donald Collier (1955), which focused primarily on the project's ceramic data, was especially relevant to my research. As one of the earliest valley-wide programs in Peru, the Virú Valley Project established its own chronology and ceramic typology for the valley. While these periods and typologies do not easily fit into those used now, some of Collier's types can be reorganized into the broader categories that are currently in use (tables 2.4 and 6.1). Table 6.2 provides a comparison of the chronologies used by the primary sources for each of the five valleys discussed here.

Table 6.1. Presence of Casma Ceramic Style Traits in the Southern Half of the North Coast

Valley	Sites	Ceramic type(s)	Incised circle-and-dot	Appliquéd serpents	Press-molded geometric	Rope design	Face-neck jars
Virú[a]	V-302, V-235, V-238, V-142, Huaca de la Cruz	Tomaval Plain, Corral Incised, San Nicolas Molded	Yes	No	Yes	No	Yes
Chao[b]	Cerro la Cruz, Huasaquito, Cerro Coronado, Cerro Pucarachico	Casma Incised, Casma Molded	Yes	Yes	Yes	Yes	Yes
Santa[c]	440 Early sites, 56 Late sites	Early and Late Tanguche	Yes	Yes	Yes	No	Yes
Nepeña[d]	102 Middle Horizon sites	Huari Norteño B, Serpentine Appliqué	Yes	Yes	Yes	Unclear	Yes
Casma[e, f]	El Purgatorio, Huanchay, Cahuacucho	Casma, Casma Incised, Casma Modeled	Yes	Yes	Yes	Yes	Yes

[a] Collier 1955.
[b] Vogel 2003.
[c] Wilson 1988.
[d] Proulx 1973; Daggett 1983.
[e] Tello 1956; Collier 1962; Fung and Williams 1977.
[f] Wilson (1995) found 245 Choloque period (AD 650–900) sites and 387 Casma period (AD 900–1100) sites in his survey of the Casma Valley and remarks on the ubiquity of the Casma Incised ceramic style during the Casma period.

Table 6.2. Valley Chronologies/Ceramic Styles Relative to Larger Andean Region Chronology

Andean chronology: Horizon System[a]	Virú Valley[b]	Santa Valley[c]	Nepeña Valley[d]	Casma Valley[e]	Far north coast styles
Middle Horizon (AD 600–1000)	Tomaval period (Corral Incised, San Nicolas Molded)	Early Tanguche, Late Tanguche	Huari Norteño A, Huari Norteño B	Choloque period (AD 650–900), Casma period (AD 900–1100)	Late Moche (IV–V), Transitional
Late Intermediate period (AD 1000–1470)	La Plata period (San Juan Molded)	Early Tambo Real	Nepeña Black-White-Red, Nepeña Black-on-White, Chimú	Manchan period (AD 1100–1532)	Lambayeque, Chimú

[a] After Rowe 1960; Silverblatt 1987; Keatinge 1988.
[b] Willey 1953; Collier 1955.
[c] Wilson 1988.
[d] Proulx 1973.
[e] Wilson 1995.

Virú Valley: Chronology and Ceramics

As defined by the Virú Valley Project, the Tomaval (ca. AD 1000–1200) and La Plata periods (ca. AD 1200–1450) correspond largely to the Late Intermediate period and were thus my chronological focus. I also gave some consideration to the Huancaco period (ca. AD 700–1000); however, the pottery types from this period do not resemble those from Cerro la Cruz and generally predate the site's occupation. Willey pointed out that the Tomaval period is distinguished from the previous period by the "most drastic shift in ceramic traditions in the entire Virú sequence," postulating "strong outside cultural influences or a change in the Valley population," although he did not say from where (1953:234). As the discussion that follows will show, the Casma polity may have been one of these outside cultural influences.

One important difference between Collier's work and my sample is the lack of burial data from Cerro la Cruz, which Collier was able to obtain for the Virú sample. This lack especially impacts our understanding of Casma fineware, since mortuary contexts often provide important information on fineware ceramics. Nevertheless, the collection of ceramics associated with habitation sites in both valleys provides fertile ground for comparison. Of course, one must remember that Collier's typology is empirical, not cultural. These types are based on identifying common characteristics among ceramic sherds and grouping those sherds together. The resulting types serve as a means to outline a relative chronology, but they do not necessarily represent individual cultures. Ceramic style, on the other hand, is presumed to correspond to a cultural group and may include several types.

After examining Collier's description and figures, I have concluded that his San Nicolas Molded type (1955:172, Figure 57) may correspond to Casma Molded, and that his Corral Incised type (1955:110, 176) may be the same as Casma Incised.[1] San Nicolas Molded ceramics are described as red to brown bowls and jars with press-molded designs in bands on the shoulders and necks of the vessels, while Corral Incised "includes Tomaval Plain jars with simple incised decoration" (Collier 1955:110, 176). The Tomaval Plain vessels also resemble some of the vessels from Cerro la Cruz and are described as gray to black molded bowls, bottles, and jars with cambered or flaring rims (Collier 1955:160). Loop and strap handles are common in Tomaval Plain and run from rim to shoulder. Collier's San Juan Molded type could also be considered similar to the Chimú Casma Molded ceramic style and consists of black or gray bowls, jars, and bottles with press-molded designs (1955:169–70, Figure 55). These designs include geometric figures, animals, and humans, and the areas between figures are often filled with raised dots or stipples (Collier 1955:169–70, Figure 55). Collier himself noted the similarities in motifs between the San Juan and San Nicolas Molded types, and that San Juan Molded first appeared at the beginning of the Tomaval period, yet he associated it primarily with the La Plata or Chimú period because of its increased frequency at that time.

Collier made two important points about the Tomaval pottery types. The first is that there is a significant shift from a predominance of redware early in the Tomaval period to a preponderance of blackware by the late Tomaval period. This shift can also be observed at the Casma sites of Cerro la Cruz and El Purgatorio, which seem to have adopted the Lambayeque polity's preference for blackware. The second important shift during this period involves the use of molds. Prior to the Tomaval period, molds were used only for making finewares, which were also sometimes hand sculpted. The presence of mold-made *domestic* ware in the Tomaval period represents a shift from Moche domestic ware, which was all handmade (Collier 1955:126). Similarly the evidence from Cerro la Cruz shows that residents there were producing mold-made domestic pottery on site in the Casma Molded style.

Collier also recognized the potential for Casma stylistic influence in the Virú Valley during the Middle Horizon when he stated that the traits most characteristic of Tomaval pottery were found widely on the north and central coasts during this period (1955:112). Since the Casma polity appears to have dominated the southern half of the north coast during the Middle Horizon, this statement indirectly points to the Casma style as the origin of some Tomaval pottery traits. Thus the Virú Valley also may have been a frontier or border zone between the Casma and Chimú polities at the time the site of Cerro la Cruz was occupied, approximately AD 900–1300, a possibility which requires further investigation. So far no Casma polity sites have been identified in Virú, but identifying a site with a certain polity also can be problematic. This is especially true in a case like that of the Casma polity, whose archaeological indicators are still not widely known, even among Andean archaeologists.

Virú Valley: Settlement Patterns and Architecture

Archaeologists can also examine settlement patterns for evidence of interpolity interaction in the Virú Valley. Willey (1953) showed that all parts of the Virú Valley system were occupied during the Tomaval period and that the only new pattern was the establishment of several sites close to the shore. He grouped site types into four major categories: living sites, ceremonial sites, forts, and cemeteries. The subtypes Willey specified for each category essentially describe the types of architecture found at each type of site (e.g., living sites may include small houses, large houses, agglutinated houses, and/or rectangular enclosures).

Many of the living sites were Irregular Agglutinated Villages, consisting of stone foundations but occasionally incorporating adobe, a construction technique similar to that found at Cerro la Cruz. In fact, some of these living sites were located on terraced hillsides (Willey 1953:237). Willey also noted several Rectangular Enclosure Compounds from this period, with those built on stone foundations outnumbering those with adobe foundations. These living sites were found on both flat and terraced ground.

In contrast to the Tomaval period, Willey described a large decrease in the number of sites occupied during the subsequent La Plata period (ca. AD 1200–1450), with a drop from 110 sites during the Tomaval period to 41 sites during the La Plata period. The number of coastal sites noted during the Tomaval period increased slightly. This decrease in sites during the La Plata period presumably corresponds to a decrease in population. Such population decline may be due to the devastation wrought by the great drought of AD 1100–1500 (Moseley 2001), as well as to the reconfiguration of people and settlements following the Chimú conquest of the valley.

The majority of living sites during the La Plata period fall into the Exposed Dwelling category, along with a few pyramid mounds and two refuge forts, plus thirteen cemeteries. Although Willey described only three Rectangular Enclosure Compounds, and no additional Great Compounds, it is possible that those compounds built during the Tomaval period may have continued to be occupied during the La Plata. These general trends in settlement patterns and architecture are consistent with the long-term developments in other north coast valleys, which also show an increase in walled compounds during the Middle Horizon and into the Late Intermediate period that coincided with a decline in the construction of large platform mounds.

The Santa Valley in Regional Context, AD 800–1350

The Santa Valley is located immediately south of the Chao Valley and is one of the largest valleys on the north coast. The primary source for both settlement pattern and ceramic data in the Santa Valley is a valley-wide survey conducted by Wilson (1988) in the early 1980s. Although Wilson stressed the limited amount of irrigable land in the Santa Valley, he admitted that the Santa River provides "over ten times the amount of water required to irrigate intensively the land associated with traditional canal networks" (1987:61). Therefore, farmers in the Santa Valley could produce two or three crops a year compared to one crop a year for the Chao Valley farmers. This is an important difference between the Santa and the valleys to the north (Chao and Virú) and south (Nepeña and Casma), which relied on limited seasonal water availability and whose inhabitants would have had more difficulty producing agricultural surpluses.

Santa Valley: Chronology and Ceramics

Wilson linked his chronology to both the Virú chronology and the Horizon system, although he did not provide absolute dates for his periods. The relevant periods for this study are the Early and Late Tanguche periods (presumably AD 600–1000), which correspond to the Virú chronology's Tomaval period and the Middle Horizon. The Early Tambo Real period (presumably AD 1000–1470) is also relevant to some extent; it corresponds to the Virú chronology's La Plata period and the Late Intermediate period.

Within the context of his survey data, Wilson stressed the greater ceramic similarities between local styles in the Santa Valley and the Virú Valley while finding almost no similarities with the Nepeña and Casma valleys.[2] Yet the Santa Valley shows evidence of Casma-style pottery, both Casma Molded and Casma Incised. Wilson's Early Tanguche period ceramics (Wilson 1988:467, Figure 238, 471, Figure 241) include some incised and press-molded examples that greatly resemble the Casma Incised and Molded styles. He recognized the circle-and-dot motif in his sample as an indicator of Casma Incised style. Some of his human effigy jars (Wilson 1988:479, Figure 247) show many similarities to the face-neck jar fragments excavated at Cerro la Cruz (see figure 5.7–5.9). While some vessel forms and design elements, such as zoned stippling, bear strong resemblance to the ceramics found at Cerro la Cruz, Wilson's sample differs in that it includes ring-base bowls, tripod bowls, and Black-White-Red painting, none of which were found at the site of Cerro la Cruz (but are found at El Purgatorio). These disparities may be due to differences in sampling, intravalley stylistic variation, or, most likely, the lack of mortuary contexts at Cerro la Cruz.

Wilson believed the Black-White-Red painted style found in his sample to be the hallmark of an Early Middle Horizon state, although he did not give this state a name other than to refer to it as the "Black-White-Red State." He suggested that this interregional polity (based in the Casma Valley) incorporated at least the Virú, Chao, Santa, Nepeña, Casma, and Huarmey valleys, and possibly the Moche and Chicama valleys as well, with a capital at the site of El Purgatorio in the Casma Valley (Wilson 1988:334). I argue, therefore, that Wilson's Black-White-Red State is the same entity as the Casma polity. Unfortunately, the Black-White-Red style, a fineware characterized by painted geometric designs in black, white, and red on redware vessels, was not represented in the ceramics found at Cerro la Cruz. Again, this could be due to the site's lack of burials, the context in which fineware ceramics are more likely to be recovered.

Most relevant for this research, however, are many of the Late Tanguche period ceramics, which are almost identical to those found at Cerro la Cruz (Wilson 1988:495, Figure 259, 497, Figure 260). These bear the incised circle-and-dot design, appliquéd spotted serpents, and bean-shaped appliqués similar to those discussed in chapters 2 and 5 as well as depicted in figures 2.4 and 2.5. Wilson's Late Tanguche sample also includes press-molded designs very similar to those found at Cerro la Cruz (1988:501, Figure 263). Thus it is reasonable to include at least some of Wilson's Early and Late Tanguche ceramics under the Casma Incised and Casma Molded styles. Some of these stylistic elements, such as the incised circle-and-dot design (1988:517, Figure 272), continue into Wilson's Early Tambo Real period. However, by the Late Tambo Real period, these motifs had all but disappeared and been replaced by the Chimú style, which corresponds to the first wave of Chimú state expansion. Of course, as Wilson pointed out, the ceramic evidence from the Santa Valley generally supports the premise of a Casma polity occupation during the Middle Horizon and into the early centuries of the Late Intermediate period. In fact, more recent work in the Santa Valley has confirmed the presence of a Tanguche (read: Casma) occupation at many Moche sites after the Moche collapse (Claude Chapdelaine, personal communication 2008).[3]

Santa Valley: Settlement Patterns and Architecture

In addition to the ceramic evidence, Wilson's major focus was on settlement patterns. He divided sites into four functional categories: habitation, defensive, ceremonial-civic, and cemetery. According to Wilson (1987:56), "Extensive defensive systems" were built in several north coast valleys, including the Moche, Virú, and Nepeña. He defined two kinds of fortresses, citadels and minor fortresses, as the primary types of defensive sites. Citadels were generally found on high peaks and characterized by massive enclosure walls with few entrances, parapets, bastions, dry ditches, and bulwark walls (to block access up gentle slopes), while minor fortresses tended to be located on narrow ridges near the valley floor and contain fewer and/or smaller versions of the same defensive structures (Wilson 1987:59). Wilson also distinguished these two types of sites by the size of habitation, with citadels showing evidence for at least one hundred people and minor fortresses as less populated. He stressed that in the Santa Valley there are no fortress sites dating to the Guadalupito period, during the Moche polity occupation (no absolute dates given), and he credited this change in architecture and settlement patterns to a Pax Mochica, or peaceful period achieved by the consolidation of the valley under Moche control. This absence of fortresses continued into the Early Tanguche period, and only two citadels are dated to the Late Tanguche period. Wilson attributed two minor fortresses and two new citadels to the Early Tambo Real period, just before the Chimú state conquest of the Santa Valley.

Wilson's classification of ceremonial sites was based on the presence of four architectural features: circular sunken courts, pyramidal and platform structures, open plazas, and large adobe-walled compounds (Wilson 1988:77). His data for the Santa Valley showed a significant decrease in the number of ceremonial sites from approximately AD 900 to AD 1350, along with a less dramatic but still significant drop in population. He found no evidence for large *huacas*, or platforms, being occupied or built after AD 900. This is precisely the time period when the site of Cerro la Cruz was established in the Chao Valley immediately north of the Santa Valley, which contains just one small structure that only resembles a platform (within Compound B3). This trend toward a reduction in large platforms appears to be characteristic of the majority of north coast sites at the end of the Middle Horizon.

Santa Valley: Great Wall System

One last important feature of the Santa Valley during the Middle Horizon is its "Great Wall" system. These walls have been tentatively dated to the

Middle Horizon and linked to defensive or boundary marking functions. Wilson described the Santa Valley walls not as one continuous system but as consisting of seven major sections (Wilson 1988:251). Based on his observations of wall construction techniques and their association with Early Tanguche period roads and settlements, he argued that the walls had been built in the early Middle Horizon and suggested that they would *not* have been an effective defensive barrier. Instead, he viewed the Great Wall system as a boundary "delineating regional sociocultural groupings and as a means of controlling extensive coastwise commerce" (Wilson 1988:254). Similar alternative (nondefensive) functions were suggested by Donald Proulx (1973) for the Great Wall system in the Nepeña Valley, as discussed below.

The Nepeña Valley and the Casma Polity

The Nepeña Valley, which lies between the Santa Valley and the Casma Valley (map 1.1), also contains extensive defensive systems. There is abundant evidence of Casma Incised ceramics in the Nepeña Valley, which date primarily to the Middle Horizon. Thus the Nepeña Valley, situated between the fledgling Casma polity and the southernmost reach of the Moche polity, may have been the first Casma frontier. The same may also prove to be true for the Huarmey Valley in the south, but that remains to be seen since unfortunately the bulk of archaeological research has been done farther north.[4] In this section, I focus on the Nepeña Valley, which has been surveyed in some detail by Donald Proulx.

Nepeña Valley: Chronology and Ceramics

Rather than establish his own chronological periods for the Nepeña Valley, Proulx (1973) utilized the Andean Horizon system (Rowe 1960) as the chronological framework for his ceramic styles. Proulx's Middle Horizon (ca. AD 600–1000) styles are named Huari Norteño A and B, followed by Nepeña Black-White-Red. His Late Intermediate period (AD 1000–1470) styles for Nepeña include Black-on-White and the Chimú style (Proulx 1973:57).

Proulx's (1973) descriptions of ceramic types were based on the assumption that the Wari state dominated the north coast during the first half of the Middle Horizon. Significantly, his description of the Huari

Norteño B utilitarian wares fits the description of the Casma Incised and Molded styles. Proulx indicated that decoration on these vessels "consists of the raised circle and dot design, zoned punctation, press molding geometric incision, and appliqué elements which are also decorated with incision or punctation" (1973:61). The appliquéd elements include snakes, lizards, and birds, all very similar to those found on ceramics at Cerro la Cruz (see, e.g., figures 2.4 and 2.5). Some of the vessel types he described for the finewares of this period are also found at Cerro la Cruz, such as blackware face-neck jars and press-molded flaring bowls.

While I concur with most of Proulx's conclusions about the evidence for Huari Norteño B (read: Casma) style ceramics, there are a few points on which we disagree. For example, Proulx suggested that the range of the Huari Norteño B style extends only from the Huarmey Valley to the Santa Valley. His suggestion excluded the Chao Valley, but as stated earlier, the Chao Valley is often excluded from these multivalley discussions. Moreover, Proulx claimed that the Huari Norteño B style is not found in the Virú Valley, which conflicts with Collier's (1955) descriptions of the Virú Valley ceramics. It is also worth noting that Proulx's sample of the Nepeña Black-White-Red style vessels came from private collections (1973:62–63) and was without provenience; therefore, he could not associate it with any utilitarian ware. However, he did suggest that the utilitarian ware of this period (at the end of the Middle Horizon) remained relatively unchanged from that of the Huari Norteño B, but with an increase in modeled elements on the exterior.

Nepeña Valley: Settlement Patterns and Architecture

Proulx argued for a "major population explosion" in Nepeña during the latter half of the Middle Horizon which he did *not* attribute to Wari "immigration" (1973:63). He also mentioned that the Nepeña Valley's 102 Middle Horizon sites were found in all parts of the valley, and that they include a number of large sites that cover more than a square kilometer in area. In a manner similar to Willey (1953) and Wilson (1988), Proulx divided sites into four categories: cemeteries, habitation sites, ceremonial sites, and forts. Significantly, Proulx stated that the most frequent type of habitation site (eleven sites) in this period are those with houses built on steep, terraced hillsides—a description that fits Cerro la Cruz. Rectangular stone compounds also dated to the Middle Horizon and were found at eight sites. In addition, one adobe compound associated with Middle Horizon sherds was discovered. Proulx believed that many canals, roads, long boundary walls, and fortifications were built during this period. These patterns could be consistent with a Casma polity florescence or expansion into the Nepeña Valley.

Proulx encountered great difficulty in distinguishing Late Intermediate period sites from Middle Horizon sites due to a lack of fineware and the continuity of such decoration as the circle-and-dot motif on utilitarian wares (Proulx 1973:65). Nevertheless, he estimated there was a total of forty-two Late Intermediate period sites. Based on the presence of what he considered Chimú-style ceramics and architectural features, he argued that the Chimú state often reoccupied Middle Horizon habitation sites and cemeteries after their conquest of the Nepeña Valley. He identified such Chimú architectural features as "carved clay arabesque decoration" and described a column carved with pelicans, mythical humans, and other motifs in the Chimú style (Proulx 1973:67). Proulx also mentioned several large rectangular compounds with interior divisions, including one that contains an *audiencia*, which resembles the royal compounds known as *ciudadelas* at the site of Chan Chan.

Proulx expressed doubt as to whether some fortifications were built during or prior to the Chimú occupation of the valley. He identified only one fortified site (PV31-29) securely within the Late Intermediate period, although both Middle Horizon and Late Intermediate period ceramics were found at the site. Proulx described it as a hill that was "strongly fortified with stone walls and ramparts" and on top of which was built an adobe stepped pyramid (1973:70). Although a few sites were built of stone, adobe was the primary building material, another hallmark of Chimú-style architecture. Interestingly, the Nepeña Valley experienced a decline in population during the Late Intermediate period similar to that of the Virú Valley.

Nepeña Valley: Great Wall System

Of special interest to this study is Proulx's discussion of the "walls of Nepeña" (1973:93–96). He compared the various sections of wall erected along the northern side of the Nepeña Valley with the Great Wall of Santa, which is also located along the north side of the Santa Valley. Unlike previous scholars who have assumed the primary function of these walls was defensive, Proulx argued for multiple functions (1973:93). While some walls may have indeed been defensive, he suggested that others were boundary markers and still others may have been erected as barriers to protect homes and fields from flash floods during ENSO events. This last function is one that I have suggested for the perimeter walls at Cerro la Cruz.

Due to their varying purposes and methods of construction, Proulx believed the wall segments were discontinuous, rather than part of one contemporary system. There are no walls on the southern side of the Nepeña Valley, suggesting that any fear of invasion was expected to have come from the north, or the Santa Valley. Scholars believe the inhabitants of the Nepeña Valley built the walls since they lie within that valley. Given that Wilson (1987) interpreted the Santa Valley fortifications as a response to a threat from the south (albeit one that came earlier in the Middle Horizon), the Nepeña Valley walls and Santa Valley fortifications may indicate conflict between these two valleys. Citing Middle Horizon architectural style and Middle Horizon sherds, Proulx hypothesized that the walls were built in the late Middle Horizon or early Late Intermediate period to defend the Nepeña residents against invasion by the Chimú state. However, given the new evidence that the Chimú southward expansion did not occur until ca. AD 1350 (Mackey 2009), the dating of these walls may actually be later. I suggest that they may have been erected during a retreat from the Casma polity's northern frontier after a confrontation with the advancing Chimú army. Of course, further research at Casma polity sites in the Santa and Nepeña valleys will be necessary to test this hypothesis.

The Big Picture: Tracing the Dynamic Frontier of the Casma Polity

As this regional comparison demonstrates, several commonalities can be found in these valleys during the Middle Horizon and early Late Intermediate period which may correlate with the Casma polity. Ceramic evidence shows the spread of decorated wares with incised and press-molded designs resembling the Casma style. The predominance of redware, a Casma-style trait, gradually becomes eclipsed by the blackware that is characteristic of the Lambayeque and Chimú polities but also present in Casma ceramics. During the Middle Horizon, habitation sites were increasingly located on terraced hillsides, and there was an increase in fortified sites. More specifically, in the five valleys from Virú south to

Casma, a total of sixty-four fortified sites have been identified for this period (Proulx 1973; Vogel 2003; Willey 1953; Wilson 1988, 1995). However, only nine fortified sites have been identified in these same valleys during the subsequent period (Proulx 1973; Vogel 2003; Willey 1953; Wilson 1988, 1995).[5] In fact, the Late Intermediate period shows a decrease not only in fortified sites but also in all sites and, presumably, in total population. Whether this population decrease was due to the Chimú state conquest, the prolonged drought, or some other cause remains to be investigated.

In terms of architecture, the construction of large platforms decreased while the building of rectangular enclosures or compounds increased. Sometimes these compounds were agglutinated, and sometimes they were separate. Stone was the most common construction material in the Middle Horizon, but adobe construction increased in the Late Intermediate period. All of these trends are extant at the site of Cerro la Cruz, and I propose that they indicate the presence of the Casma polity from at least the Casma Valley to the Chao Valley.

Two other possibilities could explain the increase in fortified sites. First, coastal populations may have been defending themselves against an aggressor from the highlands, such as the Wari state (discussed below). However, if this was the case, one might expect to find stronger evidence for coastal-highland conflict, with fortifications concentrated in the upper valleys rather than fairly evenly distributed. Second, these fortifications could have been intended to protect against intravalley warfare, with each valley remaining more or less autonomous. If this was the case, one might expect greater variation between local ceramic and architectural styles rather than widespread distribution of the Casma ceramic styles. A slight variation of this proposal, which better fits the current evidence, is that the Casma polity was not a centralized state with direct control over each valley, but instead a loose confederation of aligned local polities. Without the umbrella of protection provided by a unified state, each valley may have been generally responsible for its own defense. In addition, some of the fortresses identified in valley surveys may actually prove to be multifunctional sites similar to Cerro la Cruz. However, to fully evaluate these propositions, we need to continue our investigation of the Casma polity's political organization.

If the Casma polity did exercise control outside the Casma Valley, the evidence presented here suggests that expansion happened in gradual stages. The Nepeña Valley was probably the original frontier for the

Casma polity, lying immediately north of its heartland, the Casma Valley (map 1.1). The Culebras and Huarmey valleys may have been a southern frontier, as suggested by Mackey and Klymyshyn (1990) and supported by Prządka and Giersz (2003).

The increase in fortified sites and the construction of the Great Wall systems in both the Nepeña and Santa valleys may represent the advance of the Casma polity frontier as they gained control over the valleys to the north. If so, the dating of the Great Walls would be reversed from that suggested by Proulx (1973) and Wilson (1988), who placed the construction of the Santa Valley walls before that of the Nepeña Valley walls. This dating is difficult to determine regardless of whether the function of the walls was defensive or whether they served as boundary markers. Alternatively, if Proulx's and Wilson's dating is correct, these walls could represent the retreat of the Casma polity in the wake of the Chimú state expansion or the desire of local polities in each valley to mark the borders of their territory.

I have argued that the Chao Valley was at one point the northern frontier of the Casma polity and that it became a border zone as the Chimú state began to expand southward. Similarly, the fledgling Chimú state may have seen the Virú Valley as their southern frontier. Citing the presence of a standard Chimú *audiencia* and a small burial platform, Mackey and Klymyshyn (1990:215) have identified a possible elite center in the Virú Valley (site V-124). This suggests that as the Chimú consolidated their heartland, which consisted of the Chicama, Moche, and Virú valleys, the Virú Valley may have briefly served as their southern border, just as the Chao Valley served as the Casma polity's northern border. Although we need further evidence to draw definitive conclusions, the patterns of ceramic styles, architectural styles, and settlement systems discussed above can provide one means of deciphering the dynamic movements of geopolitical boundaries over time as expressed in material culture.

What about the Wari State?

In order to settle any doubts about the possible influence of another major Middle Horizon polity, the Wari, it is necessary to address the lack of evidence for a Wari state occupation at either Cerro la Cruz or in the Chao Valley. As discussed in chapter 2, until recently notions of Wari dominance on the north coast have rarely been challenged (e.g., Bawden and Conrad 1982; Mackey 1982; Shady 1982; Topic 1991). However, further research at sites on the north coast has failed to produce evidence to support a model for widespread Wari control. Instead, the relationship between coastal and highland populations seems to have been more focused around trade and ideology.

The mixing of highland and coastal ceramic styles farther north at sites such as Galindo (Bawden 1996) and San Jose de Moro has led to the tentative definition of a Transitional ceramic style (Castillo 2001; Castillo et al. 1997; Rucabado 2008; Rucabado and Castillo 2003). The Transitional style reflects the influences of both the Wari polychrome (e.g., Cook 1986) and Late Moche ceramic styles. But neither Wari polychrome nor the supposedly Wari-related Black-White-Red style (e.g., Wilson 1988) was found at Cerro la Cruz. Only one vessel form—which may show some highland influence—was found at Cerro la Cruz: a ceramic kero (figure 5.13). Keros are ceremonial drinking cups that appear to have originated with the Tiwanaku polity and continued under the Wari state in the highlands. This vessel form is also found in the Lambayeque, Chimú, and Inca ceramic styles. Other vessel forms loosely associated with the Wari style, such as double-spouted bottles and ring-base bowls, are not found at Cerro la Cruz.

This lack of evidence for Wari state control of the Chao Valley does not exclude the possibility of some form of interaction between Cerro la Cruz and the Wari state or other highland polities. It does suggest that the type of interaction was more related to trade than to conquest. Jennings and Craig (2001) suggested that the political economy of the Wari was centered on profiting from interregional exchange. They pointed to evidence which indicates that exchange networks increased both in their overall reach and in the amount of goods flowing within them during the Middle Horizon. They also linked these developments to the Wari state. This may explain how the vessel form of face-neck jars, which are found in the Wari and Tiwanaku styles (Janusek 2002), became incorporated into Late Moche and Transitional styles as far north as the Jequetepeque Valley (Castillo 2001). Blackware face-neck jars (figures 5.7–5.9) are found at Cerro la Cruz and at the capital city of El Purgatorio, which may demonstrate the Casma polity's participation in this exchange network.

Another possibility is that the Casma polity played a role in protecting the Chao Valley from Wari conquest. The valleys farther north, such as the Moche and Jequetepeque valleys, actually show greater Wari state influence on ceramic styles, which may reflect greater political instability in this area during the transitional period between the collapse of the Moche polity and the emergence of the Chimú state. Yet another explanation for the lack of evidence for Wari influence at Cerro la Cruz could be its peripheral status within the Casma polity. If Wari interaction was primarily with higher-level Casma centers or higher-ranking elites, perhaps Cerro la Cruz was not considered prestigious enough to warrant Wari interest or trade goods. In sum, although Cerro la Cruz has yielded relatively little evidence for interaction with the Wari polity, there is certainly evidence for some trade up the valley to the highlands. There is, however, greater indication of interactions between Cerro la Cruz and the Chimú.

The Chimú-Casma Connection: Hypotheses and Evidence

One problem in understanding the connection between the Chimú and Casma polities lies in the conflict between the culture history, which archaeologists and ethnohistorians have gleaned from the Spanish chronicles, and the archaeological evidence for expansion. According to these chronicles, the Chimú state became an empire through only two waves of conquest, the first of which Rowe dates to approximately AD 1370, followed by a second wave around AD 1460 (Rowe 1948). But archaeological evidence from the Jequetepeque Valley indicates that the Chimú state began its northward expansion around AD 1300, followed by a southward expansion around AD 1350 (Mackey 2009). The dates for the abandonment of Cerro la Cruz, around AD 1300, correspond well to the dates for the beginnings of Chimú imperialism. So how do we explain the Early Chimú stylistic influence on ceramics in the Chao Valley prior to the first wave of expansion? There are at least four possible hypotheses for this phenomenon, none of which is mutually exclusive. These hypotheses range from direct or indirect rule by the Chimú state to trade and political alliances between the Chimú state and the Casma polity.

Four important factors must be considered to evaluate these ideas: the dating of Chimú culture history, the dating of the occupation at Cerro la Cruz, the presence or absence of ceramic styles, and the architectural features found at Cerro la Cruz. In addition to the dates for Chimú imperial expansion given above, Chimú ceramic style has been broken into three primary phases: Early Chimú (AD 850–1100), Middle Chimú (AD 1100–1300) and Late Chimú (AD 1300–1470) (Topic and Moseley 1983).

Combining the ceramic chronology with the archaeological evidence for Chimú expansion shows that any site conquered by the Chimú Empire should show Middle or Late Chimú-style ceramics. Therefore, one would expect the Early Chimú ceramic style to be confined geographically to their original homelands, the Moche and Chicama valleys, except perhaps for vessels obtained through trade. In order to evaluate these ideas, the archaeological evidence to support or refute each hypothesis is discussed below.

Hypothesis 1: Direct Rule. Prior to my research, the site of Cerro la Cruz had been described as an Early Chimú state occupation by two scholars who had previously investigated the site, Cárdenas (1976, 1978) and Silva (1991, 1992). Taking their interpretations into consideration, I originally suspected that certain architectural modifications at Cerro la Cruz were likely the result of the Chimú state's conquering the area and transforming the site into a tertiary administrative center (Vogel 1999). The architectural modification in question consisted of adobe construction on stone structures, which were later shown to be foundations. This scenario would involve the stationing of at least one Chimú administrator, if not several, at Cerro la Cruz. But neither typical Chimú architectural features nor an abundance of Chimú-style ceramics were found at Cerro la Cruz. If the Chimú state ever directly occupied Cerro la Cruz, they did not leave behind significant cultural indicators of their presence, such as an *audiencia* or carinated rim ceramics, which would be expected if Chimú administrators had actually lived there. Therefore, it seems highly unlikely that the Chimú state directly occupied Cerro la Cruz.

Hypothesis 2: Indirect Rule. If Cerro la Cruz was not ruled *directly* by the Chimú state, could it have been ruled indirectly? A second possible explanation is that the Chimú state was exacting tribute from the inhabitants of Cerro la Cruz and more or less ruling the area indirectly through the local elites. Indirect rule by the Chimú state would not have required the building of distinct Chimú architectural features, such as *audiencias*, so long as the tribute was exacted according to the wishes of the Chimú ruler. Ethnohistorical sources suggest that the Chimú Empire utilized the existing power structure in their conquered territories whenever possible (e.g., Mackey 2009; Mackey and Klymyshyn 1990). In this case, the Chimú state would neither have to establish its own administrative center in the Chao

Valley nor impose its own structures on those at Cerro la Cruz. This hypothesis implies a conquest of the Chao Valley by the Chimú state *before* the first wave of expansion is believed to have occurred.

We can best investigate this hypothesis by examining the ceramic data from Cerro la Cruz. The predominance of Casma-style ceramics at the site could reflect the persistence of a utilitarian (domestic) ware used by locals after the conquest of the area. It has been suggested that local utilitarian wares had a longer continuity of use than did the fineware introduced by a governing body such as the Moche or the Chimú state (Shimada 1994). Thus the coexistence of the two styles may represent the persistence of local style in everyday activity with the addition of a foreign fineware for ceremonial or administrative purposes only. However, if the Chimú state politically controlled the area, even indirectly, one might expect to find a higher proportion of their ceramic style and architectural features, rather than only the occasional mixing of Chimú design elements with Casma style. In addition, the phase of Chimú ceramic style represented should then correspond to Middle, not Early, Chimú times in order to concur with the culture history of their expansion. Mackey and Klymyshyn (1990:213) have argued that the archaeological signature for Chimú state use of existing administrators includes the co-opting of administrative centers and the blending of Chimú and local styles, especially in architecture. If this were the case at Cerro la Cruz, then where are the standard Chimú architectural features that Mackey (1987) found to be typical of the first Chimú wave of expansion? They are notably absent. This hypothesis also conflicts with my radiocarbon dates for Cerro la Cruz (as well as those for Chimú imperialism), which place almost the entire duration of the site's occupation prior to the Chimú state's southward expansion. In fact, the Chimú state would have had to conquer the Chao Valley at the beginning of their existence as a polity, as early as AD 900.

In order for Cerro la Cruz to be an Early Chimú site, we would have to completely disregard the culture history of the north coast as defined by ethnohistorical documents, redefine the architectural indicators of the Chimú, redefine some of the ceramic indicators, and include a large geographic area under the Chimú domain from the beginning of their existence as a recognizable polity. This would mean allowing the Chimú presence at Cerro la Cruz to be defined by only a few stylistic elements in the ceramics, such as stippling and the front-facing god motif. The evidence simply does not support the idea of an Early Chimú state occupation at Cerro la Cruz.

Hypothesis 3: Autonomy. A third possibility is that the local elites had no direct affiliation with either the Casma or Chimú polities. In this scenario, the residents of Cerro la Cruz would have pursued relationships with both groups opportunistically, to their own advantage. When the Chimú polity decided to formally incorporate the area under their dominion during the first wave of expansion, the inhabitants of Cerro la Cruz would have been forcibly relocated by the invading polity.

Determining whether Cerro la Cruz was autonomous or had fallen completely under the control of the Casma polity can be somewhat difficult because our current understanding of this polity is somewhat lacking. Nevertheless, the predominance of the Casma Incised and Casma Molded ceramic styles (and the absence of a distinct local ceramic style), along with the tentative architectural signatures delineated in chapter 2, suggests a strong association with the Casma polity rather than with a completely independent local polity. If this were the case, one might expect to find a more differentiated local style of ceramics and architecture.

Hypothesis 4: Prior Alliances. One final and quite plausible hypothesis is that the people at Cerro la Cruz (or the Casma polity as a whole) had established trade relationships and/or political alliances with the Chimú state before its imperial expansion began. In this scenario, the Casma polity controls the site but maintains communication with the Chimú state until the first wave of expansion. This sort of interaction would explain the presence of small quantities of Early Chimú–style pottery at such an early date as well as the mixing of Casma and Chimú stylistic elements. It would also explain the lack of any clear Chimú architectural elements, such as *audiencias*.

Of course, none of these possibilities need be the only explanation, as alliances tend to shift over time. What began as a tributary or exchange relationship could have resulted in a standoff as the dynamics between the two polities and the individual rulers of these polities changed. Indeed, the burgeoning threat of Chimú power remains the most likely cause for the abandonment of the site in all of these scenarios.

The data suggests that the original builders of Cerro la Cruz were most likely members of the Casma polity. As detailed in the previous chapter, multiple lines of evidence support the identification of the site's establishment with the Casma polity. The Casma elites living at Cerro la Cruz enlarged and improved several of their compounds over time, especially those which appear to have been important to public administration and ritual, perhaps as a means for surviving in an increasingly competitive political environment. This demonstration of sociopolitical identity and prowess would have served to mark the inhabitants of Cerro la Cruz as members of a strong opposing polity, deserving of another state's recognition. It could also help to explain the mixing of Casma- and Chimú-style elements in the ceramics found at Cerro la Cruz. Emulation of the powerful and alliances with them, whether real or simulated, commonly help elites to maintain their positions in the regional hierarchy, at least temporarily (e.g., Ashmore and Sabloff 2002; Hyslop 1990).[6] Therefore Casma elites may have incorporated Chimú stylistic elements into their ceramics as a sign of allegiance or legitimacy.

It is intriguing, then, that at some point the Casma polity appears to have lost the political battle—and perhaps an actual military battle as well, if the scatters of slingstones found at Cerro la Cruz are indeed evidence of combat. The site appears to have been not only abandoned, but officially closed and then ritually cleansed by a burning event (described in chapter 5). Due to the nature of the construction materials (stone and adobe), which are generally not flammable, and the widespread evidence for burning throughout the compounds, this does not appear to have been an accidental fire. Therefore, the most plausible explanation at this point remains that the Casma people either chose or were forced to leave, most likely by the Chimú Empire's advance southward.

In any event, Cerro la Cruz was never occupied in the same way again. The site does not appear to have been settled by either the Chimú or the Inca Empires. With the Chimú Empire's incorporation of the Casma polity during the second wave of imperial expansion, the periphery of the empire shifted at least as far south as the Casma Valley. By approximately AD 1350, the Casma polity appears to have been completely consumed by the Chimú Empire.

The Geopolitical Landscape

In summary, the Casma polity appears to have expanded both north and south from its heartland, the Casma Valley. Although we are still learning about Casma polity sociopolitical organization, origins, and longevity, the ceramic style associated with the Casma polity appears most consistently in Middle Horizon and Late Intermediate period contexts.[7] The fall of the Moche polity near the beginning of the Middle Horizon would have provided the Casma polity with the opportunity to move north into the Santa Valley and eventually to the Chao Valley. The high number of walled compounds (nine) at Cerro la Cruz indicates that it was an important site, probably the regional administrative center.

The Chimú state appears to have had more difficulty conquering the core of the Casma polity than the periphery. They established Manchan, an important Chimú secondary center, along with ten other centers in the Casma Valley alone. Mackey and Klymyshyn (1990) argued that most sites in the Casma Valley were either co-opted by the Chimú Empire or left under the control of the local lords in a form of indirect rule. This strategy of governance could have been the means by which the Chimú state was finally able to subdue the Casma polity.

During the Late Middle Horizon, both the Casma and Chimú polities seem to have been somewhat amorphous, dispersed organizations. While there is substantial evidence that the people who settled Cerro la Cruz came from the Casma polity, they clearly intermingled with the Chimú polity. Architectural features, ceramic styles, textile technology, and imported goods at Cerro la Cruz show the cross-cutting social networks that characterize many peripheral settlements. This evidence also reflects the intermixing of peoples and ideas that occurred during the Late Middle Horizon, when the lack of a dominating centralized government seems to have fostered a variety of stylistic influences which were later suppressed or canonized into a corporate style under Chimú state control.

The site of Cerro la Cruz reflects the mixture of traits found in material culture on the north coast of Peru during the Late Middle Horizon. But in the early Late Intermediate period, when the Chimú style became codified, the material culture at Cerro la Cruz did not follow the Chimú trends. Although a few Chimú stylistic elements were integrated into ceramics at Cerro la Cruz, certain hallmarks of Chimú imperial ceramics, such as plates, tripod vessels, ring bowls, and paddle-stamping, have not been found at the site. Instead, the development of style continues on an alternate path, further evidence that it was not under direct Chimú control.

Summary

Investigations at Cerro la Cruz have recovered provocative evidence for the sociopolitical events that occurred during the Middle Horizon. The presence of perimeter walls implies a need for defense while the enlargement and embellishment of stone buildings with adobe and plaster suggests either an increase in local elites' power and prosperity or the need to convey the appearance of such. I suggest that the Casma people attempted to make a political statement of their identity and their ownership of the area in response to the rising power of what would become the Chimú state. Their incorporation of some Chimú stylistic elements into their ceramics may indicate a desire to align themselves with this foreign polity, or it may refer to a previously formed alliance. In any event, the Chimú state was eventually able to conquer the Chao Valley, and the site of Cerro la Cruz was abandoned.

Further investigations into the Casma polity may add an important dimension to our understanding of not only the Middle Horizon and Late Intermediate period but also the processes of sociopolitical change in the Andes. More specifically, the sociopolitical events documented in the archaeological record at Cerro la Cruz indicate four areas of significant change. First, the establishment of the site by the Casma polity marks the northernmost extent of their territory at that time. The radiocarbon dates obtained during my excavations provide the temporal framework for this colonization of the Chao Valley at what appears to be the height of Casma political influence on the north coast. Second, artifacts recovered from Cerro la Cruz point to ongoing interactions among coastal polities and between coastal and highland polities. Those interactions shaped material culture and style, the secularization and centralization of government, and the increasing association of economy with religion which coalesced under the Chimú Empire. Third, Cerro la Cruz provides evidence and absolute dates that correlate with the second wave of Chimú expansion and the subsequent decline of the Casma polity at the turn of the fourteenth century AD. Finally, the subsistence data from Cerro la Cruz corroborates to some degree the data on the extended drought of AD 1100–1500 and its effects on coastal polities, especially the increasing need for centralized storage and control of resources. However, it also shows that settlements in poorly watered areas like the Chao Valley were able to survive extended periods of drought, perhaps due in part to a dependence on long distance trade.

In addition, Cerro la Cruz shows some evidence for trade and exchange. Its location near the intersection of routes heading both north-south and west-east, along with the visibility granted by the height of the hillside, could have facilitated trade as well as the monitoring of travelers passing through the valley. Various goods produced at the site could have been exchanged for the foreign goods that have been found at Cerro la Cruz, which include *Spondylus* beads, the stone and turquoise jaguar pendant, the wool textile, and guanabana fruits from the jungle.

But frontiers often reflect more than the exchange of goods and raw materials. They also provide a common ground for the exchange of ideas. Interaction through trade provides exposure to various stylistic influences in ceramic designs and textile technology and sometimes the meanings and beliefs signified by those designs. This type of exchange can be peaceful or have the potential for conflict, in which case the defensive location of the settlement may have proved auspicious. Nevertheless, the cross-cutting social networks established at the site of Cerro la Cruz disappeared with the site's abandonment, most likely during the second wave of the Chimú state expansion. The impact of the Chimú movement southward ultimately proved devastating to the Casma polity.

The intention of this chapter is not only to identify the sociopolitical changes that occurred during this transitional period on the north coast but also to suggest the potential benefits of cross-cultural comparison between this case study and other Andean (or even non-Andean) societies for understanding peripheries and the people who inhabited them. The movement of geopolitical boundaries on the north coast of Peru could be compared to interpolity interactions in the Andean highlands or in other regions of the world, such as the ebb and flow of the Roman frontier, or the expansion and contraction of the Ottoman Empire.

As demonstrated in this chapter, there is considerable evidence to support some degree of control by the Casma polity in the valleys stretching from the Casma Valley north to the Chao Valley and probably at least some degree of influence in the Virú, Culebras, and Huarmey valleys. For now, this evidence exists primarily in the form of ceramic styles and their chronology, with some data on architecture and settlement patterns. However, as more is learned about the structure and organization of the Casma polity, data on architectural style and settlement patterns may provide further lines of evidence to indicate a Casma polity occupation in these valleys. Temporally speaking, the evidence from these valleys indicates relatively continuous habitation, along with the hypothesis that the Casma polity expanded north during the Late Middle Horizon and early part of the Late Intermediate period, until being conquered by the Chimú state in the fourteenth century. Nevertheless, further research at Middle Horizon and Late Intermediate period sites in these valleys would greatly assist in confirming or denying the hypotheses presented here.

7

Conclusion

Conquest and Abandonment

Peripheral areas, such as frontiers and border zones, are especially well suited to the study of cultural change and transition. This research focused on the Chao Valley as an example of the dynamic nature of geopolitical boundaries. The transformation of this periphery from frontier to border zone to conquered territory during a period of transition marked the decline of the Casma polity and the rise of the Chimú state. The approach used here examined the relationship between architecture, ceramics, and sociopolitical change through a diachronic analysis of the expansion and modification of Cerro la Cruz, a fortified hillside town on the north coast of Peru. In an attempt to understand the multivariate aspects of "life on the frontier," this study sought artifactual evidence of cultural intersections in daily life and placed the site's occupation within the context of contemporary regional settlement patterns.

Change occurred on several levels. At the site itself, change was indicated by the phases of construction and remodeling of buildings in relation to sociopolitical events, and by the incorporation of foreign elements into the Casma ceramic style. At the valley level, change occurred through the transformation of the Chao Valley from Casma polity frontier to border zone to province of the Chimú Empire. On a larger regional scale, interpolity relations fluctuated between the Casma polity and the Chimú polity as the latter expanded from local state to conquering empire. Absolute dates, in conjunction with superimposition of architectural features, analysis of ceramic styles, fortifications, and patterns of artifact deposition, provide multiple lines of evidence for these changes and for the following reconstruction of the establishment, occupation, and abandonment of the site.

Reconstructing the Events Surrounding the Establishment, Occupation, and Abandonment of the Site

The survey data from every valley, at least from Culebras north to Chao and perhaps including Virú, show that the Casma polity occupied the north coast during this period. My data indicates that the site of Cerro la Cruz was occupied for three hundred to four hundred years. Arriving in approximately AD 900, members of the Casma polity began construction of the compounds (Phase 1). The reasons for the establishment of the site of Cerro la Cruz may never fully be known, but I submit the following proposition. First, in the wake of the Moche polity collapse around AD 700, the Casma polity could have expanded northward, reaching the Chao Valley (ca. AD 890) before the end of the Middle Horizon and establishing a fortified settlement on what would become its northern frontier.[1] Second, the Chao Valley, while limited in natural resources, offered a strategic advantage for controlling trade because of the easy west-east passage from coast to highlands and north-south access from the Santa Valley to the Virú Valley (map 1.2). Third, the Casma polity might have continued their expansion north had they not encountered the southern frontier of the Chimú polity, which was gathering force and consolidating power in their heartland (the Chicama, Moche, and Virú valleys) at the end of the Middle Horizon (ca. AD 900–1000). With the rise of the Chimú state, the site of Cerro la Cruz suddenly would have had a formidable polity located to the north at the site of Chan Chan, leaving the Chao Valley at the intersection of these two territories (map 1.1). This is one possible explanation for the defensive aspects of the terraced hillside site of Cerro la Cruz, which would have served the population well as a fortification and boundary marker for the northern extent of the Casma polity. The site's location also left valuable irrigable land open for farming.

The population of Cerro la Cruz appears to have grown steadily until the site's abandonment (ca. AD 1290). Construction expanded around the hillside and out from the base of the two primary architectural zones on the southern and eastern slopes. Phase 2 of construction in Compound B3 occurred between around AD 1000 and AD 1150, while the third and final phase (Phase 3) probably corresponds to around AD 1200. These phases appear to have been completed by the same cultural group since there are no distinct changes in architectural style or other cultural indicators to suggest the incursion of an outside group. Instead, these changes appear to have been caused by an increase in population and the growing importance of the site for the Casma polity as the frontier became a border zone. The dramatic enlargements of Compound B3 during Phase 2 seem particularly indicative of an increase in the site's importance, perhaps concurrent with the ambitions of a particular local leader. In this way, the expansion and modification of the site's built environment represent one area of architectural change linked to sociopolitical events.

In terms of climatic changes, Moseley (2001) discussed the significant sociopolitical effects of an extensive drought, which affected the Andes from AD 1100 to AD 1500. The fact that the site of Cerro la Cruz not only survived the first half of the drought but actually increased in size testifies to the resourcefulness of its people. This resourcefulness may have included the ingenuity of the agriculturalists, the expertise of the fishermen, the magnitude to which the elites were able to benefit from trade through the valley, or some combination of these specializations.

During the centuries that Cerro la Cruz was inhabited, daily life was probably quite similar to that of other coastal Peruvian communities. Subsistence included a reliance on marine resources such as fish and shellfish but also incorporated staple crops such as maize, squash, cotton, and chili peppers. There is some evidence for the herding of camelids, probably llamas or alpacas, but not much for the raising of guinea pigs. The only other domesticated animals present were dogs, and wild birds may have been caught for food.

The final series of architectural changes (Phase 3) relates to the end of the site's occupation. The site seems to have been under construction up to the moment it was abandoned. Construction of compounds in Sector D was never finished, and it is possible that the final perimeter wall (Wall 1) was also never completed. Although the site of Cerro la Cruz seems to have been abandoned rather quickly around AD 1300, there is abundant evidence that the site was ritually closed during a termination event. This suggests that either the inhabitants decided to flee the advancing armies of the Chimú state rather than fight, or they indeed lost the battle implied by the stockpiles of slingstones. While I cannot determine with certainty which group conducted the ritual closing events, it seems unlikely that the Chimú forces would expend the time and effort for such rites at a site occupied by an opposing polity. Instead, it appears the leaders of the site of Cerro la Cruz either had time to close the site before they left or were granted permission to do so by the conquering general.

The Site of Cerro la Cruz as a Frontier: Evidence for Cross-Cutting Social Networks

The artifacts recovered at the site of Cerro la Cruz present several examples of the cross-cutting social networks discussed by Lightfoot and Martinez (1995). The site's residents appear to have been incorporating some elements of Chimú iconography into the local Casma ceramic style (figure 5.11). But the Casma ceramic style was not replaced by Early or Middle Chimú–style ceramics. Instead, inhabitants of the site of Cerro la Cruz produced their own version of subjects that had a long continuity in coastal styles, such as birds (especially pelicans), fish, serpents, and *Spondylus* shells (figure 5.12). I interpret this heterogeneous blend of styles as representative of multiple cultural influences, which correspond to the cross-cutting social networks typical of a periphery.

There are also some potential references to interactions with highland polities. These include one ceramic kero (figure 5.13), an unusual vessel form for the coast; llama bone; and a textile fragment made entirely of camelid wool. Coastal textiles were usually made of cotton or a mix of cotton and wool (O'Neale and Kroeber 1930; Rowe 1980). As these few examples show, the inhabitants of the site of Cerro la Cruz incorporated resources and stylistic elements from various coastal and highland traditions, possibly as a result of the trade facilitated by the Chao Valley's strategic location.

Moreover, there appears to be a connection between the Casma polity, the Chimú polity, and perhaps the Lambayeque polity in the far north. Textile style at the site of Cerro la Cruz is most similar to that of other north coast cultures such as the Lambayeque and Chimú. Similarly, the stone jaguar pendant found at the site of Cerro la Cruz bears a striking resemblance to felines portrayed in profile on Lambayeque ceramic vessels. Unfortunately, we cannot know whether the pendant was traded from the far north or whether it simply emulated the Lambayeque style. Only one *Spondylus* bead was found, but this remains a significant find because of the expense and importance of *Spondylus* in Andean cultures. *Spondylus* shells can be harvested only in the warm waters off the coast of Ecuador north to West Mexico, and therefore must have been traded south to Cerro la Cruz, probably as a finished product. These shells possess special significance for Andean peoples as symbols for blood and the food of the gods (e.g., Marcos 1977; Paulsen 1974). While the sample of potentially imported goods is rather small, this could be due to the lack of mortuary data from Cerro la Cruz. Many times, the more exotic goods tend to be found in burials rather than casually left on the surface when a site is abandoned.

In contrast to these northern influences, the predominant ceramic style at the site of Cerro la Cruz, Casma Incised, comes from the Casma Valley to the south. While the overwhelming majority of Casma ceramics found at Cerro la Cruz were redware, blackware was also present in the sample, and it included Casma stylistic elements. For example, the fragment of a stirrup-spout mold (figure 5.17) found in the ceramic workshop was made of blackware. This suggests that blackware, which became the prevalent paste in both Lambayeque and Chimú fineware styles, may also have spread northward from the south (Castillo 2001), perhaps even via the conduit of the Casma polity. The architecture at Cerro la Cruz fits generally with north coast patterns but does not include any Chimú diagnostic features, such as *audiencias*. Likewise, the occupation of terraced hillside settlements is not typical of Chimú settlement patterns but is instead similar to Late Middle Horizon sites such as Galindo. Subsistence remains clearly indicate a coastal diet, with little evidence of highland influence. Other evidence for coastal interaction is found in the abundant refuse of marine resources such as fish and shellfish, as well as a wooden harpoon (figure 5.25). Nevertheless, there is abundant evidence to prove that the site was established and occupied by members of the Casma polity and no convincing evidence to indicate a Chimú or Wari occupation.

Life on the Casma Periphery

The artifacts recovered from the site of Cerro la Cruz paint a picture of life on the edge of the Casma polity, revealing the cultural intersections and influences that shaped the lives and identities of the site's inhabitants. Data from the site of Cerro la Cruz suggest that its residents included women, men, and children of various ages, occupations (such as farming, fishing, weaving, and pottery production), and at least two levels of status, commoners and elites. The commoners lived and worked on most of the habitational terraces, while the elites resided in the larger compounds and administered the site and its surrounding area. Elites were expected to serve multiple purposes as administrators, diplomats, and religious specialists, and they most likely identified with the Casma polity, perhaps ethnically as well as politically. Not only is there a clear quantitative difference in the size and cost of the elite architecture, both in terms of labor and materials, but there is a qualitative difference in the artifacts found within the compounds as compared to those found without. Perhaps the clearest examples of this are the spindle whorls recovered: the incised and polished whorl (figure 5.27) found in Room 3 of Compound B3, as compared to the plain, unpolished clay whorl (figure 5.28) found in Test2, a terrace on the western slope of the hill.

Furthermore, artifactual evidence demonstrates that the site of Cerro la Cruz was more than simply a military outpost or fortification; it also may have served as a regional administrative center, as demonstrated by the archaeological remains of production, consumption, and ritual activities. If the site of Cerro la Cruz were a fortification for defensive purposes alone, one might expect only adult males to have been present. Instead, there is abundant evidence for many productive and consumptive tasks performed by both men and women, typical of most Andean settlements.

Without further investigation of the Casma polity and the Casma system of political organization, it is difficult to judge the degree of freedom granted to elites in their administrative duties at the site of Cerro la Cruz. Given the mixture of cultural influences reflected in the site's material culture as evidence for interaction with the neighboring Chimú and possibly highland polities, the rulers of Cerro la Cruz may have been semi-autonomous, so long as they paid tribute and/or taxes. Of course, local elites were not merely passive recipients of core actions and decisions but active agents in their own survival or defeat. The evidence from Cerro la Cruz suggests that elites there were proficient diplomats who managed to successfully negotiate the minefield of border politics for nearly four hundred years. They may have even managed to personally benefit from these interpolity relations and thereby finance the expansion of the site observed in Phase 2 of the construction sequence. Presumably, it would have been prudent for the local leaders at Cerro la Cruz to develop and maintain amiable relationships with their neighbors to the north as long as possible.

The degree to which commoners at the site of Cerro la Cruz identified with the elite administrators is also difficult to judge. While some may have been living at the site when the Casma polity arrived, the predominance of Casma designs on utilitarian pottery from the beginning of the occupation suggests that the majority of the population had traveled north to the Chao Valley to establish the site. Whether they were compelled to do so by the authorities or went freely is also subject to debate; however, the settlers were probably not kept there by force. The perimeter walls of the site of Cerro la Cruz are much more intimidating from the outside than the inside, and they appear to have served more as a means to keep out unwelcome visitors and provide protection from flooding. In addition, the ease of travel allowed by the geography of the Chao Valley may have brought travelers who decided to stay rather than pass through.

Overall, the research presented here affirms the existence and extent of the Casma polity, which appears to have experienced a florescence during the Late Middle Horizon and into the Late Intermediate period (ca. AD 900–1350). I have argued that the Casma polity was responsible for building the site of Cerro la Cruz, and that, therefore, the local elites would have been politically aligned with the Casma polity. This contradicts earlier notions, which suggested the site was an Early Chimú state occupation, or that the Wari polity controlled the north coast, including the Chao Valley, during the Middle Horizon. The evidence shows that the site of Cerro la Cruz was a fortified town on the Casma periphery, and as such it provides a useful case study to illustrate the dynamic movements of geopolitical boundaries over time.

Sociopolitical Change and Continuity at Cerro la Cruz

The architecture and other material culture recovered from the site of Cerro la Cruz support the idea of rapid sociopolitical change during the establishment and abandonment of the site, with more gradual stages of development occurring in between. However, the enlargement of the compounds, which occurred in Phase 2, may represent rapid growth in the size of the site's population or a change in the status of its leaders. I argued that the site's perimeter walls served multiple functions, ranging from defense and restriction of access to retention of soil, and protection from flooding. I also suggested that the internal organization of the two excavated compounds (Compounds B3 and D3) shows a tripartite spatial division representing domestic, public, and sacred spaces. Many of these spaces contain evidence of a termination event, or ritual closing of the site, as part of its abandonment.

Nevertheless, some questions have produced ambiguous answers. The degree to which the inhabitants of Cerro la Cruz were controlled by the Casma polity core or were semiautonomous is not yet known. Whether the local elites maintained an alliance or tributary relationship with the Early Chimú state can only be speculated at this time. The relative numbers of residents who immigrated to the Chao Valley or who were local to the area requires skeletal evidence, which is not currently available. The extent to which the Virú Valley also may have served as a border zone between the Chimú and Casma polities can only be inferred until further research is conducted. Whether the inhabitants of the site of Cerro la Cruz were forced to leave or left of their own accord is unknown. Indeed, we may never know if the battle suggested by the slingstone piles ever took place. And finally, the exact nature and organization of the Casma polity remains under investigation. The raising of new questions is not surprising for research conducted on a periphery, and hopefully this study will provide significant impetus for future research on frontiers, border zones, and the Casma polity.

Many questions remain to be answered about the nature and organization of the Casma polity. Taken within the framework of core/periphery analyses, the Chao Valley appears to have been the northern periphery of the Casma polity's domain. Thus the next stage of this investigation is focused on the core, or heartland, of the Casma polity. The Casma Valley as a whole has been extensively investigated, yet relatively little attention has been given to the Casma polity occupation of the valley. The presumed capital city at El Purgatorio has been described in Casma Valley surveys, but it has never been thoroughly investigated. My current project (Vogel 2011; Vogel, Falcón, and Pacifico 2010) seeks to remedy these omissions and provide further insight into the fundamental questions of Casma polity origins, development, social and political organization, religious activity, and interpolity interactions.

Nevertheless, a number of interesting points of inquiry remain in the Chao Valley. The "twin" site to Cerro la Cruz, the site of Huasaquito, has never been thoroughly investigated. Further excavation at Huasaquito or at Cerro Coronado, a terraced hillside site along the Pan-American Highway, would contribute to our understanding of the Casma polity occupation in the Chao Valley and perhaps add to the evidence for the crosscutting social networks that typify frontiers. The fourth Casma polity site, Cerro Pucarachico, has only recently been identified (by Jonathon Kent and Teresa Rosales of the Santa Rita B Project) and would clearly benefit from archaeological examination.

Finally, the identification and investigation of other frontiers and border zones would greatly further our understanding of the transitional periods in prehistory. Significant sociopolitical changes often occur during these periods, changes that may redefine the nature of political and social organization and reshape the everyday lives of ancient peoples. Frontiers and border zones can provide unique insights into the events of these periods and help illuminate pivotal moments in the development of complex societies.

Relevance of the Site of Cerro la Cruz for Andean Archaeology

In the broader scope of Andean archaeology, this study argues that even a small valley like the Chao can play a significant role in regional cultural developments, in this case on the north coast of Peru. In addition to providing part of what may eventually become a valley-wide ceramic sequence, this research contributes a valuable set of absolute dates for use in the regional chronology. The new information generated on the Casma polity points to its importance during the Middle Horizon–Late Intermediate period transition and adds to our limited knowledge of this group, indicating possible directions for future research. Finally, the data acquired at Cerro la Cruz provide further evidence for long-term coastal continuities in cultural evolution which were affected but not controlled by interactions with highland polities. In other words, this study supports the independent development of coastal polities while recognizing the consistent interdependence of coastal and highland peoples throughout the history of human occupation in the Andes.

The relevance of the research at Cerro la Cruz extends beyond revisions of culture history or even the newly realized importance of the Casma polity in the development of Andean civilizations. It adds to our knowledge of border zones and frontiers and the roles they play in the interpolity dynamics of precapitalist states. Correspondingly, the picture of life on the frontier as represented by the inhabitants of Cerro la Cruz aids in our conceptions of border identities, the group affiliations and social identities of people living in borderlands, whether the borders are cultural, geopolitical, or both. Border zones are fertile ground for the investigation of dynamic sociopolitical change and the cross-cutting social networks that create such change. From an anthropological perspective, the results of this research contribute to our understanding of the catalysts for culture change and how local people adapt during periods of transition.

Archaeological Contributions to the Study of Peripheries

Archaeologists must strive to achieve a balance between research at large/core sites and smaller/peripheral sites, as well as at variously sized sites in between, to correct the bias in the archaeological record, which often favors large sites with monumental architecture. Indeed, minor administrative centers and smaller polities are also important to the total picture of life in the prehistoric past. For example, it may be more feasible to try to understand the nuances of interpolity relations at smaller sites rather than at core sites, where such interactions may be masked or overwhelmed by the need to show state identity. In a similar manner, so-called lesser polities are not merely fillers to plug the gaps of prehistory between the rise and fall of larger or more well-known states. They play pivotal and significant roles in charting the course of the development of human societies and in some cases may represent the resistance of local groups to a larger authority, even to the point of toppling a great empire. The agency exerted by these groups can have lasting effects on the development of complex societies. The study of frontiers and border zones recognizes the agency of many individuals in shaping prehistory by, rather than favoring the conquerors, giving the inhabitants of the periphery a "voice."

The research conducted at the site of Cerro la Cruz in the Chao Valley has relevance both within and beyond the realm of Andean archaeology. As the events of the Middle Horizon on the north coast of Peru are being reevaluated and the culture history revised, the evidence from the site of Cerro la Cruz shows the importance of the Casma polity, a relatively unknown group, which appears to have played a pivotal role in the sociopolitical transitions between the collapse of the Moche polity and the rise of the Chimú state. Although the inner workings of the polity require further investigation, the data recovered thus far suggest that the Casma polity represents an intermediate stage between the religiously centered polities of previous periods, such as the Chavín and Moche polities, and the more secularized states that dominate the later periods of Peruvian prehistory, such as the Chimú and Inca Empires. This study attempts to synthesize our current knowledge of the Casma polity and provide the foundation for subsequent research on this group.

Identifying and examining frontiers and border zones can greatly contribute to our understanding of the development and collapse of complex societies in the New World. This area of study addresses the need to investigate smaller, more peripheral sites in addition to the larger, more popular core settlements. Similarly, the everyday lives of prehistoric people and their ability to adapt during periods of sociopolitical transition can be examined. For example, this study demonstrates the ability of prehispanic people to survive in an inhospitable environment during an extended drought, balancing the importance of climatic change and its impact on human societies with human agency and the ability to adjust to environmental challenges. Thus, from a historic or prehistoric perspective, archaeology can explore the ways in which people have adapted to fluctuating social, political, and environmental conditions.

In some archaeological research, the emphasis is on the synchronic view, a slice of life taken from one particular point in the past. In the case of Cerro la Cruz, I chose instead to emphasize a diachronic perspective, pointing out the dynamic, shifting nature of geopolitical boundaries as people moved through the landscape in response to or as initiators of sociopolitical change. While the blending of artifact styles can be seen as an analytical problem for the archaeologist, I prefer to highlight these complexities and seemingly odd combinations as manifestations of the crosscutting social networks typical of a periphery. Instead of being treated as problems to be solved or explained away, "anomalous" artifacts can be used to invoke a more flexible or perhaps even more realistic vision of the past—one that acknowledges the "messiness" of everyday life and social interaction.

Examining frontiers and border zones can be one way of correcting previous oversights by confronting the inconsistent, anomalous, and troublesome aspects of the archaeological record. Ultimately, this approach may lead us one step closer to our final goal, a deeper and fuller understanding of the human past and the possibilities for our future. After all, archaeology seeks to tell us who we are, where we come from, who we could become, and who we might have been.

Notes

Chapter 1. Introduction

1. In later chapters the multiple functions of these perimeter walls are discussed in more detail.

Chapter 2. A Time and Place of Transition

1. See Quilter 2002 and Chapdelaine 2010 for more extensive discussion of recent models for Moche political organization.

2. Ongoing investigations at the Casma capital city of El Purgatorio are aimed at fleshing out our understanding of Casma polity organization (e.g., Vogel 2011; Vogel, Falcón, and Pacifico 2010).

3. Conrad 1990; Donnan and Mackey 1978; Dulanto 2008; Keatinge 1982; Kolata 1990; Mackey 1982, 1987, 2002, 2009; Mackey and Klymyshyn 1990; Moore 1996a, 1996b; Moore and Mackey 2008; Moseley 1975, 1990; Moseley and Cordy-Collins 1990; Parsons and Hastings 1988; Pozorski 1980; Pozorski and Pozorski 1997; Rowe 1948; Shimada 1990; T. Topic 1990; Topic and Moseley 1983; Topic and Topic 1978.

4. *Chala* is the indigenous term for the arid coastal desert habitats of Peru, which support only xerophytic vegetation unless made productive by irrigation (Topic and Topic 1983:240).

5. *Yungas* is the indigenous term for the low-altitude (500–2300 m), hot, dry habitats which are characterized by scrub vegetation and cacti (Topic and Topic 1983:240). Yunga is the Quechua name for the language spoken in the northern half of the north coast, sometimes referred to as Muchic (Rowe 1948:27).

6. In addition, the vessel form she describes as a large bowl appears to correspond in my classification system to the tinaja vessel form, a large storage jar.

7. Wilson (1995) believes the site of Huanchay to have been established during the Early Intermediate period but to continue to have been occupied into the Middle Horizon.

8. It is expected that investigations at other Casma polity sites, such as my current project at the Casma capital of El Purgatorio, will augment this description (e.g., Vogel 2011; Vogel, Falcón, and Pacifico 2010).

9. Unfortunately, Fung and Williams (1977) provided no further discussion of settlement patterns; however, Wilson's (1995) survey results supported their hypothesis.

Chapter 3. Archaeological Approaches to Peripheries

1. For a useful summary of these attempts, see Hall and Chase-Dunn 1993.

2. Scholars investigating the past in this manner using world-systems theory include Amin 1980, 1989, 1991; Blanton et al. 1981; Chase-Dunn 1990, 1992; Chase-Dunn and Hall 1991, 1992, 1993, 1996, 1997, 1998; Ekholm and Friedman 1982; Frank 1990a, 1990b, 1993; Frank and Gills 1992; Gills and Frank 1990, 1991, 1992; Kohl 1978, 1979, 1989; Peregrine 1999; Renfrew and Shennan 1982; Urban and Schortmann 1999; Wallerstein 1990, 1991, 1992; and Wells 1999.

3. Although I mention some recent exceptions to the core-centered approach later in this chapter, Lightfoot and Martinez's (1995) critique still applies to the majority of core/periphery analyses in the Andes.

4. On the Roman frontier, for example, choosing to live inside or outside a wall was a declaration of one's affiliation with the Roman Empire (Samson 1992:28).

5. El Niño is the common name for the weather phenomenon referred to scientifically as El Niño–Southern Oscillation (ENSO) events. Two main changes in weather patterns characterize these events: a rise in sea water temperature, which depletes marine resources, and excessive rainfall, which can cause flooding.

6. Highland polities were also affected by the harsh terrain of the Andes, with smaller pockets of dispersed populations rather than the larger, more densely populated polities of the coast.

7. I refer to the Chimú polity as a state when discussing time periods prior to its first wave of expansion, circa AD 1300. In discussions of periods after this time, I refer to the Chimú polity as an "empire." When the timing of an event is questionable, I use the less specific term "polity" to describe the political organization of the Chimú.

Chapter 4. Investigating Peripheries

1. The terms provided here in quotes are the species' local, common names.

2. Although Moseley (1983:785) reports on the flow volume of six north coast rivers from the Santa Valley to the Zaña Valley, the flow volume for the Chao River was listed as "not available." However, the Virú River flow volume is given at 105 $m^3 \times 100^3$, and since the Chao River is smaller, one can assume that its flow volume would not exceed that of the Virú River.

3. Evidence to support this idea regarding the channeling of water may be found in various walls at the site of Cerro la Cruz, which still serve to control water and retain earth along the hillside.

4. These two samples were analyzed in a laboratory at the Pontifícia Universidad Católica del Perú in 1977. At that time, the lab may not have used the same

procedures or equipment I had access to through the National Science Foundation–University of Arizona Accelerator Mass Spectrometry Laboratory in 2002 and would therefore have produced different results.

5. Evidence for trade at Cerro la Cruz is discussed in chapter 5.

6. This site has only recently been identified as belonging to the Casma polity (and possibly later occupied by the Chimú) by Jonathan Kent and Teresa Rosales of the Santa Rita B Project (Rosales et al., Entre Casma 2008).

7. *Quincha* is a type of architecture sometimes referred to as "wattle-and-daub" and commonly used for making temporary or fragile structures. The construction technique usually involves a small stone foundation supporting cane and reed matting placed vertically into the ground and sometimes covered in mud.

8. The Moche style, also from the north coast of Peru, is renowned for depicting actual personages and ritual activities practiced by Moche people, and evidence for these personages and rituals has been excavated archaeologically (Alva and Donnan 1993; Bawden 1996; Donnan and Castillo 1992, 1994).

9. Many Andean scholars have examined various aspects of mortuary practice as representative of social identities (e.g., Carmichael 1995; Donnan 1995; Donnan and Mackey 1978; Isbell 1997; Rivera 1995).

10. The three paste types distinguished were redware, which besides its red color generally has medium-sized inclusions and is used primarily for domestic vessels; blackware, which in addition to its color has only fine inclusions and is used primarily for fineware; and tinaja, which is red in color but has large inclusions and is used only for making large storage vessels. See Vogel 2003 for the results of the room-by-room surface sherd counts.

11. Modern maize cobs are significantly larger than preconquest varieties, which are generally no more than 6–8 cm in length (Victor Vásquez, personal communication 2003).

12. The botanical and faunal analysis, which included fifty-three samples for dry sieving and fifty-three samples for flotation, was completed by Rocio Sanchez with the assistance of Silvia Saldivar and consultation from Jonathan Kent, Teresa Rosales, and Victor Vásquez. Alejandro Fernández Honores of the University of Trujillo, along with his students, conducted the flotation analysis.

13. Skeletal analysis was completed by Susan Haun Mowery, ceramic analysis by Melissa Vogel, adobe analysis by Patrick Brett, and textile analysis by María Jesús Jiménez Díaz.

Chapter 5. Life on the Edge of the Casma Polity

1. As mentioned in chapter 1, I defined a compound as a group of rooms, patios, and/or plazas enclosed by a large exterior wall. In contrast, agglutinated room clusters are distinguished by the lack of an obvious perimeter wall.

2. For descriptions of individual unit excavations, see Vogel 2003.

3. During the mapping process, I noticed that the first section of Compound D3

showed markedly different construction and organization from the other two sections although it was located within the exterior wall of the compound. Because of this difference from the rest of the compound, I numbered the rooms in this section separately, with the subdesignation "a" (e.g., R1a, R2a, R3a, etc.).

4. Thanks to the generous funding of the National Science Foundation, twelve carbon samples were analyzed by the National Science Foundation–University of Arizona Accelerator Mass Spectrometry Laboratory. For the locations from which these samples were taken, see table 2.2 or 6.12 in Vogel 2003:Table 6.12.

5. Dedicatory burials within architecture were a longstanding tradition in Andean prehistory (Nash 2009:242–43; Verano 1995:189–219) and have been found in Chimú buildings at the sites of Chan Chan, Farfán, and Pacatnamu.

6. For further discussion of this architectural form from the perspective of household archaeology, see Nash 2009.

7. For a similar comparison of Wari and Inca architecture, see Nash and Williams 2005.

8. Nash and Williams (2005:167–69) describe a few tripartite structures from Cerro Baúl, but they are quite simple and very different in design from the compounds at Cerro la Cruz.

9. Multipurpose architecture is known from Inca sites as well. Hyslop (1990:165) describes the close relationship between Inca warfare and religion, such that even "purely" military sites include religious structures.

10. An olla is a closed vessel form used for cooking. Ollas are generally globular with relatively wide mouths and short rims, and they come in a range of sizes.

11. A stirrup-spout bottle is a closed vessel form. The body is globular with a semicircular hollow handle that connects the narrow spout to the body. It may have been used to pour libations during rituals or as a funerary object.

12. A florero is a shallow bowl with a wide flaring rim.

13. A kero (also called a beaker) is a tall, cylindrical vessel made of ceramic, wood, or metal. It was used as a ceremonial drinking cup, usually for the consumption of maize beer.

14. A tinaja is the largest ceramic vessel form, used for storage of both dry goods and liquids. The paste is usually thick with many inclusions, and the mouth is generally unrestricted.

15. A grater is a bowl-shaped vessel form with deeply incised grooves in a cross-hatched pattern, believed to have been used for food preparation.

16. A jar is a closed vessel form, often greater in height than in width but sometimes egg-shaped, that was used for storage or serving.

17. Counts and percentages of each paste type listed by room can be found in Vogel 2003, Appendix II.

18. See Appendix II in Vogel 2003 for more details.

19. A waster is a misshapen ceramic vessel or sherd from such a vessel damaged during the firing process or due to poor manufacture.

20. However, Shimada (1994:199, Figure 8.14) suggests that certain marks found on the exteriors of storage vessels at the contemporaneous site of Pampa Grande may have also served as maker's marks.

21. All skeletal analysis was conducted by Susan Haun Mowery.

22. Although rodent bones were found they could not be speciated, so the presence of guinea pigs can only be inferred.

23. All textile analysis was performed by Dr. María Jesús Jiménez Díaz.

24. Although the content of modern Andean *pago* offerings is different from that found at Cerro la Cruz, the concept may be similar.

25. In the case of Tiwanaku's Akapana East, Janusek (2004:112) interpreted a layer of charcoal found beneath the top of the tumulus as a burnt offering interred during the area's final closing.

26. At sites like Chiripa, ritual burning was practiced regularly as part of a sequence of closures and rebuilding events (Bandy 2001:127; Hastorf 2008:551).

27. For a room-by-room description of the evidence for this event, see Vogel 2003.

28. In Andean tradition, *apus* are spirits that dwell within mountains and other aspects of the sacred landscape.

29. These sites include Cerro Coronado, Cerro la Cruz, Huasaquito, and Cerro Pucarachico. The site of Cerro Santa Rita may be a fifth site, but there is relatively little evidence for a Casma occupation there.

Chapter 6. The Geopolitical Landscape of the Peruvian Coast in Late Prehistory

1. See table 2.4 for a comparison of previous names for variations on the Casma ceramic style.

2. Unfortunately, Wilson often skips over the Chao Valley to discuss the comparisons between Virú and Santa valleys.

3. Although the Tanguche data collected by Chapdelaine and Pimentel's project has not yet been published, it does provide evidence for a Casma occupation of the Santa Valley (Claude Chapdelaine, personal communication 2008).

4. In fact, the few published works on the Huarmey Valley deal almost exclusively with the Preceramic and Early Horizon occupation (Bonavia 1996; Bonavia et al. 1993), with one exception addressing Huarmey Middle Horizon textiles (Prümers 1989, 1990). However, recent work in the tiny Culebras Valley (between Huarmey and Casma) has shown a clear Casma polity presence (Prządka and Giersz 2003).

5. For the names of all these fortified sites, see Table 8.4 in Vogel 2003.

6. Hyslop (1990:244–45) gives examples of how local lords under the Inca Empire sometimes imitated Inca-style architecture as a sign of their high status, thereby aligning themselves with the ruling polity.

7. Thus far, the results of the ongoing investigation of the Casma capital city, El Purgatorio, supports these assertions and is expected to provide answers to many of these questions (Vogel 2011; Vogel, Falcón, and Pacifico 2010).

Chapter 7. Conclusion

1. In fact, the Casma polity may have been partly responsible for the collapse of the southern half of Moche territory. However, this hypothesis remains to be tested as the investigation of the Casma polity continues.

Glossary

audiencia. A U-shaped room considered to be a hallmark of Chimú architectural style. These rooms are believed to have been used for administrative purposes, to receive visitors and their tribute. The goods received were stored in rooms located behind the *audiencia*, which often also controlled access to the storage areas. According to Mackey (1982), the *audiencia* developed from similar features in the Moche V period architecture at the sites of Pampa Grande and Pacatnamu.

baffled entryway. An entrance that has an obstructing wall that prevents direct entry into a room, causing anyone entering to turn around the wall to reach the inside.

border zone. The larger area (larger than the boundary itself) where territories governed by two or more separate polities meet or intersect.

boundary. The vertical plane dividing adjacent polities. It may or may not be physically marked on the ground.

bowl. A deep, rounded dish usually considered a serving vessel. Also called a *cuenco*.

burial. An feature that consists of human skeletal remains and associated grave goods. In the case of the one excavated burial at the site of Cerro la Cruz, we created a special designation (Bu1) for the pit where the skeletal remains were found, in order to keep all artifactual remains from the burial separate from the rest of the excavation unit in which it was found.

canal. A ditch that is assumed to have transported water in the past (if not at present), most likely to irrigate fields. A canal is different from a dry moat, which served primarily defensive purposes and is not believed to have carried water.

ceque. A ceremonial line or path. The *ceque* system was a radial system of forty-one sighting lines in Cuzco that integrated Inca kinship, cosmology, and calendrics (Hyslop 1990:334).

ceramic(s). A term that, based on context, refers to whole vessels, ceramic sherds, or the larger category of artifacts made from fired clay.

chala. The indigenous term for the arid coastal desert habitats of Peru, which support only xerophytic vegetation unless made productive by irrigation (Topic and Topic 1983:240).

chicha. A beer made from maize which has been important for ritual activities throughout the Andes for many centuries.

compound. A group of rooms, patios, and/or plazas enclosed by a large exterior wall. We numbered these sequentially within each sector of the site of Cerro la Cruz and labeled them with the corresponding sector letter and compound number (e.g., Sector B, Compound 3 was labeled Compound B3).

compound wall. A large exterior wall that forms the outer boundary of the space enclosed by the compound. This differs from both the perimeter wall of a site and the smaller interior walls of the rooms within the compound.

corridor. A narrow passageway delineated by walls leading from one room to another. We labeled these with a C and numbered them within each compound (e.g., Sector D, Compound 3, Corridor 3 was labeled D3C3).

ENSO events. The weather phenomenon referred to scientifically as El Niño–Southern Oscillation (ENSO) and commonly known as El Niño. The changes in weather patterns that characterize these events include a rise in seawater temperature, which depletes marine resources, and excessive rainfall, which can cause flash flooding.

face-neck jar. A jar whose neck is decorated with a modeled, incised, or painted human face or, less often, animal face.

Farfán. A Chimú regional center located in the Jequetepeque Valley.

feature. A "nonportable artifact, not recoverable from its matrix without destroying its integrity" (Sharer and Ashmore 1993:613).

firing pit. An oval-shaped pit used for firing ceramics, usually stained bright red from repeated use.

floor. A horizontal surface that, when well preserved, is relatively easy to differentiate from layers of mud created by natural processes, such as rain. In this study, plastered floors are distinguished from hard-packed soil layers, which may also have served as floors in lower-status areas. Plastered floors generally indicate a higher-status space.

florero. A distinct ceramic vessel form consisting of a shallow bowl with a flaring rim. Considered fineware.

frontier. The farthest extent of any given polity's territory, which may or may not border another polity's territory.

gateway. A deliberate opening in a perimeter wall, defined by clear corners.

grater. A bowl-shaped vessel form with deeply incised cross-hatching. Considered utilitarian ware, but its exact function is unknown.

hearth. A clearly defined fire pit containing charcoal and ashes, whose specific purpose may be undefined.

huaca. A complex Andean term with several meanings, including platform mound, sacred place, and sacred object.

jar. A vessel form greater in height than in width, with a restricted mouth, and used for storage or serving. Also called a *cantaro*.

kero. A vessel form that can be made of ceramic, wood, or metal. Considered fineware, it functions as a ceremonial drinking cup, usually for the consumption of *chicha*. Also called a beaker or cup.

level. A layer of soil in an excavation unit. We excavated natural levels according to changes in soil type and cultural remains. They were numbered from top to bottom as excavations proceeded downward and labeled with an L (e.g., B3R2U1L4 was beneath B3R2U1L2.)

mold. A hollow form into which clay is pressed to produce ceramics, sometimes incised on the inner surface to produce raised designs on the final product.

niche. An architectural feature, usually rectangular in shape, consisting of a recess in a wall and believed to have held sacred objects or ancestor mummies.

olla. A ceramic vessel form, used for cooking. Ollas come in a range of sizes and are generally globular, have incurving but relatively unrestricted mouths and short rims. They were the most frequent vessel form found at the site of Cerro la Cruz. Also called a pot.

pago. An offering to the earth and the Andean earth goddess, Pachamama. The offering may take many forms, such as *chicha* or cane alcohol poured on the ground or items with special meaning buried in a particular spot.

parapet. A bench built against the inside of a perimeter wall, such that defenders may stand on the bench to see over the wall and have the advantage of greater height than any of their attackers (Topic and Topic 1987).

patio. A small open area within a compound, thought to have been used for private activities.

perimeter wall. A wall that surrounds a site or a portion of a site. This is differentiated from a compound wall, which forms the outer boundary of one structure.

platform (mound). A raised horizontal surface resembling a truncated pyramid, which can be built in a broad range of sizes. In the Andes, platform mounds were used as temples and for burials.

plaza. A large open area enclosed within a compound, thought to have been used for more public activities.

polishing stones. A small, smooth pebble used for smoothing the wet clay coils during the production of ceramics.

polity. A culturally distinct political organization, usually identifiable primarily by archaeological indicators such as ceramic and architectural style and by settlement pattern. The level of political organization in these polities may or may not reach the level of a state, but it certainly extends beyond kinship and even ethnic ties.

quechua. (1) The indigenous term for the habitats 2,300–3,500 m above sea level which are generally frost free and suitable for rainfall agriculture (Topic and Topic 1983:240). (2) The Quechua language. (3) The ethnic group composed of native speakers of this language, who often inhabit the geographic regions called *quechua*.

quincha. A type of architecture sometimes referred to as "wattle-and-daub," commonly used for making temporary or fragile structures. The construction technique usually involves a small stone foundation supporting cane and reed matting placed vertically into the ground and sometimes covered in mud. *Quincha* structures are generally thought to be the dwellings of the lower classes.

ramp. An inclined surface used to traverse from one floor level to another.

rim. The edge of a ceramic vessel. Rims can usually be analyzed to indicate vessel form.

room. An architectural subdivision within a compound set apart by walls which may or may not have a defined doorway. Rooms were numbered sequentially from left to right and up the hillside. Each room number is preceded by the letter R for room as well as the compound number and sector letter (e.g., B3R2 identifies Sector B, Compound 3, Room 2).

sector. An arbitrary division of the site into smaller areas, primarily based on density of architectural remains. Silva (1992) divided the area encompassed by the site of Cerro la Cruz into five sectors during his survey. For simplicity and data compatibility, I use the same designations he established: A, B, C, D, and E.

slingstones. A smooth, fist-sized pebble used with a slingshot as a weapon for both hunting and combat.

spindle whorl. A small object, usually made of ceramic or stone, used to spin raw cotton or wool into thread and yarn. It is roughly circular with a central hole for attachment to a wooden spindle and is sometimes decorated.

sterile. The deepest level in an excavation unit in which no further cultural remains are found. At the site of Cerro la Cruz, this level was often the bedrock of the hillside.

stirrup-spout bottle. A ceramic vessel whose body is globular with a semicircular hollow handle connecting the narrow spout to the body. These vessels were used to pour libations during rituals or as funerary objects and are considered fineware.

strata. The definable layers of archaeological matrix revealed by excavation (Sharer and Ashmore 1993:621).

suni. The indigenous term for the grassland habitats 3,500–4,000 m above sea level in the Andes Mountains, which are prone to frost (Topic and Topic 1983:240).

test unit. An excavation not located within a compound, selected to compare areas outside of compounds to those within, which are simply referred to as units. Test units were numbered in order of their excavation preceded by the label Test (e.g., Test1) to distinguish these areas from units excavated inside compounds.

tinaja. The largest ceramic vessel form, used for storage of both dry goods and liquids. The paste is usually thick with many inclusions, and the mouth is unrestricted.

trench. An area of excavation 0.5 m wide and of varying length, depending on the distance between perimeter walls. We excavated trenches in two locations between the perimeter walls to determine if any subsurface architecture or unusual features existed in these areas. The trenches were numbered in order of their excavation (e.g., Trench1 and Trench2).

type. With reference to ceramics, a type is an empirical grouping of sherds based on common characteristics, not based on culture of origin.

unit. An area of excavation. Each excavation unit was given a number according to its order of excavation within a particular room and was labeled with the corresponding sector, compound, and room designations. Unit numbers were labeled with the letter U (e.g., B3R2U1 identifies the first unit excavated in Sector B, Compound 3, Room 2). Most units began as squares 2 m × 2 m and were extended if necessary.

ware. A "broad class [of ceramics] based on some prominent feature such as color, decorative technique, or function" (Shepard 1995:318 [1956]).

waster. A misshapen ceramic vessel or sherds from such a vessel either damaged during the firing process or resulting from poor manufacture. The presence of this artifact may indicate ceramic production.

weaving sword. A long, flat wooden implement used during weaving to separate the warp from the weft.

yungas. The indigenous term for the low-altitude (500–2,300 m) hot, dry habitats which are characterized by scrub vegetation and cacti (Topic and Topic 1983:240). Yunga, sometimes referred to as Muchic, is the Quechua name for the language spoken in the northern half of the north coast (Rowe 1948:27).

References Cited

Ackerman, Raquel
1991   The Despacho: Analysis of a Ritual Object. *Journal of Latin American Lore* 17:71–102.

Alconini, Sonia
2004   The Southeastern Inka Frontier Against the Chiriguanos: Structure and Dynamics of the Inka Imperial Borderlands. *Latin American Antiquity* 15(4):389–418.
2005   Military and Cultural Imperial Frontiers: Dynamics and Settlement Patterns of the Southeastern Inka Frontier. In *Untaming the Frontier in Anthropology, Archaeology, and History*, edited by Bradley J. Parker and Lars Rosdeth, pp. 115–46. University of Arizona Press, Tucson.
2010   Yampara Households and Communal Evolution in the Southeastern Inka Peripheries. In *Distant Provinces in the Inka Empire: Toward a Deeper Understanding of Inca Imperialism*, edited by Michael A. Malpass and Sonia Alconini, pp. 75–107. University of Iowa Press, Iowa City.

Algaze, Guillermo
1993a   Expansionary Dynamics of Some Early Pristine States. *American Anthropologist* 95(2):304–33.
1993b   *The Uruk World System: The Dynamics of Expansion of Early Mesopotamian Civilization*. University of Chicago Press, Chicago.

Alva, Walter
1986   *Salinas de Chao: Asentimiento temprano en el norte del* Peru. Kommission fur Allgemeine und Vergleichende Archaologie, Bonn.

Alva, Walter, and Christopher B. Donnan
1993   *Royal Tombs of Sipán*. UCLA Fowler Museum of Cultural History, Los Angeles.

Amin, Samir
1980   *Class and Nation: Historically and in the Current Crisis*. Monthly Review Press, New York.
1989   *Eurocentrism*. Monthly Review Press, New York.
1991   The Ancient World-Systems Versus the Modern Capitalist World-System. *Review* 14(3):349–85.

Anton, Ferdinand
1972   *The Art of Ancient Peru*. Rev. and enlarged ed. Translated by Mary Whittall. Thames & Hudson, London.

Ashmore, Wendy
1989 Construction and Cosmology: Politics and Ideology in Lowland Maya Settlement Patterns. In *Word and Image in Maya Culture*, edited by William F. Hanks and Don S. Rice, pp. 272–86. University of Utah Press, Salt Lake City.
Ashmore, Wendy, and Jeremy A. Sabloff
2002 Spatial Orders in Maya Civic Plans. *Latin American Antiquity* 13(2):201–16.
Bandy, Matthew S.
2001 Population and History in the Ancient Titicaca Basin. Unpublished Ph.D. dissertation, Department of Anthropology, University of California at Berkeley.
Bauer, Brian S.
1992 *The Development of the Inca State*. University of Texas Press, Austin.
Bawden, Garth
1977 Galindo and the Nature of the Middle Horizon in Northern Coastal Peru. Unpublished Ph.D. dissertation, Department of Anthropology, Harvard University.
1982 Galindo: A Study in Cultural Transition During the Middle Horizon. In *Chan Chan: Andean Desert City*, edited by Michael E. Moseley and Kent C. Day, pp. 285–320. School of American Research Advanced Seminar Series. University of New Mexico Press, Albuquerque.
1996 *The Moche*. Blackwell, Cambridge, Mass.
Bawden, Garth, and Geoffrey W. Conrad
1982 *The Andean Heritage Masterpieces of Peruvian Art from the Collections of the Peabody Museum*. Peabody Museum Press, Cambridge, Mass.
Bender, Barbara
1998 *Stonehenge: Making Space*. Berg Press, Oxford.
Blanton, Richard, and Gary Feinman
1984 The Mesoamerican World-System. *American Anthropologist* 86:673–92.
Blanton, Richard E., Stephen A. Kowalewski, Gary M. Feinman, and Jill Appel
1981 *Ancient Mesoamerica: A Comparison of Change in Three Regions*. Cambridge University Press, Cambridge.
Bonavia, Duccio
1996 From Hunting-Gathering to Agriculture: A Local Perspective. *Bulletin de l'Institut français d'études andines* 25(2):169–86.
Bonavia, Duccio, Laura W. Johnson, Elizabeth J. Reitz, and Glendon H. Weir
1993 Un sitio precerámico de Huarmey (PV35-6) antes de la introducción del maíz. *Bulletin de l'Institut français d'études andines* 22(2):409–42.
Bourdieu, Pierre
1973 The Berber House. In *Rules and Meanings: The Anthropology of Everyday Knowledge*, edited by Mary Douglas, pp. 98–110. Penguin, Harmondsworth, UK.
Bourget, Steve
2001 Rituals of Sacrifice: Its Practice at Huaca de la Luna and Its Representation in Moche Iconography. In *Moche Art and Archaeology in Ancient Peru*, edited by Joanne Pillsbury, pp. 89–110. Yale University Press, New Haven.

Brett, Patrick
2002 Adobe Manufacture in the Andean Past. Undergraduate thesis, Department of Anthropology, University of Pennsylvania.

Broda, Johanna, David Carrasco, and Eduardo Matos Moctezuma
1987 *The Great Temple of Tenochtitlan: Center and Periphery in the Aztec World*. University of California Press, Berkeley.

Brown Vega, Margaret Yvette
2008 War and Social Life in Prehispanic Peru: Ritual, Defense, and Communities at the Fortress of Acaray, Huaura Valley. Unpublished Ph.D. dissertation, Department of Anthropology, University of Illinois at Urbana-Champaign.
2009 Conflict in the Early Horizon and Late Intermediate Period: New Dates from the Fortress of Acaray, Huaura Valley, Perú. *Current Anthropology* 50(2):255–66.

Burger, Richard L., and Ramiro Matos Mendieta
2002 Atalla: A Center on the Periphery of the Chavín Horizon. *Latin American Antiquity* 13(2):153–77.

Cabello Balboa, Miguel
1951 [1586] *Miscelánea antárctica: Una historia del Perú antiguo*. Universidad Nacional Mayor de San Marcos, Facultad de Letras, Instituto de Etnologiìa, Lima.

Calancha, Antonio de la
1638 *Crónica moralizada del Ordén de San Agustín en el Perú, con sucesos ejemplares en esta monarquía*. Pedro Lacavalleria, Barcelona.

Carcelén Silva, José, and Orlando Angulo Zavaleta
1999 *Catastro de los sitios arqueológicos del área de influencia del canal de irrigación Chavimochic: Valle Viejo de Chao*. Instituto Nacional de Cultura, Trujillo, Peru.

Cárdenas, Mercedes
1976 *Informe Preliminar del Trabajo de Campo en el Valle de Chao*. Instituto Nacional de Cultura, Lima.
1978 *Columna Cronológica del Valle de Chao*. Pontificia Universidad Católica del Perú, Lima.
1979 *A Chronology of the Use of Marine Resources in Ancient Peru*. Publicación del Instituto Riva-Agüero No. 104. Pontificia Universidad Católica del Perú, Lima.
1998 Material diagnóstico del período formativo en los valles de Chao y Santa, costa norte del Perú. In Boletin de Arqueología PUCP 2:61–81. Pontificia Universidad Católica del Perú, Lima.

Carmichael, Patrick H.
1995 Nasca Burial Patterns: Social Structure and Mortuary Ideology. In *Tombs for the Living: Andean Mortuary Practice*, edited by Tom D. Dillehay, pp. 161–88. Dumbarton Oaks, Washington, D.C.

Castillo Butters, Luis Jaime
1989 *Personajes míticos, escenas y narraciones en la iconografía Mochica*. Fondo editorial, Pontificia Universidad Católica del Perú, Lima.
2001 The Last of the Mochicas: A View from the Jequetepeque Valley. In *Moche Art and Archaeology in Ancient Peru*, edited by Joanne Pillsbury, pp. 307–32. Center

for the Advanced Study of the Visual Arts, National Gallery of Art, Washington, D.C.

Castillo Butters, Luis Jaime, Carol J. Mackey, and Andrew J. Nelson
1997   Informe Preliminar de Investigación Arqueológica: Proyecto "Complejo Arqueologico de Moro." Campaña 1996. Instituto Nacional de Cultura, Lima.

Champion, T. C. (editor)
1989   Centre and Periphery: Comparative Studies in Archaeology. Unwin Hyman, London.

Chapdelaine, Claude
1998   Excavaciones en la zona urbana de Moche durante 1996. In Investigaciones en la Huaca de la Luna 1996, edited by Santiago Uceda, Elías Mujica, and Ricardo Morales, pp. 85–115. Facultad de Ciencias Sociales, Universidad Nacional de la Libertad, Trujillo, Peru.
2001   The Growing Power of a Moche Urban Class. In Moche Art and Archaeology in Ancient Peru, edited by Joanne Pillsbury, pp. 69–87. Center for the Advanced Study of the Visual Arts, National Gallery of Art, Washington, D.C.
2008   Moche Art Style in the Santa Valley: Between Being "à la Mode" and Developing a Provincial Identity. In The Art and Archaeology of the Moche: An Ancient Andean Society of the Peruvian North Coast, edited by Steve Bourget and Kimberly L. Jones, pp. 129–52. University of Texas Press, Austin.
2010   Recent Advances in Moche Archaeology. Journal of Archaeological Research 19, no. 2 (November): 191–231. http://www.springerlink.com/content/2114316018412264/. Accessed January 5, 2011.

Chapdelaine, Claude, Santiago Uceda, M. E. Moya, César Jáuregui, and Chanel Uceda
1997   Los complejos arquitectónicos urbanos de Moche. In Investigaciones en la Huaca de la Luna 1995, edited by Santiago Uceda, Elías Mujica, and Ricardo Morales, pp. 71–92. Facultad de Ciencias Sociales, Universidad Nacional de la Libertad, Trujillo, Peru.

Chase-Dunn, Christopher
1990   World State Formation: Historical Processes and Emergent Necessity. Political Geography Quarterly 9:108–30.
1992   The Comparative Study of World-Systems. Review 15:313–33.

Chase-Dunn, Christopher, and Thomas D. Hall
1991   Conceptualizing Core/Periphery Hierarchies for Comparative Study. In Core/Periphery Relations in Precapitalist Worlds, edited by Christopher Chase-Dunn and Thomas D. Hall, pp. 5–44. Westview Press, Boulder, Colo.
1992   World-Systems and Modes of Production: Toward the Comparative Study of Transformations. Humboldt Journal of Social Relations 18(1):81–117.
1993   Comparing World-Systems: Concepts and Working Hypotheses. Social Forces 71:851–86.
1996   World-Systems in Prehistory. In Pre-Columbian World-Systems, edited by Peter N. Peregrine and Gary M. Feinman. Monographs in World Archaeology No. 26. Prehistory Press, Madison.

1997 Rise and Demise: Comparing World-Systems. New Perspectives in Sociology. Westview Press, Boulder, Colo.
1998 World-Systems in North America: Networks, Rise and Fall and Pulsations of Trade in Stateless Systems. *American Indian Culture and Research Journal* 22(1):23–72.

Claval, Paul
1980 Centre/Periphery and Space: Models of Political Geography. In *Centre and Periphery: Spatial Variation in Politics*, edited by Jean Gottman, pp. 63–71. Sage, Beverly Hills.

Collier, Donald
1955 Cultural Chronology and Change as Reflected in the Ceramics of the Virú Valley, Perú. Fieldiana: Anthropology Vol. 43. Chicago Natural History Museum, Chicago.
1962 Archaeological Investigations in the Casma Valley, Peru. In *Akten Des 34. Internationalen Amerikanistenkongress, Wien, 1960*, pp. 411–17. Verlag Ferdinand Berger, Horn, Vienna.

Conkey, Margaret Wright, and Christine Ann Hastorf (editors)
1990 *The Uses of Style in Archaeology*. Cambridge University Press, Cambridge.

Conklin, William J.
1990 Architecture of the Chimu: Memory, Function, and Image. In *The Northern Dynasties: Kingship and Statecraft in Chimor*, edited by Michael E. Moseley and Alana Cordy-Collins, pp. 43–74. Dumbarton Oaks, Washington, D.C.

Conlee, Christina A., Jalh Dulanto, Carol J. Mackey, and Charles Stanish
2004 Late Prehispanic Sociopolitical Complexity. In *Andean Archaeology*, edited by Helaine Silverman, pp. 209–36. Blackwell, Oxford.

Conrad, Geoffrey W.
1974 Burial Platforms and Related Structures on the North Coast of Peru: Some Social and Political Implications. Unpublished Ph.D. dissertation, Department of Anthropology, Harvard University.
1990 Farfán, General Pacatnamu, and the Dynastic History of Chimor. In *The Northern Dynasties: Kingship and Statecraft in Chimor*, edited by Michael E. Moseley and Alana Cordy-Collins, pp. 227–42. Dumbarton Oaks, Washington, D.C.

Cook, Anita Gwynn
1986 Art and Time in the Evolution of Andean State Expansionism. Unpublished Ph.D. dissertation, Department of Anthropology, State University of New York at Binghamton.

Costin, Cathy Lynne
1998 Housewives, Chosen Women, Skilled Men: Cloth Production and Social Identity in the Late Prehispanic Andes. In *Craft and Social Identity*, edited by Cathy Lynne Costin and Rita P. Wright, pp. 123–44. Archeological Papers of the American Archaeological Association Vol. 8. American Anthropological Association, Arlington, Va.

Covey, R. Alan
2008 Multiregional Perspectives on the Archaeology of the Andes During the Late Intermediate Period (c. A.D. 1000–1400). *Journal of Archaeological Research* 16:287–338.

Daggett, Cheryl
1983 Casma Incised Pottery: An Analysis of Collections from the Nepeña Valley. In *Investigations of the Andean Past*, edited by Daniel H. Sandweiss, pp. 209–25. Cornell University Press, Ithaca.

D'Altroy, Terence N.
1992 *Provincial Power in the Inka Empire*. Smithsonian Institution Press, Washington, D.C.
2002 *The Incas*. Blackwell, Malden, Mass.

D'Altroy, Terence N., Ana María Lorandi, Verónica I. Williams, Christine Hastorf, Elizabeth DeMarrais, Milena Calderari, and Melissa B. Hagstrum
2000 Inka Imperial Rule in the Valle Calchaquí, Argentina. *Journal of Field Archaeology* 27(1):1–26.

Day, Kent C.
1982 Ciudadelas: Their Form and Function. In *Chan Chan: Andean Desert City*, edited by Michael E. Moseley and Kent C. Day, pp. 55–66. School of American Research Advanced Seminar Series. University of New Mexico Press, Albuquerque.

de Blij, Harm J.
1973 *Systematic Political Geography*. John Wiley & Sons, New York.

DeBoer, Warren R.
1990 Interaction, Imitation, and Communication as Expressed in Style: The Ucayali Experience. In *The Uses of Style in Archaeology*, edited by Margaret Wright Conkey and Christine Ann Hastorf, pp. 82–104. New Directions in Archaeology, Cambridge University Press, Cambridge.

DeBoer, Warren R., and James A. Moore
1982 The Measurement and Meaning of Stylistic Diversity. *Ñawpa Pacha* 20:147–62.

Dietler, Michael, and Ingrid Herbich
1998 Habitus, Techniques, Style: An Integrated Approach to the Social Understanding of Material Culture and Boundaries. In *The Archaeology of Social Boundaries*, edited by Miriam T. Stark, pp. 232–63. Smithsonian Institution Press, Washington, D.C.

Dillehay, Tom D., and Américo Gordon
1988 La actividad prehispanica de los Incas y su influencia en la Araucania. In *La Frontera del Estado Inca*, edited by Tom D. Dillehay and Patricia Netherly, pp. 215–34. Proceedings, 45 Congreso Internacional de Americanistas, Bogotá, Colombia, 1985. BAR International Series 442. British Archaeological Reports, Oxford.

Donley, Linda Wiley
1982 Swahili Space and Symbolic Markers. In *Symbolic and Structural Anthropology*, edited by Ian Hodder, pp. 63–73. Cambridge University Press, Cambridge.

Donnan, Christopher B.
1973   *Moche Occupation of the Santa Valley, Peru.* University of California Publications in Anthropology Vol. 8. University of California Press, Berkeley.
1978   *Moche Art of Peru: Pre-Columbian Symbolic Communication.* Museum of Cultural History, University of California, Los Angeles.
1992   *Ceramics of Ancient Peru.* UCLA Fowler Museum of Cultural History, Los Angeles.
1995   Moche Funerary Practice. In *Tombs for the Living: Andean Mortuary Practice*, edited by T. D. Dillehay, pp. 111–60. Dumbarton Oaks, Washington, D.C.
Donnan, Christopher B., and Luis Jaime Castillo Butters
1992   Finding the Tomb of a Moche Priestess. *Archaeology* 45(6):38–42.
1994   Excavaciones de tumbas de sacerdotisas Moche en San Jose de Moro, Jequetepeque. In *Moche: Propuestas y perspectivas*, edited by Santiago Uceda and Elías Mujica, pp. 415–24. Actas del Primer Coloquio sobre la Cultura Moche, Trujillo, 12 al 16 de abril de 1993. Travaux de l'Institut français d'etudes andines 79. Universidad Nacional de La Libertad, Trujillo, Peru.
Donnan, Christopher B., and Carol J. Mackey
1978   *Ancient Burial Patterns of the Moche Valley, Peru.* University of Texas Press, Austin.
Donnan, Christopher B., and Donna McClelland
1999   *Moche Fineline Painting: Its Evolution and Its Artists.* UCLA Fowler Museum of Cultural History, Los Angeles.
Dulanto, Jalh
2008   Between Horizons: Diverse Configurations of Society and Power in the Late Pre-Hispanic Central Andes. In *Handbook of South American Archaeology*, edited by Helaine Silverman and William H. Isbell, pp. 761–82. Springer, New York.
Earle, Timothy K.
1990   Style and Iconography as Legitimation in Complex Chiefdoms. In *The Uses of Style in Archaeology*, edited by Margaret Wright Conkey and Christine Ann Hastorf, pp. 73–81. Cambridge University Press, Cambridge.
Earle, Timothy K., Terence D'Altroy, Christine Hastorf, Catherine Scott, Cathy Costin, Glenn Russell, and Elsie Sandefur
1987   *Archaeological Field Research in the Upper Mantaro, Peru 1982–1983: Investigations of Inka Expansion and Exchange.* Monograph No. 28. Institute of Archaeology, University of California, Los Angeles.
Edens, Christopher
1992   Dynamics of Trade in the Ancient Mesopotamian "World System." *American Anthropologist* 94:118–39.
Emery, Irene
1966   *The Primary Structure of Fabrics.* Textile Museum, Washington, D.C.
Fernández Honores, Manuel A.
2002   Resultados del análisis de los restos orgánicos obtenido por flotación de Cerro la Cruz-Valle Chao. Manuscript on file, Facultad de Ciencias Biológicas, Universidad Nacional de Trujillo, Peru.

Frank, Andre Gunder
1990a A Theoretical Introduction to 5,000 Years of World System History. *Review* 13:155–248.
1990b The Thirteenth-Century World System: A Review Essay. *Journal of World History* 1:249–56.
1993 Bronze Age World System Cycles. *Current Anthropology* 34(4):383–430.

Frank, Andre Gunder, and Barry K. Gills
1992 The Five Thousand Year World System: An Interdisciplinary Introduction. *Humboldt Journal of Social Relations* 18(1):1–79.

Frazer, James G.
1979 Sympathetic Magic. In *Reader in Comparative Religion: An Anthropological Approach*, 4th ed., edited by William A. Lessa and Evon Z. Vogt, pp. 337–52. Harper & Row, New York.

Fung Pineda, Rosa, and Víctor Pimentel Gurmendi
1973 Chankillo. *Revista del Museo Nacional* 39:71–80.

Fung Pineda, Rosa, and Carlos Williams León
1977 Exploraciones y excavaciones en el valle de Sechín, Casma. *Revista el Museo Nacional* 43:111–55.

Ghezzi, Ivan
2006 Religious Warfare at Chankillo. In *Andean Archaeology III: North and South*, edited by William H. Isbell and Helaine Silverman, pp. 67–84. Kluwer Academic/Plenum, New York.

Ghezzi, Ivan, and Clive Ruggles
2007 Chankillo: A 2300-Year-Old Solar Observatory in Coastal Peru. *Science* 315(5816):1239–43.
2008 Las Trece Torres de Chankillo: Arqueoastronomía y organización social en el primer observatorio solar de América. Boletín de Arqueología PUCP 10:215–36. Pontificia Universidad Católica del Perú, Lima.

Gills, Barry K., and Andre Gunder Frank
1990 The Cumulation of Accumulation: Theses and Research Agenda for 5000 Years of World System History. *Dialectical Anthropology* 15:19–42.
1991 5000 Years of World System History: The Cumulation of Accumulation. In *Core/Periphery Relations in Precapitalist Worlds*, edited by Christopher Chase-Dunn and Thomas D. Hall, pp. 67–112. Westview Press, Boulder, Colo.
1992 World System Cycles, Crises, and Hegemonial Shifts, 1700 BC to 1700 AD. *Review* 15:621–87.

Goldstein, Paul
1993 Tiwanaku Temples and State Expansion: A Tiwanaku Sunken-Court Temple in Moquegua, Peru. *Latin American Antiquity* 4:22–47.
2000 Exotic Goods and Everyday Chiefs: Long-Distance Exchange and Indigenous Sociopolitical Development in the South Central Andes. *Latin American Antiquity* 11(4):335–61.

Gottman, Jean
1980   Confronting Centre and Periphery. In *Centre and Periphery: Spatial Variation in Politics*, edited by Jean Gottman, pp. 11–25. Sage, Beverly Hills.

Grobman, Alexander, Wilfredo Salhuana, and Ricardo Sevilla, in collaboration with Paul C. Mangelsdorf
1961   *Races of Maize in Peru: Their Origins, Evolution and Classification*. National Academy of Sciences, National Research Council, Washington, D.C.

Hall, Robert L.
1996   American Indian Worlds, World Quarters, World Centers, and Their Shrines. *Wisconsin Archaeologist* 77(3/4):120–27.

Hall, Thomas D.
1999   World-Systems and Evolution: An Appraisal. In *World-Systems Theory in Practice*, edited by P. Nick Kardulias, pp. 1–23. Rowman & Littlefield, Boulder, Colo.

Hall, Thomas D., and Christopher Chase-Dunn
1993   The World-Systems Perspective and Archaeology: Forward Into the Past. *Journal of Archaeological Research* 1(2):121–43.

Haselgrove, Colin
1987   Culture Process on the Periphery: Belgic Gaul and Rome During the Late Republic and Early Empire. In *Centre and Periphery in the Ancient World*, edited by Michael Rowlands, Mogens Larsen, and Kristian Kristiansen, pp. 104–23. Cambridge University Press, Cambridge.

Hastorf, Christine A.
2008   The Formative Period in the Titicaca Basin. In *Handbook of South American Archaeology*, edited by Helaine Silverman and William H. Isbell, pp. 545–61. Springer, New York.

Hedeager, Lotte
1987   Empire, Frontier and the Barbarian Hinterland: Rome and Northern Europe from AD 1–400. In *Centre and Periphery in the Ancient World*, edited by Michael Rowlands, Mogens Larsen, and Kristian Kristiansen, pp. 125–40. Cambridge University Press, Cambridge.

Helms, Mary W.
1993   *Craft and the Kingly Ideal: Art, Trade, and Power*. University of Texas Press, Austin.

Heyerdahl, Thor, Daniel Howard Sandweiss, and Alfredo Narváez
1995   *The Pyramids of Túcume: The Quest for Peru's Forgotten City*. Thames and Hudson, New York.

Heyerdahl, Thor, Daniel Howard Sandweiss, Alfredo Narváez, and Luis Millones
1996   *Túcume*. Banco de Crédito del Perú, Lima.

Hough, Ian
1999   Diet, Economic Specialization, and Complex Society on the North Coast of Peru. Master's thesis, Department of Anthropology, Northern Arizona University.

Hudson, John C.
1969   A Location Theory for Rural Settlements. *Annals of the Association of American Geographers* 59:365–81.

Hyslop, John
1990   Inka Settlement Planning. University of Texas Press, Austin.
Imbelloni, José
1925   Deformaciones intencionales del cráneo en Sud América. Revista del Museo de La Plata 28:329–407.
Ingold, Tim
1993   The Temporality of Landscape. World Archaeology 25(2):152–74.
Isbell, William H.
1977   The Rural Foundation for Urbanism: Economic And Stylistic Interaction Between Rural and Urban Communities in Eighth-Century Perú. Illinois Studies in Anthropology No. 10. University of Illinois Press, Urbana.
1988   City and State in Middle Horizon Huari. In Peruvian Prehistory: An Overview of Pre-Inca and Inca Society, edited by Richard W. Keatinge, pp. 164–89. Cambridge University Press, Cambridge.
1997   Mummies and Mortuary Monuments: A Postprocessual Prehistory of Central Andean Social Organization. University of Texas Press, Austin.
2008   Wari and Tiwanaku: International Identities in the Central Andean Middle Horizon. In Handbook of South American Archaeology, edited by Helaine Silverman and William H. Isbell, pp. 731–60. Springer, New York.
Isbell, William H., and Gordon F. McEwan
1991   A History of Huari Studies and Introduction to Current Interpretations. In Huari Administrative Structure: Prehistoric Monumental Architecture and State Government, edited by William H. Isbell and Gordon F. McEwan, pp. 1–17. Dumbarton Oaks, Washington, D.C.
Jackson, Margaret A.
2000   Notation and Narrative in Moche Iconography, Cerro Mayal, Peru. Unpublished Ph.D. dissertation, Department of Art History, University of California, Los Angeles.
Janusek, John Wayne
2002   Out of Many, One: Style and Social Boundaries in Tiwanaku. Latin American Antiquity 13(1):35–61.
2003   Vessels, Time, and Society: Toward a Chronology of Ceramic Style in the Titicaca Heartland. In Tiwanaku and Its Hinterland: Archaeology and Paleoecology of an Andean Civilization, vol. 1, edited by Alan L. Kolata, pp. 30–92. Smithsonian Institution Press, Washington, D.C.
2004   Identity and Power in the Ancient Andes: Tiwanaku Cities Through Time. Routledge, New York.
Jennings, Justin
2006   Understanding Middle Horizon Peru: Hermeneutic Spirals, Interpretive Traditions, and Wari Administrative Centers. Latin American Antiquity 17(3):265–85.
Jennings, Justin, and Nathan Craig
2001   Politywide Analysis and Imperial Political Economy: The Relationship Between

Valley Political Complexity and Administrative Centers in the Wari Empire of the Central Andes. *Journal of Anthropological Archaeology* 20:479–502.

Keatinge, Richard W.
1982   The Chimú Empire in a Regional Perspective: Cultural Antecedents and Continuities. In *Chan Chan: Andean Desert City*, edited by Michael E. Moseley and Kent C. Day, pp. 197–224. School of American Research Advanced Seminar Series. University of New Mexico Press, Albuquerque.
1988   Preface. In *Peruvian Prehistory: An Overview of Inca and Pre-Inca Society*, edited by Richard W. Keatinge, pp. xiii–xvii. Cambridge University Press, Cambridge.

Kent, Jonathan D.
1998   First Season's Fieldwork at Santa Rita B, Chao Valley, La Libertad Department, Northern Peru. Instituto Nacional de Cultura, Lima.

Kohl, Philip L.
1978   The Balance of Trade in Southwestern Asia in the Mid-Third Millennium B.C. *Current Anthropology* 19:463–92.
1979   The "World Economy" in West Asia in the Third Millennium B.C. In *South Asian Archaeology 1977*, edited by Maurizio Taddei, pp. 55–85. Istituto Universitario Orientale, Naples.
1989   The Use and Abuse of World Systems Theory: The Case of the "Pristine" West Asian State. In *Archaeological Thought in America*, edited by C. C. Lamberg-Karlovsky, pp. 218–40. Cambridge University Press, Cambridge.

Kolata, Alan L.
1990   The Urban Concept of Chan Chan. In *The Northern Dynasties: Kingship and Statecraft in Chimor*, edited by Michael E. Moseley and Alana Cordy-Collins, pp. 107–44. Dumbarton Oaks, Washington, D.C.
1991   The Technology and Organization of Agricultural Production in the Tiwanaku State. *Latin American Antiquity* 2(2):99–125.
1993   *The Tiwanaku: Portrait of an Andean Civilization*. Blackwell, Cambridge.

Kolata, Alan L., and Carlos Ponce Sangines
1992   Tiwanaku: The City at the Center. In *Ancient Americas: Art from Sacred Landscapes*, edited by Richard F. Townsend, pp. 317–33. Art Institute of Chicago, Chicago.

Kosok, Paul
1965   *Life, Land and Water in Ancient Peru*. Long Island University Press, New York.

Kristof, Ladis K. D.
1973 [1959]   The Nature of Frontiers and Boundaries. In *Systematic Political Geography*, edited by Harm J. de Blij, pp. 136–57. John Wiley & Sons, New York.

Kroeber, Alfred L.
1944   *Peruvian Archaeology in 1942*. Viking Fund Publications in Anthropology No. 4. Wenner-Gren Foundation for Anthropological Research, New York.

Kurjack, Edward B., and E. Wyllys Andrews V
1976   Early Boundary Maintenance in Northwest Yucatan, Mexico. *American Antiquity* 41(3):318–25.

Kuznar, Lawrence A.
1996   Periphery/Core Relations in the Inca Empire: Carrots and Sticks in an Andean World System. *Journal of World-Systems Research* 2(9):1–20.
1999   The Inca Empire: Detailing the Complexities of Core/Periphery Interactions. In *World-Systems Theory in Practice: Leadership, Production and Exchange*, edited by P. Nick Kardulias, pp. 223–40. Rowman & Littlefield, Lanham, Md.

La Lone, Darrell E.
1994   An Andean World-System: Production Transformations Under the Inca Empire. In *The Economic Anthropology of the State*, edited by Elizabeth M. Brumfiel, pp. 17–42. University Press of America, Lanham, Md.

Lanning, Edward P.
1967   *Peru Before the Incas*. Prentice Hall, Englewood, N.J.

Lattimore, Owen
1962   *Studies in Frontier History: Collected Papers 1928–1958*. Oxford University Press, London.

Lau, George F.
2001   The Ancient Community of Chinchawas: Economy and Ceremony in the North Highlands of Peru. Unpublished Ph.D. dissertation, Department of Anthropology, Yale University.
2002   Rural Complexity in the Recuay Hinterlands: The View from Chinchawas. Paper presented at the 67th annual meeting of the Society for American Archaeology, Denver.
2005   Core-Periphery Relations in the Recuay Hinterlands: Economic Interaction at Chinchawas, Peru. *Antiquity* 79(303):78–99.

Lawrence, Denise L., and Setha M. Low
1990   The Built Environment and Spatial Form. *Annual Review of Anthropology* 19:453–505.

Lightfoot, Kent G., and Antoinette Martinez
1995   Frontiers and Boundaries in Archaeological Perspective. *Annual Review of Anthropology* 24:471–92.

Lippi, Ronald D., and Alejandra M. Gudiño
2010   Inkas and Yumbos at Palmitopamba in Northwestern Ecuador. In *Distant Provinces in the Inka Empire: Toward a Deeper Understanding of Inca Imperialism*, edited by Michael A. Malpass and Sonia Alconini, pp. 260–78. University of Iowa Press, Iowa City.

Lumbreras, Luis G.
1974   *The Peoples and Cultures of Ancient Peru*. Smithsonian Institution Press, Washington, D.C.

Mackey, Carol J.
1982   The Middle Horizon as Viewed from the Moche Valley. In *Chan Chan: Andean Desert City*, edited by Michael E. Moseley and Kent C. Day, pp. 321–31. School of American Research Advanced Seminar Series. University of New Mexico Press, Albuquerque.

1987   Chimu Administration in the Provinces. In *The Origins and Development of the Andean State*, edited by Jonathan Haas, Shelia Pozorski, and Thomas Pozorski, pp. 121–29. Cambridge University Press, Cambridge.

2000   Los dioses que perdieron los colmillos. In *Los dioses del antiguo Perú*, vol. 2, edited by Krzysztof Makowski Hanula, pp. 111–57. Banco de Crédito del Perú, Lima.

2009   Chimu Statecraft in the Provinces. In *Foundations of Andean Civilization: Papers in Honor of M. E. Moseley*, edited by Joyce Marcus, Charles Stanish, and Patrick Ryan Williams, pp. 325–49. Cotsen Institute of Archaeology, University of California, Los Angeles.

Mackey, Carol J., and Alexandra M. Ulana Klymyshyn

1981   Construction and Labor Organization in the Chimu Empire. *Ñawpa Pacha* 19:99–114.

1990   The Southern Frontier of the Chimu Empire. In *The Northern Dynasties: Kingship and Statecraft in Chimor: A Symposium at Dumbarton Oaks, 12th and 13th October 1985*, edited by Michael Edward Moseley and Alana Cordy-Collins, pp. 195–226. Dumbarton Oaks Research Library and Collection, Washington, D.C.

Madry, Scott L. H., and Carole L. Crumley

1990   An Application of Remote Sensing and GIS in a Regional Archaeological Settlement Pattern Analysis: The Arroux River Valley, Burgundy, France. In *Interpreting Space: GIS and Archaeology*, edited by Kathleen S. Allen, Stanton W. Green, and Ezra B. W. Zubrow, pp. 364–80. Taylor & Francis, London.

Malpass, Michael A. (editor)

1993   *Provincial Inca: Archaeological and Ethnohistorical Assessment of the Impact of the Inca State*. University of Iowa Press, Iowa City.

Malpass, Michael A., and Sonia Alconini

2010   Provincial Inka Studies in the Twenty-first Century. In *Distant Provinces in the Inka Empire: Toward a Deeper Understanding of Inca Imperialism*, edited by Michael A. Malpass and Sonia Alconini, pp. 1–13. University of Iowa Press, Iowa City.

Marcos, Jorge G.

1977   Cruising to Acapulco and Back with the Thorny Oyster Set: A Model for a Lineal Exchange System. *Journal of the Steward Anthropological Society* 9(1/2):99–132.

McClelland, Donna

1990   A Maritime Passage from Moche to Chimu. In *The Northern Dynasties: Kingship and Statecraft in Chimor*, edited by Michael E. Moseley and Alana Cordy-Collins, pp. 75–106. Dumbarton Oaks, Washington, D.C.

McEwan, Gordon F.

1990   Some Formal Correspondences Between the Imperial Architecture of the Wari and Chimu Cultures of Ancient Peru. *Latin American Antiquity* 1(2):97–116.

2006   *The Incas: New Perspectives*. W. W. Norton, New York.

Menzel, Dorothy
1964   Style and Time in the Middle Horizon. *Ñawpa Pacha* 2:1–105.
1977   *The Archaeology of Ancient Peru and the Work of Max Uhle*. R. H. Lowie Museum of Anthropology, Berkeley.
Modelski, George, and William R. Thompson
1999   The Evolutionary Pulse of the World System: Hinterland Incursions and Migrations, 4000 B.C. to A.D. 1500. In *World-Systems Theory in Practice: Leadership, Production, and Exchange*, edited by P. Nick Kardulias, pp. 241–74. Rowman & Littlefield, Lanham, Md.
Moore, Jerry D.
1989   Pre-Hispanic Beer in Coastal Peru: Technology and Social Context. *American Anthropologist* 91(3):682–95.
1992   Pattern and Meaning in Prehistoric Peruvian Architecture: The Architecture of Social Control in the Chimu State. *Latin American Antiquity* 3:95–113.
1996a The Archaeology of Plazas and the Proxemics of Ritual: Three Andean Traditions. *American Anthropologist* 98:789–802.
1996b *Architecture and Power in the Ancient Andes: The Archaeology of Public Buildings*. Cambridge University Press, Cambridge.
2005   *Cultural Landscapes in the Ancient Andes: Archaeologies of Place*. Gainesville: University Press of Florida.
Moore, Jerry D., and Carol J. Mackey
2008   The Chimú Empire. In *Handbook of South American Archaeology*, edited by Helaine Silverman and William H. Isbell, pp. 783–807. Springer, New York.
Morris, Craig
1995   Symbols to Power: Styles and Media in the Inka State. In *Style, Society, and Person: Archaeological and Ethnological Perspectives*, edited by Christopher Carr and Jill E. Neitzel, pp. 419–33. Plenum, New York.
Moseley, Michael E.
1975   Chan Chan: Andean Alternative of the Preindustrial City. *Science* 187:219–25.
1983   The Good Old Days Were Better: Agrarian Collapse and Tectonics. *American Anthropologist* 85:773–799.
1990   Structure and History in the Dynastic Lore of Chimor. In *The Northern Dynasties: Kingship and Statecraft in Chimor*, edited by Michael E. Moseley and Alana Cordy-Collins, pp. 1–42. Dumbarton Oaks, Washington, D.C.
1992   *The Incas and Their Ancestors: The Archaeology of Peru*. Thames & Hudson, London.
2001   *The Incas and Their Ancestors: The Archaeology of Peru*. Revised ed. Thames & Hudson, New York.
Moseley, Michael E., and Alana Cordy-Collins (editors)
1990   *The Northern Dynasties: Kingship and Statecraft in Chimor*. Dumbarton Oaks, Washington, D.C.
Munizaga, Juan R.
1976   Intentional Cranial Deformation in the PreColumbian Populations of Ecuador. *American Journal of Physical Anthropology* 45:687–94.

Nash, Donna J.
2009   Household Archaeology in the Andes. *Journal of Archaeological Research* 17:205–61.

Nash, Donna J., and Patrick Ryan Williams
2005   Architecture and Power on the Wari-Tiwanaku Frontier. *Archaeological Papers of the American Anthropological Association* 14(1):151–74.

Newman, Marshall T.
1947   *Indian Skeletal Material from the Central Coast of Peru.* Papers of the Peabody Museum of American Archaeology and Ethnology Vol. 27, No. 4. Harvard University Cambridge, Mass.

O'Neale, Lila M., and A. L. Kroeber
1930   Textile Periods in Ancient Peru. *University of California Publications in American Archaeology and Ethnology,* 28(2):23–56.

ONERN (Oficina Nacional de Evaluación de Recursos Naturales)
1973   *Inventario, evaluacion y uso racional de los recursos naturales de la costa: Cuencos de los ríos Virú y Chao,* Vol. 1. Lima.

Parsons, Jeffrey R., and Charles M. Hastings
1988   The Late Intermediate Period. In *Peruvian Prehistory: An Overview of Pre-Inca and Inca Society,* edited by Richard W. Keatinge, pp. 190–229. Cambridge University Press, Cambridge.

Patterson, Thomas C.
1986   Ideology, Class Formation, and Resistance to the Inca State. *Critique of Anthropology* 6(1):75–85.
1987   Tribes, Chiefdoms, and Kingdoms in the Inca Empire. In *Power Relations and State Formation,* edited by Thomas C. Patterson and Christine W. Gailey, pp. 117–27. American Anthropological Association, Washington, D.C.

Paulsen, Allison C.
1974   The Thorny Oyster and the Voice of God: *Spondylus* and *Strombus* in Andean Prehistory. *American Antiquity* 39(4):597–607.

Peregrine, Peter N.
1999   Legitimation Crises in Prehistoric Worlds. In *World-Systems Theory in Practice: Leadership, Production, and Exchange,* edited by P. Nick Kardulias, pp. 37–52. Rowman & Littlefield, Lanham, Md.

Pillsbury, Joanne
1997   Vessel with Figures. In *The Spirit of Ancient Peru: Treasures from the Museo Arqueológico Rafael Larco Herrera,* edited by Kathleen Berrin, p. 182. Thames & Hudson, New York.

Pillsbury, Joanne, and Banks L. Leonard
2004   Identifying Chimú Palaces: Elite Residential Architecture in the Late Intermediate Period. In *Palaces of the Ancient New World,* edited by Susan Toby Evans and Joanne Pillsbury, pp. 247–98. Dumbarton Oaks, Washington, D.C.

Pozorski, Shelia
1976   Prehistoric Subsistence Patterns and Site Economics in the Moche Valley, Peru. Unpublished Ph.D. dissertation, Department of Anthropology, University of Texas at Austin.

1980   Subsistencia Chimú en Chanchán. In *Chanchán: Metrópoli Chimú*, edited by Rógger Ravines, pp. 181–93. Instituto de Estudios Peruanos, Lima.
1982   Subsistence Systems in the Chimú State. In *Chan Chan: Andean Desert City*, edited by Michael E. Moseley and Kent C. Day, pp. 177–96. School of American Research Advanced Seminar Series. University of New Mexico Press, Albuquerque.

Pozorski, Thomas, and Shelia Pozorski
1997   Cherimoya and Guanabana in the Archaeological Record of Peru. *Journal of Ethnobiology* 17(2):235–48.

Protzen, John-Pierre
1993   *Inca Architecture and Construction at Ollantaytambo*. Oxford University Press, Oxford.

Protzen, John-Pierre, and John Howland Rowe
1994   Hawkaypata: The Terrace of Leisure. In *Streets: Critical Perspectives on Public Space*, edited by Zeynep Çelik, Diane Favro, and Richard Ingersoll, pp. 235–46. University of California Press, Berkeley.

Proulx, Donald A.
1968   *An Archaeological Survey of the Nepeña Valley, Peru*. Research Report No. 2. Department of Anthropology, University of Massachusetts, Amherst.
1973   *Archaeological Investigations in the Nepeña Valley, Peru*. Research Reports No. 13. Department of Anthropology, University of Massachusetts, Amherst.

Prümers, Heiko
1989   Tejidos del Horizonte Medio del valle de Huarmey. In *The Nature of Wari: A Reappraisal of the Middle Horizon Period in Peru*, edited by R. Michael Czwarno, Frank M. Meddens, and Alexandra Morgan, pp. 188–213. BAR International Series 525. British Archaeological Reports, Oxford.
1990   *Der Fundort "El Castillo" im Huarmeytal, Peru: Ein Beitrag zum Problem des Moche-Huari Textilstils 1*. Holos Verlag, Bonn.

Prządka, Patrycja, and Miłosz Giersz
2003   *Sitios arqueológicos de la zona del valle de Culebras*. Vol. 1, *Valle bajo*. Polish Society for Latin American Studies/Andean Archaeological Mission of the Institute of Archaeology, University of Warsaw, Warsaw.

Prządka-Giersz, Patrycja
2009   Patrones de asentamiento y transformaciones sociopolíticas en la costa norcentral del Perú durante los Períodos Tardíos: El caso del valle de Culebras. Unpublished Ph.D. dissertation, Institute of Archaeology, University of Warsaw, Warsaw.

Quilter, Jeffrey
2002   Moche politics, religion, and warfare. *Journal of World Prehistory* 16(2):145–95.

Rapoport, Amos
1994   Spatial Organization and the Built Environment. In *Companion Encyclopedia of Anthropology*, edited by Tim Ingold, pp. 460–502. Routledge, London.

Redman, Charles L.
1986   *Qsar es-Seghir: An Archaeological View of Medieval Life*. Academic Press, Orlando.

Renfrew, Colin, and Stephen Shennan (editors)
1982   Ranking, Resource and Exchange: Aspects of the Archaeology of Early European Society. Cambridge University Press, Cambridge.

Rivera, M. A.
1995   The Preceramic Chinchorro Mummy Complex of Northern Chile: Context, Style, and Purpose. In Tombs for the Living: Andean Mortuary Practices, edited by Tom D. Dillehay, pp. 43–78. Dumbarton Oaks, Washington, D.C.

Rodman, Amy Oakland
1992   Textiles and Ethnicity: Tiwanaku in San Pedro de Atacama, North Chile. Latin American Antiquity 3(4):316–40.

Rosales Tham, Teresa
1999   Informe Final (Temporada 1998): Manejo Ecosustentable y Desarollo Cultural del Complejo Arqueológico Santa Rita "B." Instituto Nacional de Cultura, Lima.

Rosales Tham, Teresa, and Jonathan Kent
2000   Informe Final (Temporada 2000): Manejo Ecosustentable y Desarrollo Cultural del Complejo Arqueológico Santa Rita "B." Instituto Nacional de Cultura, Lima.

Rosales Tham, Teresa, Jonathan Kent, Victor Vásquez Sánchez, and Amanda Aland
2008   Informe Final (Temporada 2007): Manejo Ecosustentable y Desarrollo Cultural del Complejo Arqueológico Santa Rita "B"—Valle de Chao. Instituto Nacional de Cultura, Lima.

Rosales Tham, Teresa, Jonathan Kent, Victor Vásquez Sánchez, Catherine Gaither, and Jonathan Bethard
2008   Entre Casma y Chimú: Estilo cerámico y modo de vivir en el valle medio de Chao. Paper presented at Reconsiderando el Periodo Intermedio Tardío en la Costa Norte del Perú: Una Mesa Redonda en Trujillo, Perú. Sponsored by Dumbarton Oaks and la Universidad Nacional de Trujillo, June 5–7, 2008, Trujillo, Peru.

Rossen, Jack, María Teresa Planella, and Rubén Stehberg
2010   Archaeobotany of Cerro del Inga, Chile, at the Southern Inka Frontier. In Distant Provinces in the Inka Empire: Toward a Deeper Understanding of Inca Imperialism, edited by Michael A. Malpass and Sonia Alconini, pp. 14–43. University of Iowa Press, Iowa City.

Rostworowski de Diez Canseco, María
1977   Coastal Fishermen, Merchants, and Artisans in Pre-Hispanic Peru. In The Sea in the Pre-Columbian World, edited by Elizabeth P. Benson, pp. 167–88. Dumbarton Oaks, Washington, D.C.

Rowe, Ann Pollard
1980   Textiles from the Burial Platform of Las Avispas at Chan Chan. Ñawpa Pacha 18:81–147.
1984   Costumes and Featherwork of the Lords of Chimor. Textile Museum, Washington, D.C.

Rowe, John H.
1948   The Kingdom of Chimor. Acta Americana 6(1–2):26–59.
1960   Cultural Unity and Diversification in Peruvian Archaeology. In Men and Culture,

Selected Papers, 5th International Congress of Anthropological and Ethnological Sciences, edited by Anthony F. C. Wallace, pp. 627–31. University of Pennsylvania Press, Philadelphia.

Rowlands, Michael, Mogens Larsen, and Kristian Kristiansen (editors)
1987   *Centre and Periphery in the Ancient World*. Cambridge University Press, Cambridge.

Rucabado Yong, Julio
2008   Prácticas funerarias de elite en San José de Moro durante la fase transicional temprana: El caso de la tumba colectiva M-U615. In *Arqueologia mochica: Nuevos enfoques*, edited by Luis Jaime Castillo Butters, Hèléne Bernier, Gregory Lockard, and Julio Rucabado Yong, pp. 359–80. Fondo Editorial Pontificia Universidad Católica del Perú, Lima.

Rucabado Yong, Julio, and Luis Jaime Castillo Butters
2003   El periodo Transicional en San Jose de Moro. In *Moche: Hacia el final del milenio*, edited by Santiago Uceda and Elías Mujica, pp. 15–42. Actas del Segundo Coloquio sobre la Cultura Moche, Tomo I. Universidad Nacional de Trujillo and Fondo Editorial Pontificia Universidad Católica del Perú, Lima.

Russell, Glenn S.
1990   Preceramic Through Moche Settlement Pattern Change in the Chicama Valley, Peru. Presented at the 55th annual meeting of the Society for American Archaeology, Las Vegas.

Russell, Glenn S., Banks Leonard, and Jesús Briceño Rosario
1994   Cerro Mayal: Nuevos datos sobre producción de cerámica Moche en el valle de Chicama. In *Moche: Propuestas y perspectivas*, edited by Santiago Uceda and Elías Mujica, pp. 181–206. Actas del Primer Coloquio sobre la Cultura Moche, Trujillo, 12 al 16 de abril de 1993. Travaux de l'Institut français d'etudes andines 79. Universidad Nacional de La Libertad, Trujillo, Peru.

Salomon, Frank
1986   *Native Lords of Quito in the Age of the Incas: The Political Economy of North Andean Chiefdoms*. Cambridge University Press, New York.

Samson, Ross
1992   Knowledge, Constraint, and Power in Inaction: The Defenseless Medieval Wall. *Journal of Historical Archaeology* 26(3):26–42.

Schaedel, Richard P.
1951   Moche Murals at Pañamarca. *Archaeology* 4:145–54.

Schjellerup, Inge R.
1997   *Incas and Spaniards in the Conquest of the Chachapoyas: Archaeological and Ethnohistorical Research in the North-Eastern Andes of Peru*. Series B, Gothenberg Archaeological Thesis No. 7. Department of Archaeology, Gothenberg University.

Schneider, Jane
1977   Was There a Pre-Capitalist World-System? *Journal of Peasant Studies* 6(1):20–29.

Schortman, Edward M., and Seiichi Nakamura
1991   A Crisis of Identity: Late Classic Competition and Interaction on the Southeast Maya Periphery. *Latin American Antiquity* 2:311–36.
Schortman, Edward M., and Patricia A. Urban
1994   Living on the Edge: Core/Periphery Relations in Ancient Southeastern Mesoamerica. *Current Anthropology* 35:401–30.
Schortman, E. M., and Patricia A. Urban (editors)
1992   *Resources, Power, and Interregional Interaction*. Plenum, New York.
Schreiber, Katharina J.
1987   Conquest and Consolidation: A Comparison of the Wari and Inka Occupations of a Highland Peruvian Valley. *American Antiquity* 52(2):266–84.
1992   *Wari Imperialism in Middle Horizon Peru*. Anthropological Papers Vol. 87. Museum of Anthropology. University of Michigan, Ann Arbor.
2001   The Wari Empire of Middle Horizon Peru: The Epistemological Challenge of Documenting an Empire Without Documentary Evidence. In *Empires: Perspectives from Archaeology and History*, edited by Susan E. Alcock, Terence N. D'Altroy, Kathleen D. Morrison, and Carla M. Sinopoli, pp. 70–92. Cambridge University Press, Cambridge.
Shady, Ruth
1982   La cultura Nievería y la interacción social en el mundo andino en la época Huari. *Arqueológicas* 19:5–108.
Sharer, Robert, and Wendy Ashmore
1993   *Archaeology: Discovering Our Past*. 2nd ed. Mayfield, Mountain View, Calif.
Shepard, Anna O.
1995 [1956]   *Ceramics for the Archaeologist*. Carnegie Institution of Washington, Washington, D.C.
Shimada, Izumi
1990   Cultural Continuities and Discontinuities on the Northern North Coast of Peru, Middle-Late Horizons. In *The Northern Dynasties: Kingship and Statecraft in Chimor*, edited by Michael E. Moseley and Alana Cordy-Collins, pp. 297–392. Dumbarton Oaks, Washington, D.C.
1994   *Pampa Grande and the Mochica Culture*. University of Texas Press, Austin.
2000   The Late Prehispanic Coastal States. In *The Inca World: The Development of Pre-Columbian Peru AD 1000–1534*, edited by Laura Laurencich Minelli, pp. 49–64. University of Oklahoma Press, Norman.
Silva Vigo, Edgardo
1991   *Estudio de un asentamiento Chimu Temprano en el valle medio de Chao, costa norte del Peru*. Universidad Nacional de Trujillo, Trujillo, Peru.
1992   Cerro la Cruz: Asentamiento Chimú en el sector medio del valle de Chao. *Gaceta arqueológica andina* 6(22):35–49.
Silverblatt, Irene
1987   *Moon, Sun, and Witches: Gender Ideologies and Class in Inca and Colonial Peru*. Princeton University Press, Princeton.

Smith, Adam T.
2003   *The Political Landscape: Constellations of Authority in Early Complex Polities.* University of California Press, Berkeley.

Smith, Michael E.
2001   The Aztec Empire and the Mesoamerican World System. In *Empires: Perspectives from Archaeology and History*, edited by Susan E. Alcock, Terence N. D'Altroy, Kathleen D. Morrison, and Carla M. Sinopoli, pp. 128–54. Cambridge University Press, Cambridge.

Soukup, Jaroslav
1970   *Vocabulario de los nombres vulgares de la flora peruana.* Colegio Salesiano, Lima.

Stanish, Charles
2003   *Ancient Titicaca: The Evolution of Complex Society in Southern Peru and Northern Bolivia.* University of California Press, Berkeley.

Steadman, Sharon R.
1996   Recent Research in the Archaeology of Architecture: Beyond the Foundations. *Journal of Archaeological Research* 4(1):51–77.

Stein, Gil J.
1999   Rethinking World-Systems: Power, Distance, and Diasporas in the Dynamics of Interregional Interaction. In *World-Systems Theory in Practice: Leadership, Production, and Exchange*, edited by P. Nick Kardulias, pp. 153–77. Rowman & Littlefield, Lanham, Md.

2005   Introduction: The Comparative Archaeology of Colonial Encounters. In *The Archaeology of Colonial Encounters*, edited by Gil J. Stein, pp. 1–29. School of American Research Press, Santa Fe.

Stone-Miller, Rebecca, and Gordon F. McEwan
1990/1991 The Representation of the Wari State in Stone and Thread: A Comparison of Architecture and Tapestry Tunics. *RES: Anthropology and Aesthetics* 19/20:53–80.

Strong, William Duncan, and Clifford Evans Jr.
1952   *Cultural Stratigraphy in the Virú Valley Northern Peru: The Formative and Florescent Epochs.* Columbia University Press, New York.

Stuiver, M., and P. J. Reimer
1993   Extended (Super 14) C Data Base and Revised CALIB 3.0 (Super 14) C Age Calibration Program. *Radiocarbon* 35:215–230.

Tello, Julio C.
1956   *Culturas: Chavín, Santa o Huaylas Yunga y sub-Chimú.* Editorial San Marcos, Lima.

Thompson, Donald E.
1964   Postclassic Innovations in Architecture and Settlement Patterns in the Casma Valley, Peru. *Southwestern Journal of Anthropology* 20(1):91–105.

1966   Archaeological Investigations in the Huarmey Valley, Peru. In *Proceedings of the 36th International Congress of Americanists* 1:541–48. Spain.

1974   Arquitectura y patrones de establecimiento en el valle de Casma. *Revista el Museo Nacional* 40:9–29.

Topic, John R.
1990   Craft Production in the Kingdom of Chimor. In *The Northern Dynasties: Kingship and Statecraft in Chimor*, edited by Michael E. Moseley and Alana Cordy-Collins, pp. 145–76. Dumbarton Oaks, Washington, D.C.

Topic, John R., and Michael E. Moseley
1983   Chan Chan: A Case Study of Urban Change in Peru. *Ñawpa Pacha* 21:153–82.

Topic, John R., and Theresa Lange Topic
1978   Prehistoric Fortification Systems of Northern Peru. *Current Anthropology* 19(3):618–19.
1983   Coast-Highland Relations in Northern Peru: Some Observations on Routes, Networks, and Scales of Interaction. In *Civilization in the Ancient Americas: Essays in Honor of Gordon R. Willey*, edited by Richard M. Leventhal and Alan L. Kolata, pp. 237–59. University of New Mexico Press, Albuquerque.
1987   The Archaeological Investigation of Andean Militarism: Some Cautionary Observations. In *The Origins and Development of the Andean State*, edited by Jonathan Haas, Shelia Pozorski, and Thomas Pozorski, pp. 47–55. Cambridge University Press, Cambridge.

Topic, Theresa Lange
1990   Territorial Expansion and the Kingdom of Chimor. In *The Northern Dynasties: Kingship and Statecraft in Chimor*, edited by Michael E. Moseley and Alana Cordy-Collins, pp. 177–94. Dumbarton Oaks, Washington, D.C.
1991   The Middle Horizon in Northern Peru. In *Huari Administrative Structure: Prehistoric Monumental Architecture and State Government*, edited by William H. Isbell and Gordon F. McEwan, pp. 233–46. Dumbarton Oaks, Washington, D.C.

Treacy, John M., and William M. Denevan
1994   The Creation of Cultivable Land Through Terracing. In *The Archaeology of Garden and Field*, edited by Naomi F. Miller and Kathryn L. Gleason, pp. 91–110. University of Pennsylvania Press, Philadelphia.

Trigger, Bruce G.
1989   *A History of Archaeological Thought*. Cambridge University Press, Cambridge.

Urban, Patricia A., and Edward M. Schortman
1999   Thoughts on the Periphery: The Ideological Consequences of Core/Periphery Relations. In *World-Systems Theory in Practice: Leadership, Production, and Exchange*, edited by P. Nick Kardulias, pp. 125–52. Rowman & Littlefield, Lanham, Md.

Urban, Patricia, Edward Schortman, and Marne Ausec
2002   Power Without Bounds? Middle Preclassic Political Developments in the Naco Valley, Honduras. *Latin American Antiquity* 13(2):131–52.

Verano, John W.
1995   Where Do They Rest? The Treatment of Human Offerings and Trophies in Ancient Peru. In *Tombs for the Living: Andean Mortuary Practices*, edited by Tom D. Dillehay, pp. 189–228. Dumbarton Oaks, Washington, D.C.

Vogel, Melissa A.
1999 Prospección Preliminar del Complejo Arqueológico Cerro de La Cruz. Instituto Nacional de Cultura, Lima.
2000 Informe Final: Proyecto Arqueológico Cerro la Cruz 2000. Instituto Nacional de Cultura, Lima.
2003 Life on the Frontier: Identity and Sociopolitical Change at the Site of Cerro la Cruz, Peru. Ph.D. dissertation, Department of Anthropology, University of Pennsylvania. University Microfilms International, Ann Arbor.
2005 Life on the Frontier in Ancient Peru: Archaeological Investigations at Cerro la Cruz. *Expedition* 47(1):25–31.
2011 Style and Interregional Interaction: Ceramics from the Casma Capital of El Purgatorio. *Ñawpa Pacha: A Journal of Andean Archaeology* 30. Institute of Andean Studies, Berkeley.
Vogel, Melissa A., Víctor Falcón, and David Pacifico
2010 Informe Final: Proyecto Arqueológico El Purgatorio 2010. Submitted to the Instituto Nacional de Cultura, Lima.
Vogel, Melissa A., and Luis Coronado Tello
2001 Informe Final: Proyecto Arqueológico Cerro la Cruz 2001. Instituto Nacional de Cultura, Lima.
Vogel, Melissa A., and Percy Vilcherrez
2008 Informe Final: Proyecto Arqueológico El Purgatorio 2008. Submitted to the Instituto Nacional de Cultura, Lima.
2009 [2007] Proyecto Arqueológico El Purgatorio: Datos Preliminares. *Sian Revista Arqueológica* 12(18):21–32.
2009 Informe Final: Proyecto Arqueológico El Purgatorio 2009. Submitted to the Instituto Nacional de Cultura, Lima.
Wallerstein, Immanuel
1974 *The Modern World-System*. Vol. 1, *Capitalist Agriculture and the Origins of the European World-Economy in the Sixteenth Century*. Academic Press, New York.
1989 *The Modern World-System*. Vol. 3, *The Second Era of Great Expansion of the Capitalist World-Economy, 1730–1840s*. Academic Press, New York.
1990 World-Systems Analysis: The Second Phase. *Review* 13:287–93.
1991 *Geopolitics and Geoculture: Essays on the Changing World-System*. Cambridge University Press, Cambridge.
1992 Geopolitical Strategies of the United States in a Post-American World. *Humboldt Journal of Social Relations* 18(1):217–23.
Watson, Aaron, and David Keating
1999 Architecture and Sound: An Acoustic Analysis of Megalithic Monuments in Prehistoric Britain. *Antiquity* 73:325–36.
Wells, Peter S.
1999 Production Within and Beyond Imperial Boundaries: Goods, Exchange, and Power in Roman Europe. In *World-Systems Theory in Practice: Leadership, Production, and Exchange*, edited by P. Nick Kardulias, pp. 85–101. Rowman & Littlefield, Lanham, Md.

Willey, Gordon R.
1953   *Prehistoric Settlement Patterns in the Virú Valley, Perú*. Smithsonian Institution Press, Washington, D.C.
1999   Styles and State Formations. *Latin American Antiquity* 56(2):86–90.

Williams, Patrick Ryan
2001   Cerro Baúl: A Wari Center on the Tiwanaku. *Latin American Antiquity* 12(1):67–83.

Wilson, David J.
1987   Reconstructing Patterns of Early Warfare in the Lower Santa Valley: New Data on the Role of Conflict in the Origins of North-Coast Society. In *The Origins and Development of the Andean State*, edited by Jonathan Haas, Shelia Pozorski, and Thomas Pozorski, pp. 56–69. Cambridge University Press, Cambridge.
1988   *Prehispanic Settlement Patterns in the Lower Santa Valley, Peru: A Regional Perspective on the Origins and Development of Complex North Coast Society*. Smithsonian Institution Press, Washington, D.C.
1995   Prehispanic Settlement Patterns in the Casma Valley, North Coast of Peru: Preliminary Results to Date. *Journal of the Steward Anthropological Society* 23(1–2):189–227.

Zuidema, R. Tom
1983   Lion in the City: Royal Symbols of Transition in Cuzco. *Journal of Latin American Lore* 9(1):39–100.

Index

Page numbers with *f* refer to figures;
page numbers with *m* refer to maps;
page numbers with *t* refer to tables.

Abandonment of Cerro la Cruz. *See* Ritual termination event
Accelerator mass spectrometry dating. *See* Radiocarbon dating
Access patterns, 75*f*, 76*f*, 94–95, 97–100, 106
Administrative activities, evidence for, 91, 93, 136, 171, 180
Adobe and stone construction, mixture of, 34, 38, 40, 102, 103, 150; in Compound B3, 88; in Compound D3, 90; of niches, 95; of walls, 84–85
Adobe bricks, 40, 70, 85, 139, 150
Adornos, 31, 108
Agave, 127
Agglutinated structures, 34, 38, 87, 89, 105, 163; agglutinated rooms, 82, 189n1
Agricultural remains, 12, 126–27, 141
Alconini, Sonia, 54
"Algarrobo," 61
Alleys, blind, 98, 99
Anchovies, 128
Andean chronology and culture history, 18*t*, 152; revising, 18, 183
Animals. *See* Faunal context; Faunal remains

Annexes, 38, 100, 106, 150
Appliqués. *See* Ceramic designs, appliquéd
Architectural description of Compounds B3 and D3, 87–90
Architecture, types of, 6–7; of Casma polity, 33–35; in Nepeña Valley, 160–61; *quincha*, 73, 99–100, 189n7; in Santa Valley, 157–58; in Virú Valley, 154–55; Wari-style, 82, 106–7
Architecture as indicator of social status differences, 11–12, 73, 100, 107–8
Architecture as manifestation of sociopolitical change, 6–7, 175
Artifacts, special, 131–34
Artifact styles, cultural identity and, 72–73, 81, 170
Atalla, site of, 55
Audiencias, 23, 24*f*, 82, 161, 164; lack thereof at Cerro la Cruz, 167, 169, 179
Avocados, 12, 62, 126, 127, 128*t*, 141

Baffled entryways, 23, 82, 98, 107
Bags, cloth, 129*t*, 130–31
Battle, evidence for, 67, 170, 177, 182
Bawden, Garth, 21, 106
Beakers. *See* Keros
Beans, 62
Beer, maize, 81–82, 127, 138, 139
Benches, 67, 84, 93–94, 125–26
"Bichayo," 61

Blackware, 9, 162; Chimú-style press-molded, 23; face-neck jars, 109, 111–12, 160, 165; fineware, 109; paste type, 179, 189n10; press-molded flaring bowls, 160; recovered at Cerro la Cruz, 108, 114–15, 160, 179; shift toward, 154, 162; stirrup-spout molds, 118, 119f, 179; surface sherds, 108, 109–10

Black-White-Red (ceramic style), 28, 30t, 40, 157, 165; as archaeological indicator of Casma polity, 42, 157; at El Purgatorio, 109; as fineware variation, 33. See also Nepeña Black-White-Red

"Black-White-Red State," 28t, 157

Blind alleys, 98, 99

Body sherds, 77, 109

Bones. See Human skeletal remains

Border zones, 47–48, 59, 147, 164

Botanical remains. See Floral remains

Bottles: spout-and-handle, 24; stirrup-spout, 24, 109, 110; Tomaval Plain, 153

Boundaries, 3–4, 7–9, 47–48

Bourget, Steve, 92

Bowls (*cuencos*), 40, 110; Casma Incised, 27f; Casma-style redware, 108; Chimú, 24; Chimú Imperial ring, 171; Early Tanguche ring-base and tripod, 156; fineware, 109; florero, 109, 190n12; gourd, 40; grater (see Graters); Huari Norteño B press-molded flaring, 160; San Juan Molded, 153; San Nicolas Molded, 153; Tomaval Plain, 153; Wari ring-base, 165

Bricks, adobe, 40, 70, 85, 139, 150

Buenavista, 60, 61f, 74, 81, 109, 124

Built environment, importance of, 6–7, 49–51

Burger, Richard L., 55

Burials, Casma-style, 40, 42. See also Human skeletal remains

Cactus, 61

"Carrizo," 61

Camelids, 92, 126, 128, 139, 177, 178

"Caña brava," 61

Canals, irrigation, 52, 60, 62, 70, 74, 86–87; Chavimochic system, 63, 74

Cane, 94, 95, 96, 100, 127

Cantaros, 110t. See also Jars

Cárdenas, Mercedes, 28t, 63, 65–66, 67, 167

Case-and-fill construction, 40, 85, 103

Casma ceramic styles: Casma Incised, 27–33, 30t; Casma Modeled, 27, 30t; Casma Molded, 27, 28, 30f; provenience by valley, 30t

Casma polity: architecture and settlement patterns, 33–34; capital city of El Purgatorio, 35–42; ceramic styles, 27–33; geographic and temporal extent, 26–27; mortuary practices, 40, 42; occupation of Cerro la Cruz, 176–77; political organization, 34–35

Casma Valley, 36m, 37f

Castillo Butters, Luis Jaime, 20, 72, 165, 179, 189n8

Ceramic designs, appliquéd: birds, 160; Casma Incised redware, 29, 31, 108; Huari Norteño B, 160; late Tanguche period, 157; lizards, 160; recovered at Cerro la Cruz, 114, 116f, 117f, 139; serpents, 30t, 31–33, 108, 151t; snakes, 139, 160; in southern half of north coast, 151t

Ceramic designs and motifs: appliquéd (see Ceramic designs, appliquéd); circle-and-dot (see Circle-and-dot motif); front-facing god, 114, 115f; lizards, 114; maritime and coastal styles, 24, 115, 178; rope, 31, 108, 115f; serpents, 114; *Spondylus*, 24, 115, 116f, 178

Ceramic molds, 12, 81, 110t, 118–22, 154; press-molded exterior decoration of, 122; stirrup-spout, 118, 119f, 179

Ceramics, press-molded, 150, 151t, 162; blackware, 24; Chimú, 23–24; Early

Tanguche, 156; flaring bowls, 160; Huari Norteño B, 159–60; Late Tanguche, 157; recovered at Cerro la Cruz, 160; redware, 33; San Juan Molded, 153; San Nicolas Molded, 153, 162; Tanguche, 30*t*

Ceramics, surface distribution of, 90–92, 91*t*, 109–10

Ceramics recovered at Cerro la Cruz: ceramic decoration, 114–17; predominant vessel forms, 110–14; surface collection of, 77, 90–92, 91*t*, 109–10

Ceramic styles: Casma Incised, 27–33; Casma Molded, 27, 28, 30*t*; Chimú, 23–25; Moche, 189n8; press-molded (*see* Ceramics, press-molded); Serpentine Appliqué, 30*t*, 31–33, 108, 151*t*; Transitional, 111*f*, 112, 152*t*, 165; Wari, 165

Ceramic vessel forms, 110–13. *See also* Bottles; Bowls (*cuencos*); Floreros; Graters; Jars; Molds, ceramic; Ollas; Plates; Tinajas

Ceramic workshops, 12, 80*f*, 108, 118–19*f*, 123, 138; in administrative centers, 72

Cercaduras. See *Ciudadelas*

"Ceremonial road," 68, 74

Cerro la Cruz, 2*m*, 3*f*, 41*f*, 61*f*; functions of, 66–68, 145–47; occupation by Casma polity, 176–77; plan view, 64*m*, reasons for location, 68–71, 145–46, 176

Chamber-and-fill construction. *See* Case-and-fill construction

Channeling of water at Cerro la Cruz, 63, 188n3

Chao River, 63, 63; flow volume of, 188n2

Chao Valley, 13*m*; as Casma polity periphery, 147; faunal and floral context, 61–62; geographical setting, 60–61; land use in, 62–63; previous research on, 65–68

Chase-Dunn, Christopher, 43, 44

Chavimochic canals, 60, 63, 74

Chavín (ceramic style), 33, 66

"Chavín Horizon," 55

Chicha. *See* Maize beer

Chili peppers, 62, 126, 141

Chimú-Casma connection, hypotheses and evidence, 166–70

Chimú polity, 188n7; architecture and ceramics, 23–25; emergence and collapse, 22–23; geographic and temporal extent, 23; political organization, 25

Chinchawas, site of, 55

Chitons, 126

Chronology and ceramics, 152*t*; of Nepeña Valley, 159–60; of Santa Valley, 156–57; of Virú Valley, 152–54

"Chucluy," 62

Ciperácea, 127

Circle-and-dot motif, 114*f*; in Casma ceramic styles, 29, 33, 108, 111; in Serpentine Appliqué style, 33, 66, 150, 151*t*, 156, 157, 160

Ciudadelas, 106, 161

Climatic conditions in Chao Valley, 61

Cloth bags, 129*t*, 130–31

Collier, Donald, 27–28, 29, 30*t*, 34, 108, 150, 153–54, 160

Compounds B3 and D3: architectural description, 87–90; construction of, 176–77; functions and significance, 105–8; intrasite access patterns, 97–100; niched rooms, 95–97; reception areas, 93–94; sequence of construction, 104–5; storage rooms, 94–95, 141, 143; termination evidence, 142–45; tripartite division of space, 75*f*, 76*f*, 78–79, 90–93, 181

Construction sequence, 104–5

Construction techniques: compounds, 102–3, terraces, 100–102

Consumption, evidence of, 81–82, 126–28, 140–41

Coprolites, camelid, 126, 128, 139

Core/periphery analyses, 43–46
Corral Incised, 30*t*, 151*t*, 152*t*, 153
Corridors, 98, 99
Cotton, 12, 126, 127, 141, 177; offerings, 135, 136; raw, 138; shroud, 125; textiles, 129, 130, 178
Crabs, 12, 126, 131
Craft production, degree of control over, 72
Craig, Nathan, 165
Cranial modification, 125
Crayfish, river, 62
Cross-cutting social networks, evidence of, 147, 171, 178–83; frontiers as, 45
Cuencos. See Bowls (*cuencos*)
Cultural identity, artifact styles and, 72–73, 81–82, 170
Culture history: and chronology, Andean, 18*t*, 152; of north coast, 17–42, revising, 18, 183, 184

Daggett, Cheryl, 28*t*, 30*t*, 31, 33, 108
D'Altroy, Terence N., 54
Dedicatory burials, 190n5. See Human skeletal remains
Deer, 62
Denevan, William M., 101
Dillehay, Tom D., 54
Distribution of surface ceramics, 90–92, 91*t*, 109–10
Dogs, domesticated, 12, 126, 128, 177
Donnan, Christopher B., 138
Doorways, 97, 98, 99, 100, 136; baffled, 23, 82, 98, 107; "step-over," 94–95
Dry moats. See Canals, irrigation
D-shaped architectural structures, 82

Early Tanguche (ceramic style), 30*t*, 151*t*, 152*t*, 156, 157
El Niño–Southern Oscillation (ENSO) events, 69, 146, 162; availability of resources following, 62; effects of, 63, 74, 85, 89, 162, 188n5
El Purgatorio, 2*m*, 36*f*, 38*f*, 39*f*; research on, 28*t*-29*t*, 35–42, 182, 187n2
Enclosed rock outcrops, 92–93
Excavations at Cerro la Cruz, 64*m*; methods, 78–81; strategy, 73–74

Face-neck jars, 111*f*, 112*f*, 113*f*; blackware, 109, 111–13, 160, 165; recovered at Cerro la Cruz, 109, 111–13, 156, 160, 165; recovered at El Purgatorio, 165; Transitional, 111*f*
Faunal context, 61–62
Faunal remains, 12, 126–28, 177
Feasting, evidence of, 81–82, 94, 127, 141, 144
Featherwork, 139
Fernández Honores, Manuel A., 128, 131–33
Fineware ceramics, 72, 108–9
Fires. See Ritual termination event
Firing pits, 12, 108, 118–19*f*
Fish, 12, 126, 129*t*, 139, 140, 177, 179
Floral context, 61–62
Floral remains, 12, 126–28, 177
Flor de arena, 127
Floreros, 109, 190n12
Food remains, 94, 126–28, 129*t*, 141, 144, 177
Fortification, Cerro la Cruz as, 66–68, 145; problematizing, 10–11, 50, 146, 148, 180
Foxes, 62
Front-facing god motif, 114, 115*f*
Frontiers, 3–4, 46–47; of Casma polity, 162–64; of Inca Empire, 53–54; of Pre-Inca Andes, 54–56
Frontier theory, 5–6; application to Cerro la Cruz, 56–58; built environment and, 49–51

Fronto-occipital modification, 125
Functions: of Cerro la Cruz, 66–68, 145–47; of Sections, 90–93
Fung Pineda, Rosa, 28, 33–34, 35, 71

Geography, political: Andean archaeological record and, 5–6, 59; implications of, 51–52
Geopolitical boundaries, importance of examining, 8–9
Geopolitical landscapes, 7–9, 171–74; Casma polity frontiers, 162–64; Chimú-Casma connection, 166–70; and lack of evidence for Wari state occupation, 164–66; Nepeña Valley, 159–62; Santa Valley, 155–59; Virú Valley, 150, 151–55
Giersz, Miłosz, 164
Glossary, 193–97
Goldstein, Paul, 55
Gordon, Américo, 54
Gourds, 126, 127, 129t, 131, 141
Grama, 127
Graters, 109, 110, 115, 117f, 190n15
Great Wall systems, 48, 158–59, 161–62, 164
Greens, wild, 127, 141
Guanabanas, 126, 127
Guañape, 30t
"Guayabas" (guavas), 126, 127, 141
Guinea pigs, evidence for, 127, 177, 191n22

Hacienda Buenavista. *See* Buenavista
Hair, human, packets of, 137
Hall, Thomas D., 44
Harpoons, wooden, 131–33, 179
"Huarangos," 61, 128
Huari Norteño A, 152t, 159
Huari Norteño B, 29, 30t, 151t, 152t, 159–60

Huarmey Incised, 28, 30t
"Huayabillo," 61
Huaylas Yunga, 28, 30t
Human effigy jars, 156
Human skeletal remains, 93–94, 124–26
Hyslop, John, 51, 190n9, 191n6

Iconography, Chimú, 24, 114, 178
Identity, artifact styles and cultural, 72–73, 81–82, 170
Imperial Chimú stylistic indicators, 23–25
Inca Empire, frontiers of, 53–54
Intentional burning, 141–45
Internal tripartite division of space, 75f, 76f, 78–79, 90–93, 181
Intrasite access patterns, 75f, 76f, 94–95, 97–100, 106

Jackson, Margaret A., 122
Janusek, John Wayne, 73, 191n25
Jars, 109, 110, 190n16; *cantaro*, 110t; face-neck (*see* Face-neck jars); human effigy, 156; rope-necked, 114, 115f; storage (*tinaja*), 82, 109, 110, 115, 117f, 139, 187n6, 190n14
Jar stoppers (*tapas*), 133
Jennings, Justin, 55, 165
Jewelry, 140–41, 178
Jiménez Diaz, María Jesús, 130
Juvenile burial. *See* Human skeletal remains

Keatinge, Richard W., 18
Kent, Jonathan D., 61–62, 65, 128, 182, 189nn6,12
Keros, 115, 116f, 165, 178, 190n13; as evidence for production of maize beer, 82, 139
Klymyshyn, Alexandra M. Ulana, 23, 26, 28t, 164, 168, 171

Kosok, Paul, 63
Kroeber, Alfred L., 30*t*

Lambayeque polity. *See* Sicán polity, emergence and collapse of
Late Tanguche (ceramic style), 30*t*, 151*t*, 152*t*, 157
Lau, George F., 55
Layouts: interior maps of Compounds B3 and D3, 75*m*, 76*m*; plan view of Cerro la Cruz, 64*m*
"Lechuzas," 62
Levels of ritual, spatial and social, 135–38
Lightfoot, Kent G., 14, 45, 46, 147, 178, 188n3
Lizards, 62
Llamas. *See* Camelids
Location of Cerro la Cruz, reasons for, 176; control, 68–69, 145–46; protection, 68–69, 145–46; subsistence, 68–69, 70; visibility, 68–69, 70, 145, 146
Lúcuma, 126, 127

Mackey, Carol J., 24, 25, 26, 28*t*, 164, 168, 171
Maize, 12, 62, 126, 127, 177; in association with textiles, 129*t*, 136; construction fill, 40, 142; as evidence of *chicha* production (*see* Maize beer); in feast remains, 141; as offerings, 135, 136; stalks and cobs, 40, 189n11
Maize beer, 81–82, 127, 138, 139
Maker's marks, 12, 102, 138–39, 141, 191n20; in ceramic workshop, 123–24
Mapping, preliminary, 74–77; room numbering, 189n3
Marcos, Jorge G., 178
Marine resources, evidence for harvesting of, 12, 126, 127–28, 139, 140
Martinez, Antoinette, 45–46, 147, 178
Material culture styles as indicators of cultural affiliation, 23, 59, 82
Matos Mendieta, Ramiro, 55

McEwan, Gordon F., 106, 141–42
Metallurgy, 139
Mishpingo, 94, 125, 128, 141
Moats, dry. *See* Canals, irrigation
Moche polity, emergence and collapse of, 5, 20–21, 106, 190n1
Molds, ceramic, 12, 81, 110*t*, 118–22, 154; press-molded exterior decoration of, 122; stirrup-spout, 118, 119*f*, 179
"Molle," 61
Mollusks, 12, 126
Moore, Jerry D., 107
Moseley, Michael E., 21, 177, 188n2
Mowery, Susan Haun, 125
Multifunctionality of compounds, 11, 74, 107, 136, 148, 181
Mussels, 126, 128, 138

Nash, Donna J., 190n8
Needles, copper, 133, 141
Nepeña Black-on-White, 30*t*, 152*t*, 159
Nepeña Black-White-Red, 30*t*, 152*t*, 159, 160
Nepeña Valley in regional context: chronology and ceramics, 159–60; Great Wall system, 161–62, 164; settlement patterns and architecture, 160–61
Niches. *See* Rooms: niched

Offerings, 92, 126, 129*t*
Ollas, 40, 109, 110, 190n10; Casma Incised, 27*f*, 29; Casma-style, 32*f*, Casma-style redware, 108, 111; Chimú-style press-molded blackware, 23
ONERN (Oficina Nacional de Evaluación de Recursos Naturales), 60, 62, 70
Owls, ground, 62

Pacae, 126, 127, 130
Pagos. *See* Offerings

Parapets, 10, 66–68, 84, 145, 158
Paste types, 189n10
Patios. *See* Annexes
Pendants: *mishpingo* seed, 94, 125, 128, 141; stone jaguar, 133, 173, 178
Perimeter walls, 84–86, 181; function and significance of, 50–51; multiple purposes of, 74
Peripheries: archaeological approaches to, 43–58; archaeological indicators of, 48–49; implications of, 4–6; methodological concerns in study of, 59–60, 71
Pimentel Gurmendi, Víctor, 28*t*, 191n3
Pits, firing, 12, 108, 118*f*–19*f*
Plants. *See* Floral context; Floral remains
Plates, 109; flat-bottomed, 111
Polishing stones, 12, 188
Political organization, 29*t*, 46; of Casma polity, 34–35; of Chavín polity, 55; of Chimú Empire, 25; of Moche state, 20–21
Politicogeographical analyses, 5–6, 59; implications of, 51–52
Population growth in Cerro la Cruz, 176–77
Porotic hyperostosis, 125
Post-excavation analysis, 81–83
Pots. *See* Ollas
Pottery. *See* Ceramic designs and motifs; Ceramic styles; Ceramic vessel forms
Pozorski, Shelia, 67–68
Pozorski, Thomas, 67–68
Pre-Inca Andean frontiers, 54–56
Preliminary survey, 74
Press-molded ceramics, 150, 151*t*; blackware, 24; Chimú, 23–24; Early Tanguche, 156; flaring bowls, 160; Huari Norteño B, 159–60; Late Tanguche, 157; redware, 33; San Juan Molded, 153; San Nicolas Molded, 153

Productive activities, evidence of, 138–40
Proulx, Donald A., 28–29, 30*t*, 159–62, 164
Prządka, Patrycja, 164

Quincha architecture, 73, 86, 99–100, 189n7

Radiocarbon dating: Casma-style burials, 42; Cerro la Cruz, 9, 18, 19*t*, 66, 82–83, 104–5, 168; Chimú expansion, 25; El Purgatorio, 27
Ramps, 94, 97–98
Reception areas, 93–94
Reconnaissance and preliminary survey, 74
Redware: Black-White-Red, 157; Casma styles, 29, 108; olla, 111; paste type, 189n10; recovered at Cerro la Cruz, 108, 109, 111, 179; shift away from, 153–54, 162
Reeds, 61
Research at El Purgatorio, 28*t*–29*t*, 35–42, 182, 187n2
Research design, 74–81: excavation methods, 78–81; reconnaissance and preliminary survey, 74; sampling strategies, 78; survey and mapping, 74–77
Research objectives at Cerro la Cruz, 10–11
Research on Casma polity, previous, 26–42
Rim sherds, 91, 110, 116, 117*f*, 124*f*
Ritual at Cerro la Cruz, 135–38
Ritual termination event, 141–45, 177
Road, ceremonial. *See* "Ceremonial road"
Rodents, 12, 62, 126, 191n22. *See also* Guinea pigs, evidence for
Rodman, Amy Oakland, 73
Roofs, fallen, 94, 95, 96, 142, 143
Rooms: niched, 95–97, 135–36, 143, 144; storage, 94–95, 141, 143
Rope, 129*t*, 131

Rope designs, ceramic, 108, 115*f*
Rope-necked jars, 114, 115*f*
Rosales Tham, Teresa, 65, 128, 183, 189n6
Rowe, John H., 166

Salomon, Frank, 53
Sampling strategies, 78
San Juan Molded, 30*t*, 152*t*, 153
San Nicolas Molded, 30*t*, 152*t*, 153
Santa (ceramic style), 28, 30*t*
Santa Rita B, 65, 128
Santa Valley in regional context: chronology and ceramics, 156–57; Great Wall system, 158–59, 164; in regional context, 155–59; settlement patterns and architecture, 157–58
Sardines, 126
"Sauce" (*Salix* sp.), 61
Schjellerup, Inge R., 54
Sea urchins, 12, 126, 128
Sechín (ceramic style), 28, 30*t*
Sections: division of rooms into, 75*f*, 76*f*, 78–79, 90–93; functions of, 90–93
Sectors, división of Cerro la Cruz into, 36–40, 64, 87, 105; Sector B, 78; Sector D, 68, 78, 79, 108, 177; Sector E, 135–36
Sequence of compound construction, 104–5
Serpent designs, ceramic, 114; Serpentine Appliqué style, 31–33, 108
Serpentine Appliqué (ceramic style), 30*t*, 31–33, 108, 151*t*
Settlement patterns, 6–7; Casma polity, 33–35; Nepeña Valley, 160–61; Santa Valley, 157–58; Virú Valley, 154–55
Shells, *Spondylus*, 92, 173, 178
Sherd densities, 77, 90–92, 94, 109–10. *See* Surface collection of diagnostic ceramics
Sherds, 31*f*, 114*f*, 115*f*
Shimada, Izumi, 21, 103, 142, 191n20
Sicán polity, emergence and collapse of, 21

Silva Vigo, Edgardo, 68, 69, 86–87, 88, 96, 135, 146, 167
Skeleton, recovered. *See* Human skeletal remains
Slingstones, presence of, 67, 145, 182
Smith, Adam T., 7–9
Snakes, 62
Social networks, evidence of cross-cutting, 147, 171, 178–83; frontiers as, 45
Social status differences, architecture as indicator of, 11–12, 73, 100, 107–8
Sociopolitical change, architecture and spatial organization as manifestation of, 6–7
Soil samples, 82, 189n12
Sorghum, 62
Spatial organization as manifestation of sociopolitical change, 6–7, 175
Special artifacts, 131–34
Spindle whorls, 12, 133–34, 138, 180
Spondylus, 92, 173, 178
Spondylus ceramic designs, 24, 115, 116*f*, 178
Squash, 12, 126, 127, 141, 177
Stairways, 98
Stein, Gil J., 45, 46
"Step-over" doorways, 94–95
Stirrup-spout bottles, 24, 109, 110n11
Stirrup-spout molds, 118, 119*f*, 179
Stoppers, jar (*tapas*), 133
Storage jars. *See* Tinajas
Storage rooms, 94–95, 141, 143
Strategic location, Cerro la Cruz as, 68, 146–47
Stratigraphy, 68, 78, 80
Stronghold and showplace, Cerro la Cruz as, 145–48
Styles, ceramic. *See* Ceramic styles
Stylistic indicators, Imperial Chimú, 23–25
Subsistence in Cerro la Cruz, 177, 179. *See* Faunal remains; Floral remains
Surface ceramics, distribution of, 90–92, 91*t*, 109–10

Surface collection of ceramics and botanical remains, 77
Surface collection of diagnostic ceramics, 77, 90–92, 91*t*, 109–10
Survey and mapping, 74–77; previous, 65–68
Sweet potato, 62

Tanguche ceramic styles: Early, 30*t*, 151*t*, 152*t*, 156, 157; Late, 30*t*, 151*t*, 152*t*, 157
Tapas (jar stoppers), 133
Tello, Julio C., 27, 28, 30*t*, 35, 40
Terraces, 11–12, 38, 39*f*, 40, 64, 77, 87, 90; construction of, 100–102; intrasite access patterns, 97–100; test units placed on, 79
Test units, 66, 78, 79, 88–89, 90, 118
Textiles, 129–31, 141, 178
Thompson, Donald E., 28, 30*t*, 35
Tinajas, 82, 109, 110, 115, 117*f*, 139, 187n6, 190n14. *See also* Jars
Toads, 62
Tomaval Plain, 151*t*, 153
Topic, John R., 52, 66–68, 86, 14
Topic, Theresa Lange, 52, 66–68, 86, 146
Topography: of Cerro la Cruz, 63–64; of Chao Valley, 60–61
Torsion, 130
Trade, evidence of, 12, 69, 115, 141, 178
Transitional (ceramic style), 111*f*, 112, 152*t*, 165
Treacy, John M., 101
Trees, 61, 128
Trenches, stratigraphic, 68, 78, 80
Tributaries of Chao River, main, 60
Tripartite division of space in Compounds B3 and D3, 75*f*, 76*f*, 78–79, 90–93, 181

Units, 75*f*, 76*f*, 95*f*, 96*f*, 97*f*, 140*f*; Burial 1, 125; locations of, 79
U-shaped architectural structures. See *Audiencias*
Utilitarian wares, 72, 108–9

Variations on Casma polity ceramic styles, 27–33, 30*t*
Vegetation in Chao Valley. *See* Floral context
Vessel forms, ceramic, 110–13. *See also* Bottles; Bowls (*cuencos*); Floreros; Graters; Jars; Molds, ceramic; Ollas; Plates; Tinajas
Virú Valley in regional context: chronology and ceramics, 152–54; settlement patterns and architecture, 154–55

Wallerstein, Immanuel, 44, 51, 188n2
Walls, functions of, 50–51
Walls, great. *See* Great Wall systems
Walls, perimeter, 84–86, 181
Wari polity, 55; emergence and collapse of, 19–20; lack of evidence for state control, 164–66
Wasters, 12, 118, 190n19
Water, Chao Valley sources of, 60, 63, 70
"Wattle-and-daub" architecture. *See Quincha* architecture
Weave, patterns of, 130
Weaving swords, 133, 138
Weeds, 126, 127
Whorls, spindle, 12, 133–34, 138, 180
Willey, Gordon R., 150, 152, 154–55
Williams, Patrick Ryan, 190n8
Williams León, Carlos, 28, 33–34, 35, 188n9
Wilson, David J., 28*t*, 30*t*, 34, 69, 151*t*, 155–59, 162, 164, 187n7, 188n9, 191n2
Wool. *See* Textiles
Workshops, ceramic, 80*f*, 118*f*–19*f*; at Cerro la Cruz, 12, 79, 87, 108, 118–23, 138; in administrative centers, 72
World-systems theory, 43–46; political geography and, 51–52

Yarn. *See* Textiles

"Zapote," 61, 131

Melissa A. Vogel is associate professor of anthropology at Clemson University in South Carolina.

www.ingramcontent.com/pod-product-compliance
Lightning Source LLC
Chambersburg PA
CBHW031434160426
43195CB00010BB/726